Society and Politics
in
The Acts of the Apostles

SOCIETY AND POLITICS
IN
THE ACTS OF THE APOSTLES

Richard J. Cassidy

ORBIS BOOKS

Maryknoll, New York 10545

The Catholic Foreign Mission Society of America (Maryknoll) recruits and trains people for overseas missionary service. Through Orbis Books Maryknoll aims to foster the international dialogue that is essential to mission. The books published, however, reflect the opinions of their authors and are not meant to represent the official position of the society.

Unless otherwise indicated, all biblical citations are from the Revised Standard Version

Indexes prepared by James Sullivan

Library of Congress Cataloging-in-Publication Data

Cassidy, Richard J.
    Society and politics in the Acts of the Apostles.

    Bibliography: p.
    Includes index.
    1. Bible. N.T. Acts—Criticism, interpretation,
etc.   2. Sociology, Biblical.   3. Politics in the Bible.
I. Title.
BS2625.2.C38   1987   226'.6067   87-15259
ISBN 0-88344-568-9
ISBN 0-88344-567-0 (pbk.)

DEDICATION

To Philip Scharper (d. May 5, 1985) who was by reason of personal faith, and also perhaps by reason of the office he held, a modern-day Theophilus.

To the members of the Day House, Detroit Peace, and Covenant for Peace communities whose trial testimonies and prison experiences continue a tradition of Christian witness first described in the pages of Acts.

And to Luke himself for the care and the comprehensiveness of his two volumes, writings composed out of allegiance and given for the sake of faith, writings whose portrayal of Christian discipleship has so immeasurably enriched us all.

Contents

Preface

Because the present book has been in preparation, at least remotely, since the completion of *Jesus, Politics, and Society* in 1976, many people have helped to shape its development. As with my previous books, the steady support which I have received from my family and from close friends has been an influence conditioning the entire endeavor from beginning to end. For this love and this friendship I am deeply grateful.

I also wish to thank a number of individuals and communities who have assisted me in specific ways. I first talked about such an undertaking with Fr. Dean Brackley, SJ, a number of years ago in Berkeley. More proximate encouragement for continued Lukan studies was given me by my colleagues on the Catholic Biblical Association's Luke-Acts Task Force from 1982 through 1987. Members of the seminar on Acts that I offered at St. John's Seminary during the Spring of 1983 also contributed to my developing outlines as did Fr. Charles Morris, the faculty research assistant for that year.

As a priest of the Archdiocese of Detroit, I am particularly grateful to Archbishop Edmund Szoka for an assignment during 1985 and 1986 that allowed me to devote extra time and energy to writing. In an almost classic sense, Archbishop Szoka has thus served as the patron for this work. I am also grateful to Fr. Robert Byrne, rector, and the faculty, students, and staff of St. John's Seminary for the hospitable and encouraging surroundings which they constituted for me during this last period of intense writing. Mrs. Jean McGarty, the director of St. John's Library, responded graciously to several of my special requests during this interval and Mrs. Dorothy Christensen, the manager of the seminary bookstore, efficiently supervised the distribution of drafts of the manuscript to students in the 1986 Luke-Acts course.

During the summers of 1985 and 1986, I was pleased to return for short stays in the familiar surroundings of The Graduate Theological Union in Berkeley. The splendid G.T.U. library and its effective staff once again afforded me access to resources not easily available elsewhere. And I was again welcomed into the warm community life present at the Jesuit School of Theology.

While the responsibility for the positions eventually taken is my own, I wish to acknowledge that I have benefitted from insights that three distinguished scholars—Msgr. Warren Holleran, Dr. Edward Hobbs, and Dr. David Daube—shared with me at different points during the writing. David Doby, Francis George, Lin Baum, and Catherine Costello have also provided me with much appreciated assistance regarding the visuals and the visual format of the book. The title, *Society and Politics in the Acts of the Apostles,* evolved during the course of an enjoyable conversation with Msgr. Joseph Gremillion at Notre Dame in the summer of 1985.

To all of the above friends and colleagues, as well as to others not named, I again extend my sincere thanks. In addition, I wish to underscore at this time the special gratitude which I feel toward those to whom this book is dedicated.

1

Jesus and the Roman Order in Luke's Gospel

The primary objectives of the present study are first to analyze Luke's social and political descriptions in the Book of Acts and second to put forward some reflections about Luke's purposes in writing his two-volume work. Since it would, however, be extremely difficult to appreciate what Luke presents as the social and political stance of the first Christians without taking into account what he presented in his Gospel regarding Jesus' own stance, it is imperative to begin with an overview of the Gospel.

1. THE SOCIAL AND POLITICAL STANCE OF LUKE'S JESUS*

In analyzing and reflecting over what Luke's account conveys concerning Jesus' relationship to the existing social order, there are two dimensions which need explicit attention. The first dimension concerns the social stance which Luke shows Jesus adopting. The second concerns the portrayal given with respect to Jesus' interaction with the political authorities and specific political issues such as taxation.

Clearly Luke's reports about Jesus' interactions with Herod Antipas and his description of Jesus' conduct before Pontius Pilate are important for any assessment of Jesus' stance vis-à-vis the Roman order. No less important are the various elements present in his social stance. For the approach of Luke's Jesus toward the poor and the infirm (as well as his approaches in the other areas to be discussed below) reveal the degree to which his social stance can be considered to be compatible with the social patterns of Roman-administered Judea and Galilee.

---

*The presentation here and in the subsequent sections of this chapter generally follows the lines of the analysis given, in more detailed fashion, in the author's *Jesus, Politics, and Society: a Study of Luke's Gospel.*

A. Concern for the Sick and the Poor

An unmistakable feature of the Jesus described in Luke's account is that he displays a specific and consistent concern for the sick and the poor. Early in the Gospel, in the context of making an auspicious return to his own home town, Jesus associates himself with the following verses from the Book of Isaiah:

> The Spirit of the Lord is upon me, because he has anointed me to preach good news to the poor. He has sent me to proclaim release to the captives and recovering of sight to the blind, to set at liberty those who are oppressed, to proclaim the acceptable year of the Lord [4:18–19].

Later, when John the Baptist's disciples approach to ask him who he is, Jesus' response again emphasizes the importance that he places upon ministry to the sick and the poor:

> Go and tell John what you have seen and heard: the blind receive their sight, the lame walk, lepers are cleansed, and the deaf hear, the dead are raised up, the poor have good news preached to them. And blessed is he who takes no offense at me [7:22–23].

Subsequently, in the course of a series of teachings given with reference to banquets, Luke portrays Jesus making the following appeal regarding the handicapped and the poor:

> He said also to the man who had invited him, "When you give a dinner or a banquet, do not invite your friends or your brothers or your kinsmen or rich neighbors, lest they also invite you in return, and you be repaid. But when you give a feast, invite the poor, the maimed, the lame, the blind, and you will be blessed, because they cannot repay you. You will be repaid at the resurrection of the just" [14:12–14].

In addition to these passages in which Luke shows Jesus expressing a concern for the poor in the context of concern for those who suffer from various diseases and infirmities (see also 14:21), there are also several passages in which he shows Jesus focusing upon the situation of the poor. Perhaps the best-known of these passages is the beatitude in which Jesus proclaims that the poor are blessed (6:20). Luke also shows Jesus telling the parable of Lazarus and the rich man in which neglect of the poor is a central issue (16:19–26) and portrays him explicitly instructing a rich ruler to sell all that he has and "distribute to the poor" (18:22).

B. Affirmation for Other Less Regarded Groups

In addition to the particular concern which Luke describes Jesus according to the infirm and the poor, the evangelist also shows him giving affirmation to several other groups that were, to varying degrees, denied full acceptance within the prevailing social context. Among the groups which fall into this general category are Samaritans, Gentiles, women, tax collectors, and sinners.

With respect to Samaritans there are two instances within the Gospel in which Jesus makes extremely positive reference to Samaritans. The first reference occurs in the well-known parable with which Jesus answered a lawyer's question about who should be considered a neighbor. Jesus' response (10:30–37) dramatically indicated the universal range of the commandment to love one's neighbor. What is more, in positioning a Samaritan as the model figure in his story, Jesus provided an immediate concrete application of this universalism.

Would it not have been possible to illustrate a neighborly response to the roadside victim with a Jewish passerby positioned in the model role? The fact that a Samaritan was given such prominence carried with it the implication that conduct relevant for God's kingdom would also be found among the Samaritans.

The second positive reference to Samaritans occurs in Luke's seventeenth chapter. There Luke indicates that, as a consequence of Jesus' intervention, ten lepers were healed from their disease. However, upon receiving this cure, only one of the ten, a Samaritan, returned to give thanks to Jesus. In response Jesus commended the Samaritan's faith, remarking as he did so that this "foreigner" was the only one of the ten who returned (17:11–19).

In the other passage within the Gospel dealing with Samaritans (9:51–55) Jesus is portrayed as rejecting his disciples' call for retributive action against a Samaritan village, a proposal made after the village has refused to receive Jesus. Here the Samaritans are not portrayed positively, but Jesus does make it clear that he wants to make a break with traditional retributive attitudes concerning Samaritans.

The negative attitude of the disciples presented in this passage is not untypical of the negative attitudes of Jews toward Gentiles that are indicated in other passages of the Gospel. In several of these passages Jesus is portrayed as trying to broaden the horizons of those in his audience in regard to the Gentile peoples and their cities and territories. For example, to the distress of his own townspeople in Nazareth, Jesus makes reference to the fact that the prophet Elijah was sent to sustain a widow in the land of Sidon and to the fact that the prophet Elisha presided over the healing of the Syrian leader, Naaman (4:26–27).

In the same vein, it is significant that in 8:26–29 Jesus passes into the country of the Gerasenes and there dramatically cures a possessed man. Subsequently, Luke also portrays Jesus warning his Jewish hearers that their birthright is no guarantee of entry into the kingdom of God. Rather, it is possible for them to be thrust outside while . . . "men will come from east and west and north and south, and sit at table in the kingdom of God" (13:29).

In this context, it is also appropriate to mention the extremely favorable response to a Roman centurion that Luke describes Jesus giving in 7:1–10. As conquerors who imposed their rule and their taxes upon Judea, the Romans were disliked and resented by most Jews. Yet, when word of the centurion's request reached him, Luke portrays Jesus responding favorably.

Luke states that Jewish intermediaries commended the centurion's request for his servant's healing and that these intermediaries indicated to Jesus that this particular centurion loved the Jewish people and had even built them a synagogue. Luke reports that Jesus went with these messengers back to the centurion's house only to be met by other friends bringing the message that the centurion did not believe it necessary for Jesus to come to his house but that his word alone would be sufficient to heal the servant. It is at this point that Luke reports Jesus' praise for the centurion's great faith and also the healing of his servant.

In assessing the approach that Luke's Gospel describes Jesus following in regard to women, it should be noted that Luke portrays several instances in which Jesus praised conduct by women and indicated that their behavior served as an example. This is the case in 7:44-50 when Jesus bestowed praise and forgiveness on the woman who, in contrast to his inhospitable host, washed and anointed his feet. It is also the case in 21:1-4 where Jesus praised the generosity of the poor widow in giving to the temple and stated that, compared with the others donating, she "has put in more than all of them."

Several of the parables reported by Luke also present a woman's activity or commitment in a highly favorable light. In one of them, the kingdom of God is likened to a woman's activity in leavening flour (13:20-21). In another the joy of a woman at having searched for a lost coin and found it is used as an image of God's own rejoicing over a sinner who repents (15:8-10). In a third, the persistence of a widow in seeking justice from an unjust judge is presented as an encouragement for the disciples' own persistence in prayer (18:1-8).

Luke's note that Jesus included women among the group of disciples traveling among the towns and villages of Galilee and his note that these women provided for the financial needs of the group out of their own resources (8:1-3) are also important elements in the picture that he presents of Jesus' attitude toward women. Since Luke nowhere states that any of the women listed were related to Jesus or the apostles by marriage or family bonds, the implication seems to be that these women were operating as persons with a high degree of identity and independence.

These same characteristics of personal identity and independence are also implied in the Mary and Martha account of Luke 10:38-42. Jesus receives the hospitality offered by the two sisters and he is pleased to have Mary listening intently to his teaching. Also his response to Martha is not in any way demeaning to her; rather it is a gentle rebuke respectfully given.

Although Luke only once mentions any teaching by Jesus with regard to the permanence of marriage, the impact of this brief teaching is in the direction of increased security for women in their marriages. Verse 16:18 reads as follows: "Every one who divorces his wife and marries another commits adultery, and he who marries a woman divorced from her husband commits adultery." Under the prevailing patterns a man could divorce his wife and take another at his own discretion. In contrast this teaching by Luke's Jesus equates such divorce and remarriage with adultery.

With regard to those Jews who collected taxes for the Romans and others similarly regarded as sinners by respectable segments of Jewish society, Luke's Gospel provides clear indications that Jesus affirmed the possibility that they too might enter the kingdom of God and also their potential for serving as examples to others.

Clearly, Jesus' calling of a tax collector named Levi as one of the apostles is one indication that such a social standing did not preclude an invitation to the kingdom of God. And Luke's subsequent report that Jesus actually sat at table with a number of tax collectors at a banquet which Levi prepared is still another (5:27-29). Luke indicates that the Pharisees found such conduct by Jesus scandalous. On this occasion they reproach Jesus for his behavior by challenging his disciples (5:30) and in two later passages their criticism is also mentioned (7:34; 15:1-3).

Luke shows Jesus initially responding to this criticism by stating that he had come to call to repentance not the righteous, but rather sinners (5:32). Later on he also reports Jesus' words that many tax collectors had acknowledged God's plan by accepting baptism from John (7:29). Still later he portrays Jesus relating a parable, one reminiscent of the parable of the Good Samaritan, in which a tax collector is actually featured as a model figure for humility (18:9-14).

This capacity for a repentant tax collector to serve as a model for discipleship is also illustrated in the encounter that Luke portrays taking place between Jesus and Zacchaeus, a chief tax collector in the area of Jericho (19:1-10). After Zacchaeus has indicated the dramatic steps he has taken with respect to restitution and sharing with the poor, Jesus' final words are the following: "Today salvation has come to this house, since he also is a son of Abraham. For the Son of man came to seek and to save the lost."

C. The Use of Material Possessions

A particularly striking feature of the Gospel of Luke is the frequency with which Jesus addresses the related subjects of simplicity in living, the sharing of material possessions and the perilous status of the rich. These subjects are addressed in Jesus' parables and other teachings and in two significant encounters which occur toward the end of the Gospel.

Various passages in the Gospel convey the impression that Jesus himself lives simply and unpretentiously. In 9:58 he remarks to a potential disciple that "foxes have holes, and birds of the air have nests; but the Son of man has nowhere to lay his head." And although his enemies make the charge against him that he is a "glutton and a drunkard," Luke portrays Jesus matter of factly dismissing this criticism (7:33-35). In terms of financial support during his public ministry, the only information that Luke provides is the report in 8:3 that a number of women who traveled with Jesus provided for the group out of their own resources.

In Luke's account of the Sermon on the Plain, a series of woes follows upon the initial series of blessings. The blessing, "Blessed are you poor" (6:20), was noted above. Corresponding to it is the woe, "Woe to you that are rich" (6:24). And, as the Gospel narrative moves forward, Luke depicts Jesus giving a number of teachings that relate to the subject of material possessions and riches. In the challenging words contained in the parable of the second barn, Jesus warns against the accumulation of material resources (12:15-21). Instead of being anxious over how they are to acquire the resources they need, the disciples should be more trusting in God's providence (12:22-32). Indeed, Jesus exhorts them to sell their possessions and give alms (12:33).

As noted above, in regard to the subject of material possessions, the basic approach of Luke's Jesus is that surplus possessions, possessions over and above what is necessary for one's life, are dangerous for true discipleship. In chapter sixteen Luke shows Jesus presenting a striking parable in which a rich man comes to a woeful end for neglecting to use his riches on behalf of the beggar Lazarus (16:19-26). And two chapters later he shows Jesus presenting a serious challenge to a rich ruler by telling him that he cannot be a disciple unless he sells his possessions and distributes the money to the poor. It is at the end of this passage that the words occur, "How hard it is for those who have riches to enter the kingdom of God! For it is easier for a camel to go through the eye of a needle than for a rich man to enter the kingdom of God"(l8:18-25).

In several descriptions of events in Jesus' ministry, Luke does portray Jesus accepting hospitality from or cooperating with those who are rich, but there is virtually nothing in any of these descriptions that is inconsistent with the stance Luke has indicated in the passages just considered. The case of Zacchaeus, referred to in the preceding section, is a case which illustrates this point. In his description Luke shows Jesus actually seeking hospitality from Zacchaeus, but his initiative comes in the light of Zacchaeus' words that he will give half of his goods to the poor and restore fourfold to anyone he has defrauded (19:1-10). In Luke's account Zacchaeus thus marks a dramatic contrast with the rich ruler whose encounter with Jesus was described one chapter earlier in the narrative. For when that official heard Jesus' teaching about distributing his possessions to the poor, "he became sad, for he was very rich" (18:23).

D. Service and Humility

Luke indicates that Jesus was concerned to instruct the disciples with respect to service and humility at several junctures. A consideration of the passages in which these subjects are treated shows that Jesus provided negative as well as positive applications of these qualities, using as his reference points the practices of religious and political figures.

In both the ninth and twenty-second chapters, Luke indicates that disputes arose among the disciples as to which of them was the greatest. In the first instance Luke reports that Jesus took a child to his side and stated that the response which any of them gave to such a child was a measure of their greatness. He concluded this intervention with the words, "for he who is least among you all is the one who is great" (9:48b).

In the latter case (22:24–27), Luke describes a more extended response. First Jesus begins by criticizing "the kings of the Gentiles" for lording it over their subjects and appropriating for themselves the title "Benefactor." He then admonishes the disciples not to follow such an approach: "But not so with you; rather let the greatest among you become as the youngest and the leader as one who serves." He then concludes by adverting to the fact that he himself has continually been present to the disciples as a servant: "For which is the greater, one who sits at table, or one who serves? Is it not the one who sits at table? But I am among you as one who serves."

In these latter two passages Jesus' emphasis upon humility and service was in response to a quarrel over greatness. Luke also portrays Jesus upholding these qualities in other contexts as well. Positively, in 17:7–10, Jesus instructs the disciples regarding a dedicated service that does not require thanks. Indeed, those who render such authentic service should consider it no more than their duty.

Negatively, in 11:43 Luke reports Jesus' criticism of the Pharisees for seeking the best seats in the synagogues and salutations in the marketplaces. Jesus makes a similar criticism of the scribes in 20:45–47, citing them for the above practices, for wearing long robes and making long prayers for the sake of pretense, and for seeking the best seats at banquets.

This last type of behavior is also singled out by Jesus in one of the parables that Luke presents in chapter fourteen. Luke relates that Jesus told this parable (14:7–11) after he had observed guests choosing the places of honor at a banquet. This parable ends with words similar to those in one of Jesus' earlier admonitions to the disciples (see 9:48b): "For every one who exalts himself will be humbled, and he who humbles himself will be exalted." The later parable of the Pharisee and tax collector (18:9–14) concludes with almost these same exact words and, in the parable proper, the Pharisee's self-righteousness is scored and the humility of the tax collector is praised.

E. Opposition to Injustice and Corruption

With respect to the subject area of injustice and corruption, Luke reports that Jesus twice made sympathetic reference to the plight of widows trying to secure justice. In addition to citing the scribes for the failings delineated above, Jesus also censured them as a group "who devour[s] widows' houses" (20:47).

The other reference to widows' justice comes in the context of the parable that Luke recounts in 18:1–5. The parable is primarily told for the purpose of encouraging steadfastness in prayer. However, the image Jesus utilizes is that of a widow who finally secures justice from an unjust judge as a result of her perseverance.

With respect to other forms of injustice and corruption present in the society of Jesus' day, a careful reading of Luke's account reveals that Jesus' most vigorous interventions were made against the abuses taking place at the Jerusalem temple and against the Jerusalem chief priests in particular.

Further reflections on Jesus' "protest" at the temple and his ringing attack upon the chief priests will be presented in the concluding section of this chapter. At this point it is sufficient to note that it was anger over economic corruption that provided the impetus for Jesus' dramatic intervention. As Luke describes the scene (19:45–46), Jesus' fiery words were: "It is written, 'My house shall be a house of prayer'; but you have made it a den of robbers."

The term "den of robbers" carries with it the meaning that the dishonest and corrupt practices of "robbers" were taking place on a significant scale at the temple. The fact that Luke describes Jesus actually driving out "those who sold" while he made this charge further contributes to the impression that Jesus' intervention was vigorous and filled with emotion.

The same two qualities also describe the character of Jesus' response when Luke shows him controverting with the chief priests in two of the following scenes (20:1–19). After effectively countering the chief priests' challenge to his authority, Jesus continued on to tell a forceful parable identifying the chief priests and their allies as "wicked tenants" who had violated the trust which had been placed in them.

Luke reports that the chief priests were not slow to grasp that Jesus had mounted a serious attack upon them and their practices. He concludes his account of Jesus' parable by stating: "The scribes and the chief priests tried to lay hands on him at that very hour, but they feared the people; for they perceived that he had told this parable against them" (20:19).

F. Rejection of Violence against Persons

Taken together Luke's report of Jesus' conduct at the temple and his report of Jesus' verbal attack upon the chief priests provide a picture of someone capable of vigorous, forceful intervention. Yet as assertive and even intimidating a figure as these descriptions make Jesus out to be, Luke does not portray him as engaging in or sanctioning physical violence against persons. It is important to underscore this point.

In addition to these two passages, there are two other passages in Luke's Gospel which are sometimes cited in support of the interpretation that Jesus envisioned or condoned violence. The first such passage is 12:49–53 where Jesus tells the disciples that he has come to cast fire upon the earth and that grave divisions, even within families, will result. Here the distinction between controversial teachings which give rise to heated controversy and actual support for the use of violence should be kept in mind.

The well-known passage of Luke 22:35–38 in which the disciples bring forth two swords in response to Jesus' admonition, "And let him who has no sword sell his mantle and buy one," also has been misinterpreted as indicating support for violence. This particular passage is treated at length in *Jesus, Politics, and Society,* and the conclusion reached there is that Luke has portrayed the disciples so misunderstanding the symbolic sense of Jesus' words that they literally, and mistakenly, produce two swords.

Luke relates that in response to the disciples' misinterpretation, Jesus stated "It is enough," thereby abruptly ending his effort to provide them with counsel about the dangers that were imminent. Luke then narrates a sequence of words and events that are extremely important for an appreciation of Luke's Jesus as a figure of nonviolence:

> While he was still speaking, there came a crowd, and the man called Judas, one of the twelve, was leading them. He drew near to Jesus to kiss him; but Jesus said to him, "Judas, would you betray the Son of man with a kiss?" And when those who were about him saw what would follow, they said, "Lord, shall we strike with the sword?" And one of them struck the slave of the high priest and cut off his right ear. But Jesus said, "No more of this." And he touched his ear and healed him [22:47–51].

Clearly this passage indicates not only a rejection of a defensive use of the sword but also an immediate direct effort to heal the consequences of a sword's use. In Luke's account it is this passage, along with Jesus' words from the cross, "Father, forgive them; for they know not what they do" (23:34), that best identify Jesus as a figure who lives out in his own personal practice the teachings of forgiveness and love, even of enemies.

The teachings, "But I say to you that hear, Love your enemies, do good to those who hate you, bless those who curse you, pray for those who abuse you" (6:27–28) and "If your brother sins, rebuke him, and if he repents, forgive him; and if he sins against you seven times in the day, and turns to you seven times, and says, 'I repent,' you must forgive him" (17:3–4), had been given by Luke's Jesus earlier in the Gospel. Now, in the final days of his ministry, Luke shows Jesus observing these teachings to the limit.

An additional point regarding Luke's portrait of Jesus as one who rejected the use of violence is that Luke does present Jesus as fully cognizant of the violent practices present in the society around him. According to Luke's account Jesus was aware of the violence that his cousin John the Baptist had undergone at the hands of Herod Antipas (9:7–9,19). And in 13:1–3 he is informed of a massacre of Galileans by the governor Pilate. On the other end of the political spectrum, Luke's note that Jesus selected Simon, a member of the Zealot party, as one of the apostles (6:15) also suggests that Jesus was familiar with the program of the Zealots for armed insurrection against Roman rule.

The portrait of Jesus which emerges from Luke's various reports is thus that of someone who knew of the various forms of violence utilized by others. Yet at the same time, it is also the portrait of someone who heralded a response to the enemy accomplished without violence.

G. Prayer and the Sovereignty of God

On the occasion of his baptism (3:21), many times during his public ministry (5:16; 6:12; 9:18; 9:28–29; 11:1; 22:32; 22:41–42), and at the time of his death on the cross (23:34; 23:46), Luke portrays Jesus deeply engaged in personal prayer. In addition, Luke also relates that, on more than one occasion, Jesus encouraged the disciples to pray (11:5–8; 18:1–8; 22:40,46) and that, in response to the disciples' request for instruction in prayer, he gave them "the Lord's prayer" as a model (11:1–4).

These instances of prayer and encouragement in prayer all testify to the fact that the Jesus of Luke's Gospel was convinced that all of life and all of life's activities, including his own, were dependent upon God.

Early in the Gospel, in describing the visit of Mary, Joseph, and the young Jesus to Jerusalem, Luke portrays Jesus stating that he must be in his Father's house (2:49). Subsequently, in describing Jesus' baptism, Luke indicates that the Holy Spirit descended upon Jesus and that a heavenly voice spoke the words, "Thou are my beloved Son . . ." (3:22). By such indications Luke's narrative emphasizes at the outset that his relationship with God will be the foundation of Jesus' life and ministry. The many subsequent descriptions which Luke provides of Jesus in prayer further illustrate and testify to the powerful influence of this relationship upon Jesus.

The numerous instances in which "the kingdom of God" is a reference point for Jesus' ministry in Luke serve to strengthen the impression that Jesus believes in and operates in terms of God's concerns. Luke frequently portrays Jesus describing what the kingdom of God is like and how it arrives. Indeed, the kingdom of God is the concept that Luke's Jesus uses in describing the central thrust of his ministry (4:43; 9:60; 16:16; 22:16,18).

In addition to praying to God frequently and describing his activities with reference to God's kingdom, the Jesus of Luke's Gospel also appeals to the gracious behavior of God when exhorting his hearers to embrace some of the difficult standards to which he is calling them.

The first example of such an appeal occurs in 6:35–36 where Jesus encourages the love of enemies on the grounds that such conduct is an appropriate imitation of a God who is kind to those who do not themselves show kindness. A similar example can be found in 12:22–31. There Jesus instructs the disciples not to be anxious regarding material possessions because the God who provides for the needs of the lilies of the fields and the birds of the air will surely provide the disciples with what is necessary.

The foregoing considerations regarding Luke's presentations of Jesus praying to God and making reference to the kingdom of God serve as an effective bridge to an analysis of Luke's presentation of Jesus' interactions with various political authorities. For in presenting him in prayer to God and engaged in activities pertaining to the kingdom of God, Luke has portrayed Jesus as consistently expressing an appreciation for God's sovereignty. This same appreciation for God's sovereignty is also a critical factor in one of the principal political issues that Luke describes Jesus facing, i.e., the issue of Roman taxes (20:20–26).

As argued at length in *Jesus, Politics, and Society,* Luke's account of Jesus' dialogue with the spies who were sent to entrap him does not reveal whether or not Jesus himself actually paid Roman taxes. Nor does it reveal him taking a definite position on whether it was right for other Jews to pay these taxes. Rather the force of Jesus' reply, "Then render to Caesar the things that are Caesar's and to God the things that are God's" (20:25), was to bring those present into reflection and dialogue regarding "the things of Caesar" and "the things of God."

What things does Caesar have in his own right? What things does Caesar control that do not ultimately belong to God? For Jesus in Luke's Gospel are not the "things of God" such things as a concern for the infirm and the poor, the spirit of service and humility, the incorporation of those with lesser status into the life of the community, the sharing of material possessions, and the rejection of violence?

In effect the thrust of Jesus' answer in Luke is to imply that there is a prior question which must be answered before the question of paying tribute can be properly assessed. How adequately and how effectively are the "things of God" being adverted to and being fostered in the "things" for which Caesar has a degree of responsibility? That is the question which must be answered first. In effect, Jesus' reply, as Luke presents it, is calling for an evaluation of Caesar's stewardship in terms of the things of God.

In terms of the political alignments of the day, such a position with respect to Roman taxes would not have been satisfactory to the Zealots. Clearly, for the members of that movement, the only desirable answer would have been to oppose unambiguously any further payment of taxes to the Roman oppressors.

It also should be emphasized that the answer which Luke reports was far from acceptable to the Romans. The Romans were not interested in reflective dialogue about whether the things of Caesar were consistent with, and serving, the concerns of God. The Romans operated in Palestine in terms of the sovereignty of Rome, and they regarded the regular and prompt payment of taxes as standard procedure. For them a dialogue to assess Rome's "things" in the light of God's was a proposal for disloyal and potentially dangerous talk.

While considerations about the sovereignty of God are not as explicitly present in the three other Lukan passages in which Jesus has contact with or reference to the political authorities, the issue of allegiance is present to a remarkable degree in all three of them. In one instance the allegiance described is Jesus' allegiance to his own appointed course despite possible action against his life. In the second, the disciples' allegiance to Jesus' name will result in their persecution. In the third, the disciples must retain their allegiance to Jesus' model of service and not be influenced by the model of those political figures who function in terms of domination.

The first principal passage in which the issue of allegiance is present occurs in Luke's thirteenth chapter. The entire passage reads as follows:

> At that very hour some Pharisees came, and said to him, "Get away from here, for Herod wants to kill you." And he said to them, "Go and tell that fox, 'Behold, I cast out demons and perform cures today and tomorrow, and the third day I finish my course. Nevertheless I must go on my way today and tomorrow and the day following; for it cannot be that a prophet should perish away from Jerusalem' " [13:31–33].

By including such a report within his narrative, Luke alerts his readers to the fact that Jesus does not attach undue emphasis to the concerns and the directives of the existing political authorities. Herod Antipas is the Roman-appointed ruler for Galilee and, in the Roman ordering of things, his negative attitude toward Jesus would be a factor to be taken seriously. Yet, as Luke presents it, Jesus' reply is far from subservient and conciliatory. Indeed the sobriquet "fox" carries with it an unmistakable note of deprecation and scorn.

The concept of maintaining allegiance to one's course despite persecution by the political authorities is also present in Jesus' words to the disciples in Luke's twenty-first chapter. Jesus is addressing them concerning a time of great upheavals (21:12–15) and he indicates that they can expect to be handed over to "synagogues and prisons" and brought before "kings and governors." When this happens they are not to waver or become fearful about their witness to Jesus' name. Rather they are to stand firm in their testimony and Jesus himself will give them a wisdom which none of their adversaries will be able to withstand.

A passage which has already been referred to in a previous section also speaks to the present subject of allegiance. In words which Luke records in 22:24–27, Jesus indicates to the disciples that they must not be influenced by the existence of a domination-oriented approach in the world around them. For such is the approach practiced by the "kings of the Gentiles" and those rulers who adopt the title "Benefactor."

In showing him trying to keep the disciples from being seduced by a "domination model" of behavior, Luke once again portrays a Jesus whose own approach is not influenced by the practices of the political rulers around him.

The series of responses which Luke portrays Jesus making at the time of his trials also serves to indicate that Jesus does not automatically defer to the political rulers appointed by the emperor or to the procedures they were accustomed to follow. Luke portrays Jesus on trial before the Jewish Sanhedrin, before the governor, Pilate, and before Herod Antipas. He shows Jesus making slightly different responses within each of these settings; but at no time do his descriptions depict Jesus taking any particular account of the high offices held by those who interrogated and judged him.

In describing the trial which took place before the Sanhedrin, Luke shows Jesus giving two antagonistic responses to his interrogators' questions:

> And they said, "If you are the Christ, tell us." But he said to them, "If I tell you, you will not believe; and if I ask you, you will not answer. But from now on the Son of man shall be seated at the right hand of the power of God." And they all said, "Are you the Son of God, then?" And he said to them, "You say that I am" [22:66b–70].

In describing the first part of the trial before Pilate, Luke reports that, after Pilate heard the three charges brought by the members of the Sanhedrin, he asked Jesus a single question: "Are you the King of the Jews?" (23:3). Though Pilate held supreme power of life and death, Jesus' reply was terse and non-deferential: "You have said so" (23:3).

As Luke describes the scene before Herod Antipas, Jesus was even less cooperative: "So he questioned him at some length; but he made no answer" (23:9).

In describing the remainder of the trial before Pilate, Luke does not indicate that Pilate asked Jesus any further questions. Nor does he indicate that Jesus volunteered any comments to Pilate or any of the others who were present. Keeping in mind that a fuller analysis of Luke's reports of Jesus' arrest, trial, and execution will be given below, it is sufficient here merely to note that, especially in the trials before Pilate and Herod Antipas, Jesus' participation was minimal. He answered tersely and noncommittally to Pilate's single question and to Herod's questions he answered not at all.

It is thus the case that, in describing Jesus' responses and teachings regarding the existing political authorities, Luke puts forward the portrait of someone who is concerned with identifying and preferring the "things of God." Jesus is in general far from awed with the various political rulers and on one occasion he is openly disdainful toward Herod Antipas. He is not overtly antagonistic toward the Roman governor or toward Roman taxes; but, on the other hand, there is nothing in his approach that signals subservience. In regard to the chief priests and their allies on the Sanhedrin, Luke's reports portray Jesus as highly critical of them. It will be indicated below that the result of this criticism was death on a Roman cross.

2. THE NATURE OF THE CONFLICT BETWEEN LUKE'S JESUS AND THE ROMAN ORDER

The outcome of Jesus' death on a Roman cross is a stark reality confronting anyone seeking to assess the impact of Jesus' ministry. Did Jesus directly challenge the Roman presence in Judea? Did he present such a danger to Roman rule that, in order to safeguard Rome's interests, the governor had to order his execution? Questions of this kind emerge when an effort is made to explain how Jesus' life came to an end in crucifixion.

A. The Character of Roman Rule

Before seeking to investigate what light Luke's account sheds upon these matters, it is desirable to present a few brief considerations regarding the character of the order that the Romans sought to achieve in their provinces.

The Romans were above all concerned to achieve stability within their territories and to maintain secure borders. These features of stability and security were the conditions for two other related objectives. That the people of the provinces would make regular payment of a large number of taxes was a matter of fundamental importance to the Romans. They also desired to promote profitable trade exchanges between the provinces and Rome and to this end sought improved channels of transportation and communication.

In considering the impact of these objectives upon the provincial peoples, it should be borne in mind that the Roman provincial system was designed, in its origins and operations, for the benefit of the Roman conquerors. While the system did afford certain advantages and benefits to the peoples of the territories, it was not intentionally designed to promote their well-being. Rather, the system as a whole was premised upon the advantage of those who had prevailed, with any degree of benevolence to the vanquished as a by-product.

As a means of fulfilling their objectives within a particular province the Romans frequently enlisted the aid of indigenous leaders and leadership groups. In the furtherance of their aims the Romans were also prepared to grant the people of the conquered areas a considerable latitude in their social, economic, religious, and even political practices.

At the time of Jesus, the Roman arrangements for the area of Palestine relied primarily upon a Roman governor based in Jerusalem and Caesarea, and also provided a role for Herod Antipas as the tetrarch of Galilee. Similarly, the Romans accorded a considerable role to a high priest and to a Sanhedrin council in Jerusalem.

B. Points of Contact between Jesus and the Political Authorities

With respect to Jesus' contacts with Herod Antipas, Luke records two incidents, one of them relatively mild in its implications, the other more severe. At the beginning of his ninth chapter Luke indicates that reports of Jesus' activities in Galilee reached Herod. Particularly because some were suggesting to him that Jesus was John the Baptist or Elijah or a prophet, Herod was perplexed and wanted to see him personally (9:7–9).

Luke's second report involving Herod Antipas and Jesus has already been referred to above. It is the passage (13:31–33) in which some Pharisees report to Jesus that Herod is seeking to kill him. These Pharisees do not indicate what motives Herod now has for wanting Jesus dead, but Luke portrays Jesus taking their report seriously. However, until Jesus enters Jerusalem, there is nothing further in Luke's narrative regarding any additional contact between Jesus and Antipas.

It is thus the case that, despite some notes regarding Herod's attitude toward Jesus, Luke's Gospel does not indicate that Jesus' actual point of conflict with the Roman order occurred in his dealings with Herod Antipas. The same conclusion does not emerge from the reports that Luke provides concerning Jesus' conflict with the chief priests of Jerusalem.

As indicated above the high priest and the chief priests of Jerusalem played important roles in the Roman arrangements for the administration of Judea. They played these roles by reason of their influential positions at the Jerusalem temple and by reason of their standing as leading members of the Sanhedrin.

Under the Roman governors the Sanhedrin was recognized as a council possessing extensive jurisdiction in matters pertaining to Jewish law. Since these laws continued to have great influence upon ongoing Jewish life, the Sanhedrin's role was considerable. The Roman leadership also recognized the paramount importance of the Jerusalem temple in Jewish faith and life. One sign of this recognition was the extraordinary step taken by Augustus in allowing Jews throughout the empire to collect and transport an annual contribution for the upkeep of the temple.

If the Romans fostered their own objectives by tolerating the prerogatives of the temple and the Sanhedrin, they also enacted arrangements designed to prevent either of these centers of activity from becoming too autonomous. Their principal provision in this regard was to follow Herod the Great's practice of personally appointing priests to the office of high priest.

Since the high priest was the highest official at the temple as well as the president of the Sanhedrin, the Romans could hope to exercise a considerable influence upon the functioning of both institutions by virtue of a single appointment. Formerly the office of high priest was hereditary and lifelong. The Romans accepted neither of these traditions. During the time of the governors, a given priest only held the office of high priest for a period of a few years and the right to hold office could not be inherited.

It is also significant that, in their appointments to the office of high priest, the Romans did not select priests from the authentic Zadokite line. Instead they conferred the office upon various priests from four lesser priestly families. Again, such a policy reduced the likelihood of a situation in which, from the Roman point of view, too much power would be concentrated in the person of the high priest. That such an approach was greatly resented by a certain segment of the Jewish populace is seen from the fact that, upon their successful revolution in A.D. 66, the Zealots executed the reigning high priest and determined his successor by means of a lottery for which only Zadokite priests were eligible.

Given the fact that the priests whom the Romans appointed as high priests did not have hereditary title to the office, it might be thought that, owing their offices to the Roman governors, they would obsequiously seek to promote

Rome's interests. In actual practice, they frequently did conduct themselves in a manner that was supportive of Rome's general objectives. But not always. For, in gradually gaining control of the high offices of the temple and the Sanhedrin, the four families of chief priests seemingly acquired a secure base of power. And it can be seen that in practice they provided strong opposition to more than one Roman policy and proved to be formidable adversaries of more than one Roman governor.

It is an interesting feature of Luke's narrative that Jesus does not come to the attention of the high priest and the other chief priests until he has finished his Galilean ministry and traveled to Jerusalem. Earlier in the Gospel Luke has reported that the Pharisees, sometimes joined by their scribes, opposed Jesus for blaspheming (5:21), for associating with tax collectors and sinners (5:30; 15:2), for picking corn on the sabbath (6:2), for healing on the sabbath (6:7; 14:3), for not washing before a meal (11:38), and for his teaching about riches (16:14). Further, Luke indicates that on some of these occasions, Jesus responded with severe counter-criticisms and in 11:39-52 he portrays Jesus making a vigorous denunciation of the Pharisees and lawyers for their hypocritical and legalistic practices.

However, in all of these controversies with the Pharisees, no mention is made of any involvement by the chief priests. Indeed, were it not for the fact that Jesus had earlier expressed a prophecy that he would suffer at the hands of the priests and their allies (9:22), the reader of Luke's Gospel would be completely startled by the events that ensue when Jesus eventually enters Jerusalem and first comes into contact with the chief priests.

There is no difficulty in determining from Luke's account what it was that the chief priests found so abhorrent about Jesus. In contrast to what Luke describes as the reason for the opposition of the Pharisees and their scribes, the chief priests' opposition was engendered by the attack which Jesus made upon their administration of the temple and by his attack upon them personally as "wicked tenants." The passages in which these two incidents occur have been analyzed in a preceding section. What needs to be stressed here is that it was these two attacks which set in motion the chain of events that resulted in Jesus being denounced to the Roman governor.

The situation Luke describes is thus a fairly complex one. Jesus did not come to Pilate's attention for his teachings regarding concern for the poor, the sick, and other marginal groups, for his teachings on the use of material possessions, for his emphasis upon service and humility, for his allegiance to the "things of God," or for his teachings against the use of violence.

Nor was Jesus denounced to Pilate because the chief priests were particularly concerned about his teachings regarding the payment of taxes or his general attitude toward Roman rule. Rather, according to Luke, the reason why Jesus was brought to trial before Pilate lies in the attacks that he made upon the chief priests and their administration of the temple. According to Luke, it was these attacks which provided the actual point of conflict between Jesus and the Roman order in Judea.

In light of these considerations, it is now possible to respond to the questions that were initially posed at the beginning of this section. These questions addressed the issue of whether Jesus directly questioned the Roman presence in Judea or actively challenged the order that the Romans sought to maintain there. Luke's account is clear on both of these matters: while he did engage in heated controversy with the chief priests of Jerusalem, Jesus never directly challenged the Roman presence in Judea and the overall character of Roman rule there.

In stating such a conclusion it is important to emphasize that, while it is a correct response to the questions that were originally framed, this conclusion does not reflect the richness or the full meaning of what Luke has presented. For, in addition to indicating that Jesus did not directly confront the issue of Roman presence and the Roman system in Judea, Luke's account simultaneously indicates that there was the *potential* for such a confrontation.

The Jesus that Luke presented to his readers is thus a figure significantly at variance with the values and the patterns in terms of which the Romans built their empire. Luke's Jesus opts for the sick and the poor; the Romans rewarded the strong. Luke's Jesus stresses humility and service; the Romans took pride in their own superiority. Luke's Jesus stresses the sharing of surplus possessions; the Romans enacted oppressive taxes in order to increase their wealth. Luke's Jesus emphasizes the sovereignty of God; the Romans affirmed pagan gods and the persona of the emperor. Luke's Jesus rejects the use of the sword; the Romans built an empire based upon violence.

As indicated above Luke's account indicates his attack upon the chief priests was the *point of conflict* between Jesus and the Roman order. But Luke's descriptions also provide ample notice that a more extensive *basis for conflict* existed. Indeed, one of the great ironies of the story that Luke describes is that Pilate, the guardian and administrator of Roman rule for Judea, did not see anything in Jesus that was dangerous to Roman interests.

C. The Circumstances of Jesus' Death

> The chief priests and the scribes and the principal men of the people
> sought to destroy him; but they did not find anything they could do, for
> all the people hung upon his words [19:47b–48].

In the verses just cited, Luke describes the reaction of the chief priests and their allies to the protest that Jesus had just made at the Temple. Luke then portrays a somewhat complicated series of exchanges and events as the priests pursue their objective and finally secure Jesus' death.

In the verses which immediately follow (20:1–8), Luke indicates that the chief priests, scribes, and elders came up to Jesus and asked him to justify by what authority he had done these things. The sense of Luke's narrative at this point is that they are referring to Jesus' action of driving out from the temple those who sold and his charge that the temple had been made into a "den of robbers." Luke indicates that Jesus countered by asking them a question about John the Baptist's authority, a question they themselves would not answer.

It is at this juncture that Luke portrays Jesus renewing his attack. In this instance it comes by means of the stinging parable concerning "wicked tenants" (20:9–18). Luke then reports the following reaction: "The scribes and the chief priests tried to lay hands on him at that very hour, but they feared the people; for they perceived he had told this parable against them" (20:19).

Luke continues by stating that the chief priests and their allies then watched Jesus and sent spies to entrap him with the question concerning Roman taxes. They had a plan, Luke reports, to "take hold" of what Jesus might say and "deliver him up to the authority and jurisdiction of the governor" (20:20). This is the first time that mention is made of the priests' desire to have Jesus executed by Pilate, but it is this outcome that they ultimately achieve.

Not immediately, however. For Luke reports that they were not able to catch Jesus by the answer that he gave (20:26) and that Jesus also proved adept at parrying another entrapping question that was put to him by some Sadducees (20:27–40).

At this point Luke reports an interval in which Jesus proceeded to teach within Jerusalem and within the temple itself (20:41–21:38). However in 22:2 he reports that the priests had not, in fact, abandoned their plot: "Now the feast of Unleavened Bread drew near, which is called the Passover. And the chief priests and the scribes were seeking how to put him to death . . ." (22:1–2). Luke indicates that at this point the priests received help from an unexpected source: Satan having entered into him, Judas went to the chief priests and temple officers to discuss arrangements for betraying Jesus (22:3–4).

Luke indicates that the chief priests were glad to have Judas' help (22:5–6) and his description of Jesus' arrest suggests that they could not wait to apprehend him (22:47–53). After describing the arrest Luke then reports that Jesus was taken to the high priest's house (22:54) and that he was beaten and mocked while he was held there (22:63–65).

The fact that Jesus was then brought before the assembly of the Sanhedrin (22:66–71) has already been alluded to in a preceding section when it was emphasized that Luke portrayed Jesus responding combatively to the questions he was asked. Luke then reports that the whole company of those present took Jesus before Pilate and once there commenced to denounce him vigorously (23:1–2).

The charges that Luke portrays the chief priests pressing against Jesus were formulated in such a way that a governor charged with upholding Rome's interests in the province would consider them highly serious: "We found this man perverting our nation, and forbidding us to give tribute to Caesar, and saying that he himself is Christ a king" (23:2). These charges insinuated that Jesus was guilty of directly challenging Roman rule in Judea. However, as analyzed above, nothing in Luke's earlier descriptions ever portrayed Jesus as taking such an explicit anti-Roman approach.

As noted in the preceding section, there is no indication in Luke's Gospel that

Pilate ever heard of Jesus up until this point in the narrative. As Luke then reports the sequence of events, Pilate responded to the situation facing him by asking Jesus a question that would have had the effect of allowing Pilate to determine whether Jesus saw himself in conflict with Rome's rule. Pilate's question: "Are you the King of the Jews?" (23:3a). Jesus' answer: "You have said so" (23:3b). Pilate's assessment: "I find no crime in this man" (23:4).

In describing such a rapid process of interrogation and assessment, Luke does not indicate to his readers the basis on which Pilate reached his judgment that Jesus was innocent. Seemingly, the response that Luke portrays Jesus making would not have been particularly helpful to Pilate in his effort to assess the situation. There is, however, no ambiguity about the verdict that Luke portrays Pilate reaching: Jesus is not dangerous to the cause of Roman rule in Judea.

Up until this juncture, Luke has portrayed the chief priests steadfastly and diligently seeking Jesus' death. With Judas' help they have proceeded with their plan to hand Jesus over to the governor. They have held their own trial and formulated charges ideally suited to persuade Pilate that Jesus is dangerous. Now Pilate's surprising verdict has brought them up short. What course of action is now open to them? As Luke describes it, their response at this point is to refuse to accept Pilate's verdict:

> But they were urgent, saying, "He stirs up the people, teaching throughout all Judea, from Galilee even to this place" [23:5].

It is at this point that Luke narrates a sequence of events that may have proved disconcerting to any of his early readers who held an image of Roman governors as strong individuals, not easily manipulated. Luke first relates that Pilate decided to send Jesus to Herod Antipas. He reports that the basis for such a step was that Jesus was from Galilee; but, in reporting this decision, Luke seems also to indicate that the chief priests' bold challenge to his verdict has made an impact upon Pilate.

Luke indicates that the chief priests accompanied Jesus to Herod and that they were "vehemently accusing him" there (23:8–11). He describes the priests exerting similar pressure in the next scene when Jesus is back again before Pilate.

It was in this last session before Pilate that the priests finally succeeded in realizing their objective. Initially, Pilate continued to voice the opinion that Jesus was innocent and indicated his intention to release him (23:14–16). However, Luke shows that the chief priests then proceeded to orchestrate such an outcry for Jesus' death that Pilate, despite one final protestation regarding Jesus' innocence, finally acceded to their wishes (23:18–25).

It is a feature of Luke's account at this point that for several verses (23:26–31) it is not fully clear to the reader what specific arrangements Pilate has determined for Jesus' death. As the narrative unfolds, however, it gradually becomes apparent that the arrangements are crucifixion by Roman soldiers under the direction of a centurion. Luke indicates that this centurion was himself of the opinion that Jesus was innocent (23:47). Nevertheless, the death of Jesus, intensely desired by the chief priests and their allies, was finally achieved—crucifixion on a Roman cross, supervised by a Roman centurion acting on orders from a Roman governor.

The inscription attached to the cross (23:38) specified the grounds on which Pilate was ordering Jesus' crucifixion. The meaning of the words "The King of the Jews" was that Jesus had been found guilty of challenging Roman rule in Judea. The inscription alleged that Jesus had striven to be, or had made himself out to be, a ruler of the Jews in opposition to Caesar. Under Roman rule such activity was treasonous and punishable by death.

In terms of Luke's account the outcome of Jesus' trial before Pilate can be summarized in the following way. Pilate did not believe the chief priests' charges that Jesus was guilty of challenging Roman rule and his inclination was to release him. However, the chief priests, for their part, refused to accept such an outcome and kept pressuring Pilate for a death verdict. Pilate gradually and reluctantly bowed to their pressure and, in the end, he ordered Jesus' execution. To provide formal justification for this step, Pilate turned 180 degrees from his original assessment and asserted that Jesus was, in fact, dangerous to Roman rule in Judea. Thus, although he seemed to believe to the end that Jesus was innocent, Pilate agreed to execute him on the basis provided by the charges that the chief priests had formulated against him.

2

The Social Stance of the Apostles and the Jerusalem Community

The purpose of the present chapter and those which follow is to analyze Luke's reports concerning the social and political stance adopted by the first disciples in carrying forward as witnesses of Jesus. What were the leading elements in the social and political stance of Jesus' disciples as they began to give witness to him? To what degree do Luke's accounts indicate correspondence between the disciples' social and political stance and that of Jesus? These and related questions will be investigated in light of the analysis made in the preceding chapter and in light of the descriptions that Luke has provided in Acts, his second volume.

Inasmuch as the first chapters of Acts describe in some detail the life of the community of disciples at Jerusalem as well as many initiatives undertaken by Peter and the apostles, it is appropriate that the social and political stance of the members of this group be examined first.[1] Subsequent chapters will focus upon the social and political stance of Paul, the figure who dominates the second half of Acts.

1. THE SOVEREIGNTY OF GOD AND PRAYER

In describing the life of the Jerusalem community in the early chapters of Acts, Luke provides many indications that the apostles and the other disciples were extremely conscious of God's sovereign power. It is almost a commonplace to state that Luke shows them to have been greatly influenced by their experience of the risen Jesus and constant in their proclamation that it was by God's power that Jesus was raised. Secondly, Luke also portrays the disciples experiencing God's power in the healings and miracles that attended their own ministry. Thirdly, in reporting their many forms and occasions of prayer, he again shows them acknowledging the greatness and power of God.

In passages at the end of the Gospel as well as at the beginning of Acts, Luke indicates that the disciples' faith in the risen Jesus was strengthened by a number of appearances. In his description at the end of the Gospel, he portrays

21

the apostles initially refusing to believe the testimony of Mary Magdalene and the other women that Jesus had been raised (24:10–11). However, subsequently, as a result of Jesus' appearance to the disciples on the road to Emmaus (24:13–32) and to Peter (24:34), the eleven and those with them came to believe. Luke then describes how Jesus appeared to this entire group in a startling fashion and how he instructed them and designated them as his witnesses before being lifted from their sight (24:36–53).

Similarly, at the beginning of Acts, Luke relates that the risen Jesus appeared to the apostles and instructed them over a period of forty days prior to his ascension (1:3–11). After reporting the selection of Matthias as Judas' successor (1:12–26), he then describes the events of Pentecost, indicating that the Holy Spirit came down powerfully upon those who were assembled (2:1–4).

It was only after this powerful experience of the Holy Spirit that Peter and the others began to proclaim the resurrection (2:14–36). However, Luke's narrative shows that once they began to give testimony, they did so with great conviction. Luke reports that, in his initial speech on Pentecost, Peter twice proclaimed that Jesus had been raised by God's power and he shows him making a similar proclamation in three other instances in the early chapters of Acts (3:12–26; 4:8–12; 5:29–33). Later, in chapter seven, Luke also shows Stephen testifying to the risen Lord, indicating that, by a vision, he could see Jesus present at God's right hand (7:56).

In terms of what they reveal regarding Peter and the disciples' appreciation for the sovereignty of God, the passages just noted are extremely important. For clearly, one significant implication of the bold proclamations that God has intervened to raise Jesus to new life is that those making them have a deep appreciation for the sovereignty of God.

According to Luke's account, the power and sovereignty of God were also a part of the Jerusalem community's experience as a consequence of the many wondrous signs that occurred around and through the apostles.[2]

In 2:43 Luke states that many miracles and signs were done through the apostles and in 3:2–11, he describes how a man who was a cripple from birth was healed by Peter "in the name of Jesus Christ of Nazareth." Subsequently in 5:12–16 he indicates again that many signs and wonders were done among the people at the hands of the apostles and relates that the sick were even carried into the streets so that at least Peter's shadow might fall upon them. Still another healing by Peter, this time a cure of a man paralyzed eight years, is recorded in 9:32–35.

In addition to the just mentioned healings involving Peter, Luke indicates that Stephen also accomplished miracles and great works among the people of Jerusalem (6:8). Similarly, he also reports that Philip, another of the seven, worked a number of miracles in Samaria, including the cures of several paralytics and cripples (8:4–8). Peter is, however, in this part of Acts, the person through whom and around whom God's power is focused. Luke reports that he was the one who passed judgment on both Ananias and Sapphira before they fell instantly dead (5:1–11) and his role as a conduit of God's power was even more dramatically manifested when he prayed and successfully raised Tabitha to life (9:36–42).

Finally, Luke provides two other notices concerning God's sovereign power when he describes two interventions by an angel of the Lord, first to deliver all of the apostles from prison and later Peter alone. In the first deliverance the angel opens the prison gates and instructs the apostles to go and teach in the temple (5:19–21). In the second, the angel frees Peter from the chains binding him to his guards and takes him past two guard posts and the prison gates to freedom (12:6–11).

The references to prayer in the early chapters of Acts also testify to the disciples' appreciation of God's sovereignty. Luke indicates that, after Jesus' ascension but prior to Pentecost, the apostles and those with them in the upper room joined continuously in prayer (1:14). He also indicates that Peter and the larger group of disciples prayed to the Lord for guidance in determining a successor for Judas (1:24).

In describing the life of the Jerusalem community after Pentecost, Luke provides several notices regarding the members' dedication to prayer. In 2:42 he states that those who were converted on Pentecost remained faithful to "the prayers" and in 2:47 he indicates that they were frequently "praising God." In a subsequent circumstantial note he also indicates that Peter and John sometimes went to the temple for prayer at the ninth hour (3:1).

A striking example of the larger community at prayer is given in 4:24–30. According to Luke's report Peter and John were interrogated by the chief priests and then released. After they rejoined the community, the entire group prayed exuberantly and spontaneously, thanking God and praising the fulfillment of God's plan in Jesus. In describing the atmosphere of the situation, Luke relates that "when they had prayed, the place in which they were gathered together was shaken; and they were all filled with the Holy Spirit and spoke the word of God with boldness" (4:31).

Two other indications of the place of prayer in the ongoing life of the community are provided when Luke describes the steps that the twelve took in arranging for seven others to assume a leadership role within the community. In their speech before the entire community the twelve indicated that they would continue to devote themselves to prayer (6:4). Then, after those present had chosen Stephen and the others to fulfill this role, the apostles prayed over them as they laid their hands upon them (6:6).

Finally there are three additional notes regarding prayer in the chapters before Paul becomes the central figure of Acts. Luke reports that, when Peter and John were sent to Samaria in response to Philip's witness there, they prayed for the Samaritans to receive the Holy Spirit (8:15). In the same context Luke also shows Peter upbraiding Simon for his efforts to purchase the power of the apostles; Peter tells him that he must repent and pray to the Lord for forgiveness (8:22). Finally, Luke also indicates that, at the time when Peter was imprisoned by King Herod, the members of the church prayed for him unceasingly (12:1–5,12).

2. CONCERN FOR THE SICK AND THE POOR

In the preceding section Luke's reports regarding Peter's healing of a man crippled from birth (3:2–11) and his cure of a man paralyzed eight years (9:32–35) were noted. Mention was also made of the passage indicating that the sick were carried into the streets so that at least Peter's shadow might fall on them (5:15). It should now be noted that Luke ends his description of this latter practice with the following statement: "The people also gathered from the towns around Jerusalem, bringing the sick and those afflicted with unclean spirits, and they were all healed" (5:16).

Taking account also of the report that Philip healed many in Samaria who were paralyzed and lame (8:7), it can easily be seen that Luke portrays the members of the Jerusalem community directing a considerable amount of their attention and their ministry toward those who were sick or in some way infirm. It is thus the case that there is substantial continuity between Jesus' approach to the sick, as Luke describes it in the Gospel, and the approach followed by Peter and others in the Jerusalem community as Luke portrays their approach in Acts.

Given the analysis that Luke's descriptions show substantial continuity between Jesus' approach and that of the Jerusalem community with respect to such areas as the sovereignty of God, prayer, and ministry to the sick, it is noteworthy that Luke does not indicate such continuity with respect to concern for the poor.

Indeed a surprising fact is that the Greek word for the poor, *ptōchos*, does not appear at all within the text of Acts. Inasmuch as the Gospel has portrayed Jesus using this term nine times (and also responding favorably when Zacchaeus indicates that he will give half of his goods to the poor), the absence of this term in Acts is somewhat startling.[3]

The closest that Luke comes to describing a concern for the poor is in 4:34 when, in describing the sharing of the Jerusalem community, he states that "there was not a needy person among them." Part of the difficulty in rendering Luke's exact meaning in this passage arises from his use of the term *endeēs*. Strictly speaking this word has the meaning of "in want" or "in need,"[4] and presumably this is the reason that the translators of the RSV have settled upon the word "needy" in their translation. Nevertheless if the passage is understood to refer to material wants and needs, there is a basis for concluding that, without using the term *ptōchos*, Luke still wished to indicate that no members of the Jerusalem community were living in circumstances of economic want.

However, as a part of the effort to respect the nuances in the description that Luke has given here, attention should also be given to what he has and has not indicated. He has not stated that the members of the community were making contributions to the poor, nor has he stated that they were inviting the poor to share in the community's activities (two of the teachings that he attributed to

Jesus in the Gospel). In contrast, he has simply stated that *within the community,* arrangements were enacted so that no one of the members was in need or in economic want.

3. THE USE OF MATERIAL POSSESSIONS

In the early chapters of Acts, Luke portrays Peter responding to three different situations in which money is a factor, and it is significant that he is not favorably disposed toward money or its uses in any of these cases.

It is perhaps not surprising that, in the comment Luke shows him making regarding Judas (1:15-20), Peter expresses a disdain for Judas' behavior. This disdain is primarily focused upon Judas' betrayal, but it also extends to Judas' conduct in seeking to use the money of betrayal for his own profit. Peter relates that Judas bought a field "with the reward of his wickedness," adding immediately that Judas thereupon fell headlong into it (presumably from a roof), spilling his bowels and his blood upon it.[5]

The second instance in which Luke presents Peter making a comment regarding money occurs in 3:1-9, a passage primarily concerned with the healing of a crippled man. This man was positioned at the gate of the Temple to ask for alms. Peter's initial response to the situation was to tell the man: "I have no silver and gold . . ." (3:6). However, he then indicates that he will give the man something far more valuable, healing in the name of Jesus.

Another aspect of the power that Peter and the apostles possessed is also involved in the dispute which Peter subsequently engages in with Simon Magus. Luke states that when Simon saw that the Holy Spirit was given through the laying on of the apostles' hands, he offered them money to purchase this power (8:18-19). According to Luke Peter's response was to upbraid him sharply: "Your silver perish with you, because you thought you could obtain the gift of God with money!" (8:20).

By way of synthesis, it can be stated that, at least to some extent, the three foregoing passages serve to indicate that, within the early chapters of Acts, there is a certain skepticism about the purposes for which silver and gold might be useful. In addition, Luke also provides six other passages which shed light on a related issue, the disposition of resources already possessed. Four of these passages pertain to the practice of holding such resources in common. The fifth regards the practice of a daily "ministry" within the community and the sixth describes how the community at Antioch sent famine relief to the disciples who lived in Judea.

The two passages in which Luke describes the Jerusalem Christians' practice of a "community of goods" occur respectively in chapters two and four:[6]

And all who believed were together and had all things in common; and they sold their possessions and goods and distributed them to all, as any had need [2:44-45].

Now the company of those who believed were of one heart and soul, and no one said that any of the things which he possessed was his own, but they had everything in common. . . . There was not a needy person among them, for as many as were possessors of lands or houses sold them, and brought the proceeds of what was sold and laid it at the apostles' feet; and distribution was made to each as any had need [4:32, 34–35].

A close analysis of the passage from chapter two indicates that Luke describes the community's practice in terms of three elements. First, he states that the members of the community held all things in common. Secondly, they sold their possessions and goods. Thirdly, a distribution was made to any needy in the community.

Each of these elements is also present in the description that Luke gives in chapter four. Each is, however, described in a slightly different way.[7] In the second passage Luke repeats his earlier statement that the community members had all things in common, but also includes the amplifying note: "no one said that any of the things which he possessed was his own." He also indicates that the "possessors of lands or houses" sold these items. In contrast with the previous general report ("all who believed . . . sold their possessions and goods"), this second account is more precise.

Thirdly, while repeating that a distribution was made to the needy of the community, Luke now provides the additional note that this distribution took place after the proceeds were brought to the apostles.

Luke's latter summary also mentions one element not present in his first description. In chapter two he did not describe the situation which resulted from the community's adherence to these practices; however, in chapter four he clearly indicates the outcome. It was the outcome discussed in the preceding section, an outcome in which "there was not a needy person among them. . . ."

In the verses which follow upon the summary of chapter four, Luke narrates two incidents that, in contrasting ways, serve to accentuate the description of community life he has just provided. Luke first describes the actions taken by (Joseph) Barnabas. According to his description, Barnabas's conduct is a concrete illustration of the larger patterns which Luke has just summarized: "[Barnabas] sold a field which belonged to him, and brought the money and laid it at the apostles' feet" (4:37). It should be noted at this point that Barnabas, first mentioned by Luke in this passage, reappears in chapter nine to introduce Paul to the apostles and in chapter thirteen serves as Paul's companion on Paul's first great missionary journey.[8]

In contrast with Barnabas, Luke presents Ananias and Sapphira as much less loyal to the community's practices. According to his report in the verses which follow next (5:1–11), Ananias and Sapphira jointly sold a piece of property. However, instead of bringing the entire proceeds from the sale to the apostles, Ananias, with his wife's knowledge, held back some of the proceeds and only brought a part of what he had realized to the apostles.

In the vigorous response that Luke portrays him making first to Ananias and then to Sapphira, Peter heralds their duplicitous behavior not merely as a lie to the community but as a lie to the Holy Spirit and to God. He argues that they were not bound to sell their property and, that even upon selling it, they were not obligated to bring the money to the apostles.

However, because they tried to convey the impression that they were adhering to the community's practices regarding possessions while in reality they were not, their behavior had the effect of undermining these practices.[9] Indeed, part of the explanation for what they have done is that Satan had filled Ananias' heart and influenced him to do it. Although Peter's comments within this passage have a certain elliptical character to them, such a reconstruction seems to reflect the nuances and the inferences of what Luke has presented.

Based upon this and the preceding passages, the overall sense of Luke's account is that a "community of goods" under the auspices of the apostles was widespread within the Jerusalem community. However, it is worth noting that Peter's comments in this passage suggest that the practice of disposing of one's possessions was voluntary and not strictly or immediately mandated. If this is indeed the sense that Luke wishes to convey here, then his later passing notice that Peter went to the house of John Mark's mother when he was miraculously freed from prison (12:12) should not be regarded as being inconsistent with his general portrayal of the community's practice.[10]

The next passage in Acts in which reference is made to the allocation of resources within the Jerusalem community occurs in chapter six during the course of Luke's report about the appointment of the seven, a group that included Stephen and Philip.

When Luke's description of how and why the seven were appointed is analyzed, the assumption is usually made that they were to have responsibility for overseeing a daily distribution of food. And indeed, Luke does make it clear that controversy had arisen because of a charge that the Greek-speaking widows had been neglected in some such daily activity.

It may well be the case that Luke does wish to indicate that a breakdown in a daily distribution of food was the source of the controversy. However, it should not be ruled out that he actually wished to indicate that the breakdown had occurred in some other type of daily ministry. To a considerable degree, the interpretation hinges on his use of the word *diakonia* in verse 6:1. In this verse the RSV translates *diakonia* as "distribution" but the more usual translation for this term is "ministry."[11]

Regardless of how *diakonia* is best translated and understood, what is incontrovertible about the present passage is that Luke is providing still another note about the attitude of commonality which existed within the Jerusalem community. Whether he is implying that this commonality pertained to the sharing of food or some other form of daily sharing, it is clear that he is describing a practice which is consistent with the portrayal that he has made in other passages concerning the Jerusalem community's attitude toward sharing. In this instance, while the apostles cannot personally remedy the problem which has developed, they propose the appointment of the seven as a means of alleviating the situation.

The final passage bearing upon the Jerusalem community's use of its material resources occurs in 11:28–30. There Luke states that, because of a famine that took place during the reign of Claudius, the disciples in Antioch sent "relief" (*diakonian*) to the members who were living in Judea. Luke further indicates that the Antiochian disciples contributed according to the level of their prosperity and that they sent their contributions to the Jerusalem elders in care of Barnabas and Paul.

A somewhat surprising feature of this passage is Luke's statement that the disciples sent their contributions to the "elders." Since it becomes clear that he is referring to the "elders" in Jerusalem, Luke's readers may well be led to ask why the contribution was not remanded to the apostles or to the seven. For, up until this time, Luke has not mentioned any other leadership group within the Jerusalem community. Indeed, while Paul and Barnabas are in Jerusalem completing this assignment, Luke's narrative actually focuses upon James and Peter and no mention is made of any group of "elders." Subsequently, Luke reports that Paul and Barnabas completed their mission and returned to Antioch (12:25). There is no further mention of any elders in Jerusalem until chapter fifteen when Barnabas and Paul's *second* trip to Jerusalem is narrated.[12]

Another aspect of this passage that has proved troubling to many commentators is the fact that Luke's description of the process for raising these contributions does not seem to correspond well with the descriptions that Paul gives in his own writings concerning his personal efforts to raise support for the Jerusalem church. According to 1 Corinthians 16:1–4, 2 Corinthians 8–9, and Romans 15:25–33, Paul himself was deeply involved in encouraging and supervising a collection on behalf of the Jerusalem community. These accounts seem to clash with Luke's description of a seemingly spontaneous effort by the Antiochian disciples, an undertaking in which Paul's main role (shared with Barnabas) was to carry the collection to Jerusalem.[13]

In previously published works, New Testament scholars have made extended analyses comparing the Acts collection passage with the relevant Pauline passages. Some have reached the conclusion that the two accounts can be reconciled, while a number of others hold that Luke's version inaccurately portrays the events in which Paul was actually involved.

As interesting as such analyses may be, they lie almost entirely outside the scope of the present study, a study concerned to understand carefully and precisely the descriptions that Luke has actually set forth in his writings. In contrast with other works drawing comparisons between what Luke has portrayed in Acts and Paul has described in his own writings, the present work does not seek to move beyond the boundaries of Luke's two volumes. And, indeed, within this boundary, it has the particular concern of analyzing those passages which portray the disciples' social and political outlook.

For similar reasons, only a brief comment can be made regarding the hypothesis which states that, historically, the Jerusalem disciples' practice of community goods resulted in a breakdown in economic life that necessitated Paul's collection.

Neither in the passages analyzed above nor in any other passages within Acts does Luke indicate that there was any causal connection between the practice of community of goods and the situation of the Judean disciples during the time of famine. While the narrative of Acts does indicate that the disciples in Judea suffered greater distress under the famine than those in Antioch, it does not in any way suggest that the distress they suffered was due to their practice of holding all things in common.

It is thus the case that studies which assert a "failure" or a "breakdown" in the Jerusalem community's economic practices are making assertions that go considerably beyond what Luke himself has presented.[14] It is indeed possible to theorize that the initial economic practices of the apostolic community in Jerusalem ended in failure. However, such is not the portrayal given by Luke within Acts; and, as a prelude for constructive theorizing, it is important that the viewpoint of Luke's narrative be carefully respected.

4. AFFIRMATION FOR OTHER LESS REGARDED GROUPS

As indicated in the preceding chapter, Luke's Gospel presents Jesus adopting a positive stance toward such less regarded groups as women, Samaritans, Gentiles, and tax collectors and sinners. Indeed, in some instances, the behavior of members of these groups is actually cited by Jesus as model conduct in terms of the kingdom of God.

Within Acts a somewhat different picture emerges. The first three groups— women, Samaritans, and Gentiles—all appear within the narrative; but, particularly in the latter two instances, the principal issue which Luke portrays the apostles and the other leaders of the Jerusalem community addressing is whether members of these groups are to have full standing as Christian disciples.

With respect to the fourth group, tax collectors and sinners, it is remarkable that no mention is made of any member of these groups throughout all of Acts. As noted above, Luke frequently portrayed Jesus in the company of tax collectors and sinners and, on more than one occasion, showed him affirming them for their humility and their willingness to seek repentance. Yet *telōnai* and *hamartōloi*—the Greek words for tax collectors and sinners—do not occur in the text of Acts and there are no descriptions of members of these groups in other terms.[15]

With respect to the situation of women in the early church, Luke indicates that, unlike the case of Samaritans and Gentiles, women were participating members right from the beginning. He reports that Mary, Jesus' mother, and other unnamed women were present with the eleven in the upper room following Jesus' ascension (1:14) and he also seems to indicate that women disciples experienced the outpouring of the Holy Spirit on Pentecost.[16] Later he reports that numbers of women as well as men became believers as the community grew in Jerusalem (5:14) and then in Samaria (8:12). And, in addition, the passage in chapter six in which the seven were appointed in response to the claim that Greek-speaking widows were being neglected also testifies to the presence of a significant number of women members.

Still more testimony to the integral presence of women within the early communities emerges from Luke's reports that Paul was concerned to arrest Christian women as well as men when he was persecuting the church. In 8:3, in a reference to Paul's activities in Jerusalem, Luke states that he dragged off both men and women and committed them to prison. Then in 9:1-2 Luke relates that Paul asked the high priest for letters to the synagogues at Damascus "so that if he found any belonging to the Way, men or women, he might bring them bound to Jerusalem."

Luke's extended report concerning the death and raising to life of Tabitha, a Christian disciple at Jaffa, also testifies to the impact of women upon the early Christian communities.[17] Luke states that "she was full of good works and acts of charity" (9:36) and indicates that, at her death, she was greatly mourned by all of the disciples including many widows for whom she had provided.

Indeed, so great was their grief that, upon learning that Peter was in the area, they sent for him. Luke then describes how Peter raised Tabitha back to life and presented her to those who had been mourning. This is the first instance of such an event narrated within Acts.

According to chapter eight of Acts, the gospel was first preached to the Samaritans in the time of upheaval which followed Stephen's martyrdom and Paul's persecutions. Luke indicates that Philip, one of the seven, was among those who left Jerusalem and that he went to a Samaritan city and began preaching to the inhabitants (8:5).

Mighty works accompanied Philip's preaching and Luke narrates that many Samaritans accepted baptism from him (8:12). Hearing of this, the apostles sent Peter and John to Samaria and Luke indicates that, as a consequence of the prayers of the two apostles, the Samaritans received the Holy Spirit (8:15-17).

Since Luke then reports that Peter and John preached the gospel to many other villages of Samaritans on their way back to Jerusalem (8:25), Luke's readers easily gain the impression that large numbers of Samaritans were becoming members of the Christian way. This impression is subsequently confirmed by Luke's report in 9:31 concerning the growth of the church. There, without any intimation that the Samaritans are in any way lesser members, Luke relates that the church "throughout all Judea and Galilee and Samaria had peace and was built up."[18]

With respect to the process by which Gentiles became members of the Christian way, the account in Acts is both more extended and more nuanced than in the instance of the Samaritans. Within chapters eight, nine, and ten, it is possible to distinguish three stages in the early church's gradual acceptance of Gentiles.

The first stage can be seen in the report that Luke gives at the end of chapter eight concerning Philip's conversation with, and ultimate baptizing of, an Ethiopian eunuch. While it cannot be stated with complete certitude that this Ethiopian was a Gentile, such an interpretation is probable.[19] On this supposition, Philip's baptism of the eunuch should be seen as extending the boundaries of the Christian movement another step beyond the Samaritans. The possibility that Luke also understood Philip's act as the extension of baptism to a member of another race should also be considered.[20]

Luke's descriptions of the visions sent first to Cornelius and then to Peter and his reports concerning Peter's speech and the outpouring of the Holy Spirit leading to Cornelius's baptism constitute the second stage in the "opening to the Gentiles." Without commenting upon all of the elements that are present in Luke's descriptions, it should be noted that Peter's speech expressly indicates that the Gentiles have standing with God: "Truly, I perceive that God shows no partiality, but in every nation any one who fears him and does what is right is acceptable to him" (10:34–35).

Constituting the third stage in the outward movement toward the Gentiles is the explicit support of the apostles and the other members of the Jerusalem community detailed in chapter eleven. Luke reports that when Peter returned to Jerusalem he at first had to face criticism for his association with Cornelius (11:2–3); however, Peter's account of what had happened satisfied his critics and resulted in general approval. Luke states that those present ended by glorifying God and saying: "Then to the Gentiles also God has granted repentance unto life" (11:18).

Although there are later passages and chapters in Acts in which Luke indicates that controversies developed over the specific arrangements under which Gentiles were to be admitted into the church, the assessment contained in the passage just cited, the assessment that Gentiles were indeed eligible to be disciples of Jesus, continued to be upheld. This being the case, when Luke's account in Acts is scrutinized from the standpoint of how the Jerusalem church responded to women, Samaritans, and Gentiles, the answer is remarkably similar in all three cases. Abstracting from the particular circumstances that Luke presents in each case, the basic thrust of his narrative is that, contingent upon their faith in the risen Lord, women, Samaritans, and Gentiles were all welcomed into the church as full disciples.

5. SERVICE AND HUMILITY

With reference to the qualities of service and humility within the lives of the members of the Jerusalem community, it is significant, first of all, that Luke does *not* portray the apostles or any of the other members ever striving after greatness. And positively, there are several passages which describe the apostles' stance as that of humble servants including one passage which highlights their willingness to suffer dishonor in Jesus' name.

In Acts 4:24–31, Luke narrates a prayerful outpouring which occurred after

Peter and John had been released by the Sanhedrin. All of those present affirmed in prayer that what had been prophesied by God's servant David about Jesus, the Holy Servant, had been fulfilled.[21] They then prayerfully referred to themselves as God's *douloi* ("servants") and asked God's blessing to speak with boldness.

Inasmuch as Luke had previously shown Jesus using the term *douloi* in his encouragements to the disciples to be good servants, the fact that the same word is now used by the disciples indicates a degree of continuity between the approach of Jesus in the Gospel and that of the disciples in Acts.

Luke's description in chapter eight of the events concerning Simon the Magician, already referred to above, also sheds light on the subjects of greatness and service. In describing Simon Luke utilizes the word *megas* ("great") in interesting fashion. First he states that Simon went about among the Samaritans saying that he himself was somebody "great" (8:9). Luke then states that the least and the greatest among the Samaritans accorded recognition to Simon as having the power of God which is "great" (8:10). From these verses and from those following in which Simon tries to purchase the power of the Holy Spirit from Peter and John, Luke's account makes it clear that Simon is someone seeking status and power.

In contrast Luke shows Peter and John distancing themselves from Simon's outlook and conduct. His narrative implies that the apostles are rejecting not only Simon's means but also his objective of trying to maintain and increase his status. While they do not specifically criticize Simon for his aspirations, it is clear from Luke's narrative that they themselves are not interested in seeking such "greatness."

The phenomenon of the apostles rejecting greatness and embracing service is also portrayed in two other passages within Acts. In chapter ten, when the Roman centurion, Cornelius, fell at Peter's feet in homage, Luke states that Peter assertively rejected such a gesture stating: "Stand up; I too am a man" (10:25-26). Even more illustrative is the response that Luke attributes to the apostles in chapter five after they had been flogged. He reports that they rejoiced in the fact that they were worthy to undergo whipping and "to suffer dishonor" (*atimasthēnai*) for the name of Jesus (5:41).

6. OPPOSITION TO INJUSTICE AND CORRUPTION

As summarized in chapter one, Luke portrayed Jesus holding the chief priests responsible for dishonesty at the temple and indicting them as wicked tenants to be turned out of office. Luke then described the measures taken by the priests and their allies to secure Jesus' death.

Within Acts Luke does not, except for a faint echo contained in the charges against Stephen, show the apostles and disciples carrying forward with Jesus' criticism of the chief priests' dishonest practices at the temple.[22] This is not to say, however, that Acts portrays amicable relations between the disciples and the priests. For, far from depicting a situation of peace and toleration, Acts shows the apostles and Stephen becoming steadily more direct in charging the chief priests and their allies with the death of Jesus.

Whether Luke's Gospel shows some segments of the populace of Jerusalem taking an active role in calling for Jesus' death is a question that has been addressed from several different perspectives in recent years. While Luke does include descriptions that, at face value, seem to indicate that others from Jerusalem joined in the final outcry for Jesus' crucifixion, it is the judgment of the present writer that Luke actually portrays the chief priests and their Sanhedrin allies dominating the proceedings against Jesus and only indicates minimal involvement by other members of the Jewish populace.[23]

Given the difficulties involved in interpreting Luke's trial narrative on this point, it is significant that, in the early chapters of Acts, Luke portrays Peter operating on the assumption that a significant number of people within Jerusalem did in fact play a role in Jesus' crucifixion. Yet the matter is still far from being simple. For, after first showing Peter twice criticizing his audiences for their role in Jesus' death, Luke twice shows Peter and then finally Stephen focusing the blame upon the chief priests and their associates on the Sanhedrin with no mention being made of the role of the inhabitants of Jerusalem or even of Pilate himself.

In all, then, there are five passages in the early chapters of Acts in which significant attention is directed to the unjust killing of Jesus. The first of these occurs within the setting of Peter's Pentecost address to the assembled crowds. In it, as already noted, Peter charges his hearers with having played a role in Jesus' death. "Men of Israel" is his opening form of address and he then tells his hearers that " . . . this Jesus, delivered up according to the definite plan and foreknowledge of God, you crucified and killed by the hands of lawless men" (2:22–23).

As these verses indicate, Peter's speech contains certain nuances which partially mitigate the harshness of the charge being made. Peter refers to the Roman role in Jesus' crucifixion and he also indicates that this tragic event was in accordance with a plan of God.[24] Nevertheless, the speech clearly does indict his audience and Luke subsequently reports that, when those assembled asked Peter and the apostles what they should do, Peter replied that every one of them should repent and be baptized for the forgiveness of their sins (2:38).

The second Acts passage in which Peter holds his hearers responsible for the death of Jesus has the same general structure (direct charges accompanied by references to mitigating factors) as the passage just considered. After Peter and John had miraculously cured the man who had been crippled from birth, Luke relates that people gathered spontaneously and that Peter began to address them. Again using the term "Men of Israel," Peter stated that the crippled man had been cured because God had glorified God's servant Jesus. Regarding Jesus and their conduct toward him, Peter then stated that it was Jesus "whom you delivered up and denied in the presence of Pilate, when he had decided to release him. But you denied the Holy and Righteous One, and asked for a murderer to be granted to you, and killed the Author of life . . ." (3:13–15).

In this instance, Peter's reference to Roman involvement in Jesus' death does not in any way exonerate his hearers. However, in the next verse Peter does affirm that his hearers acted in ignorance and also adverts to the role played by their rulers (3:17). An additional qualifying factor is also alluded to in the following verse when Peter again expresses the view that these events were the fulfillment of what God had foretold by the prophets (3:18).

The third Acts passage referring to the unjust death of Jesus is different from its predecessors in several respects. The reference once again occurs in a speech by Peter. However, in this instance Peter and John are under arrest and Peter is addressing an assembly of the chief priests, the scribes and the elders.[25]

In this speech Peter only briefly mentions the death of Jesus; but, in contrast with his previous speeches, he now places responsibility for the crucifixion entirely upon those groups present before him. Luke depicts him telling them, almost matter-of-factly, that the man for whose healing they have been arrested was healed "by the name of Jesus Christ of Nazareth, whom you crucified, whom God raised from the dead . . . " (4:10).

After relating that Peter and John's self-assurance made an impression upon the Sanhedrin and after reporting the apostles' concluding words regarding obedience to God (words to be analyzed in the following chapter), Luke indicates that the council members decided to give Peter and John a warning and release them (4:13-21a). Luke then adds the note that the Sanhedrin took such a mild course of action because of the popular support that the apostles enjoyed as a result of the healing (4:21b).

One chapter later, Peter and the apostles are again in a situation of jeopardy before the Sanhedrin. Luke indicates that the high priest had arrested the apostles out of jealousy (5:17); but, during the council hearing, the charges are that the apostles have filled Jerusalem with teaching about Jesus and that "you intend to bring this man's blood upon us" (5:28).

In reply to the high priest's charges, Luke portrays Peter countering with a charge of his own. Speaking directly to the Sanhedrin members, with no reference to the involvement of the Romans or any other mitigating factors, Peter asserts that God had indeed raised Jesus "whom you killed by hanging him on a tree" (5:30).

Luke reports that, when the council members heard Peter's reply, "they were enraged and wanted to kill them" (5:33). But, as a consequence of Gamaliel's intervention, the lesser punishment of flogging was decreed (5:40). It is thus the case that, although Luke presented Peter, without any qualification, affixing the blame for Jesus' death upon the chief priests and their allies, no harm greater than flogging befell the apostles.

The same comparatively mild outcome does not materialize in the third case in which direct charges are made against the high priest and those associated with him on the Sanhedrin. The person leveling the charges in this instance is Stephen. The circumstances of Stephen's arrest and the charges against him will receive treatment below. However, what is of immediate significance is that, according to Luke's account, Stephen's speech was hardly a defense against the charges which had been made against him but actually aggressively indicted the Sanhedrin members themselves for the murder of Jesus.

As Luke reports it, Stephen's attack upon the high priest and the Sanhedrin members did not come until the end of his speech. Indeed, because his speech commented upon so much of Israel's previous history before unveiling its attack, the ringing denunciation with which Stephen ends has sometimes not been properly appreciated.[26] But, in effect, Stephen's extended treatment of Israel's previous history functions to anticipate in advance possible counter arguments by the Sanhedrin members and leaves them particularly vulnerable to Stephen's forceful closing indictment.

When the body of Stephen's speech is read not so much as a defense but rather as an extended prologue to an attack, it can be seen that his comments concerning Joseph and Moses establish the point that the great figures of Israel's past were not exempt from rejection. Secondly, his descriptions also establish that God's activity on behalf of Israel continued despite such setbacks. A third point in the body of the speech concerns the temple. Stephen reviews the origins of the "tent of witness" in Israel's desert experience and then notes that Solomon was actually the one to construct the temple even though David had wished to build it. Stephen then emphasizes that, while a temple was built, it must be remembered that "the Most High does not dwell in houses made with hands" (7:48).

Luke indicates that, after Stephen had finished describing these and related events in Israel's history, he addressed the words which follow to those present:

> You stiff-necked people, uncircumcised in heart and ears, you always resist the Holy Spirit. As your fathers did, so do you. Which of the prophets did not your fathers persecute? And they killed those who announced beforehand the coming of the Righteous One, whom you have now betrayed and murdered, you who received the law as delivered by angels and did not keep it [7:51–53].

It should be noted that, in the Greek, Stephen's speech contains the nouns "betrayers" and "murderers" and that the RSV's use of verb forms in translating these terms slightly diminishes the sharpness of Stephen's charges.[27] However, even the RSV translation leaves no room for misreading the inflammatory character of Stephen's criticism. For Stephen has clearly charged that his hearers stand in continuity with the worst elements of Israel's past. And they themselves are even more reprobate than their fathers, for their fathers murdered the prophets, whereas they themselves have now betrayed and murdered the Righteous One.[28]

In order to respect the preciseness of Luke's account, it should be noted that Stephen's original opponents were not the chief priests and their allies on the Sanhedrin but rather certain Jews from the Synagogue of the Freedmen and others from Cilicia and Asia (6:9).[29] Because Stephen worked miracles and great signs among the populace and then bested his adversaries in debate, they charged Stephen with speaking blasphemously (6:11) and secured *false* witnesses to testify: "This man never ceases to speak words against this holy place [the temple] and the law; for we have heard him say that this Jesus of Nazareth will destroy this place, and will change the customs which Moses delivered to us" (6:13–14).

Although Luke does not portray Stephen directly addressing the charges against him, Stephen seemingly indirectly takes account of them in his speech, making reference both to the temple and the traditions of Moses. It must be said, however, that Stephen's stance of "qualified loyalty" regarding the temple would not have served well against the charges which had been presented. While his comments do bespeak an appreciation for the role of the temple within Israel's history, his concluding assertion that God does not dwell in houses made with human hands would not have proved helpful against the charge that he was persistently speaking against the temple and predicting its demise.

It is also possible to view Stephen's speech as communicating a "qualified loyalty" with respect to other aspects of Israel's traditions. As Luke presents him, Stephen respects the tradition of Joseph and Moses but cannot remain silent about the abuses perpetrated by others who have walked in that tradition.

At this juncture it should be noted that the precise attitude of Jesus' disciples toward the temple is an issue of some complexity within the Lukan writings. Luke has portrayed Jesus' stand against dishonesty at the temple and he has now portrayed Stephen proclaiming that God does not dwell in houses of human construction. Subsequently, he will report that Paul also was charged with teaching against the temple (see 21:28 and below). However, within the rest of Acts, none of Jesus' other leading disciples is ever associated with a stance that is critical of the temple.

Indeed, within Acts the apostles and disciples are never portrayed questioning the validity of temple worship or the honesty of the chief priests' administration of that institution. Rather, the principal charge that the apostles and disciples make against the chief priests is the charge that they have murdered Jesus.

7. REJECTION OF VIOLENCE AGAINST PERSONS

In analyzing Luke's narrative for indications of the Jerusalem Christians' stance toward the use of violence, it is useful to distinguish between the community's internal and external relations. While Luke's portrait does not suggest any glaring discrepancy between the disciples' behavior in the two spheres, it is in the latter sphere that they have to contend with coercion and ultimately with the use of lethal force.

In describing the internal life of the Jerusalem disciples, Luke portrays a largely strife-free and harmonious community. Such harmony is highlighted in the two summaries of community life given in 2:43–47 and 4:32–35 where it is stated that the disciples were so united that they practiced a community of goods. Other passages, such as 4:23–31 which describes an exultant common prayer, also contribute to Luke's portrait of harmonious relations.

As noted above the conduct of Ananias and Sapphira stands in contrast to the generosity and sincerity of the other disciples. And, as noted above, Luke relates the sudden death of first the one and then the other spouse. Yet, in his account of the episode, he reports no vengeful attitude or righteous satisfaction on the part of the disciples. Rather the two sentiments he describes at the conclusion are fear and reverence, fear and reverence toward God for having intervened in such a way (5:11).

One additional note concerning the disciples' internal life concerns the absence of the term for "forgiving" (*aphiēmi*) from Luke's descriptions in the early chapters of Acts. Within the Gospel Jesus has instructed his followers in forgiveness on several occasions; but, now within Acts, Luke does not make use either of the term or the concept in describing the common life of the disciples. It will be shown below that Stephen practices a radical forgiveness of his enemies, but this single momentous exception makes the general silence of Acts on the subject of forgiveness even more striking.

With respect to the amount of violence directed toward the Jerusalem community from the outside, the narrative of Acts indicates that increasingly violent measures were adopted by the high priest and the Sanhedrin in response to the disciples' activities. In chapter four Luke indicates that Peter and John were arrested, kept in custody over night, and formally interrogated the next day (4:1–7). In chapter five he reports that the high priest arrested and jailed all of the apostles and then relates that as an alternative to putting them to death, the Sanhedrin decided to have them flogged (5:17–18,40).

Following the whipping of the apostles, the next act of violence that Luke reports is the murder of Stephen. The incendiary character of Stephen's speech was analyzed in the preceding section. The reaction that Stephen's speech engendered should now be considered. Luke describes the anger of the council members and their violent outburst against Stephen in the following terms:

> . . . they were enraged, and they ground their teeth against him . . . they cried out with a loud voice and stopped their ears and rushed together upon him. Then they cast him out of the city and stoned him [8:54, 57–58].

In terms of the rejection of violence against persons, it is significant that, in recounting the harsh treatment they suffered, Luke does not indicate that the disciples undertook any retaliatory actions or even allowed themselves to harbor vengeful attitudes. Rather, as noted earlier, the apostles' response to their treatment was to rejoice that they were counted worthy to suffer such dishonor.

To an even greater degree, the response given by Stephen to those stoning him also stands as an example of a disciple of Jesus forswearing any vengeful or retaliatory attitude. While Luke presents Stephen mounting an extremely aggressive attack upon the high priests and the other Sanhedrin members, he also indicates that Stephen extended forgiveness to his opponents even as they were in the act of stoning him:[30]

> And he knelt down and cried with a loud voice, "Lord, do not hold this sin against them" [7:60].

Although the term "love of enemies" does not occur within Acts, these instances of nonvengeful responses offer solid evidence for the conclusion that the conduct of the disciples within Acts follows closely upon the practice of Jesus within the Gospel. There are also two additional elements which support such a conclusion.

In the first place it should be noted that, within the whole of Acts, Luke never portrays the disciples possessing or utilizing swords or any other instrument of violence.

Luke indicates that, after Stephen's martyrdom, a great persecution arose against the church in Jerusalem. In 8:3 he relates that Paul was ravaging the church, entering house after house and dragging men and women off to prison. Then in chapter twelve Luke indicates that another persecution was begun by Herod: "About that time Herod the king laid violent hands upon some who belonged to the church. He killed James the brother of John with the sword; and when he saw that it pleased the Jews, he proceeded to arrest Peter also" (12:1-3). However, in describing the response of the disciples to these violent actions, Luke never indicates that they contemplated taking up the sword or responding with any other form of violence. Rather in the case of Saul's persecution, he indicates that, except for the apostles, the members of the Jerusalem church left the city and were scattered through Judea and Samaria. In the persecution begun by Herod he indicates that the disciples responded by praying earnestly for Peter's deliverance.

The final element to be considered in respect to the early church's rejection of violence is Peter's use of the term *eirēnē* ("peace") in his speech at Cornelius' house in the tenth chapter of Acts.[31] As Luke presents it, Peter indicated to Cornelius and the others of his household that the message of Jesus was a message of peace (10:36).

In itself this single reference to peace as an element of Jesus' preaching is perhaps not of great significance. However, it is a note that fits well with the other aspects that Luke has elaborated concerning the pacific outlook and stance of the Jerusalem community and functions as one more sign of the connection between the peaceful stance of Jesus in the Gospel and that of the disciples in Acts.

3

The Political Stance of the Jerusalem Community

In analyzing Luke's reports concerning the interactions of the disciples with various political authorities it is important to recognize that Luke does not portray the disciples' political stance as something apart from, or unrelated to, their social stance. Rather he portrays the political conduct of the community members occurring in the midst of, and in the context of, their ongoing social patterns.

As a consequence the analysis which is presented below should not be considered in abstraction from the analysis made in the preceding chapter. Together these two chapters describe the overall social and political approach of the apostles and the disciples gathered with them in Jerusalem.

1. THE ROLE AND INFLUENCE OF THE JERUSALEM SANHEDRIN

Within Acts Luke initially makes mention of the Sanhedrin's activities at the beginning of chapter four. In 4:1 he indicates that groups associated with the Sanhedrin, "the priests and the captain of the temple and the Sadducees," came and arrested Peter and John. He then describes "the rulers and elders and scribes" going into session the next day in order to interrogate them (4:5).

It is a significant feature of Luke's account at this point that he takes time to indicate that Annas continued in the office of high priest and that positioned on the Sanhedrin with him were "Caiaphas and John and Alexander, and all who were of the high-priestly family" (4:6).[1] It should be recalled that he also provided a contextual note that John the Baptist's ministry began "in the high-priesthood of Annas and Caiaphas" at 3:2 in the Gospel.

After completing their interrogation of the two apostles, the Sanhedrin members released them with a warning (4:21). That was not, however, the end of the matter. For subsequently in chapter five the high priest and council members arrest all of the apostles and put them in jail (5:18). Then, after the

39

apostles miraculously escape and are rearrested, members of the Sanhedrin take a full range of measures against them: first, they interrogate them, then they deliberate over a judgment and a course of action; finally, before releasing them, they beat the apostles and charge them not to speak further about Jesus (5:27–40).

In addition to these descriptions of the Sanhedrin's activities against the apostles, Luke also portrays this body acting vigorously against Stephen in chapter seven. This case has already been analyzed above with reference to the charges against Stephen and his speech in reply. Here what needs to be emphasized is that Luke portrays the Sanhedrin as having the power for interrogating Stephen and judging his conduct (6:12–7:1).

From the character of Luke's description, it is not clear whether he considered Stephen's execution to be the product of "lynch law" or whether he understood the Sanhedrin to be exercising a special prerogative for issuing and carrying out death sentences.[2] In either case his account of Stephen's death represents still another instance in which he portrays the Sanhedrin exercising a momentous amount of power.

The conclusion which thus emerges is that the early chapters of Acts portray the Sanhedrin in general, and the high priests in particular, as having a considerable range of jurisdiction and a considerable amount of discretionary power. This is an important insight and a proper appreciation for it now will also significantly advance the interpretation of Luke's reports, later in his narrative, concerning the trials of Paul.

Nevertheless, it should not be thought that the Acts narrative somehow portrays the Sanhedrin as a completely independent or autonomous entity. Quite the contrary. For as Luke's account begins to move forward, it becomes increasingly apparent that the Sanhedrin's power and influence fall within the larger framework of Roman dominion and Roman rule.

Interestingly, in contrast with the precise information that Luke supplies regarding the ruling high priests, Acts makes no mention of the Roman governors between Pilate and Felix and it is not until 11:28 that the reigning Roman emperor, Claudius, is mentioned. However, in chapter twelve, Herod Agrippa I's position as king and his capital powers are both indicated; and, in the following chapters, mention of other Roman officials is so frequent that Roman control, not only of Palestine, but also of Asia Minor, Greece, and the other territories of the Mediterranean area is unmistakably portrayed.

It should be noted, in closing, that there are more subtle questions concerning the role of the Sanhedrin within the larger framework of Roman rule that cannot be answered on the basis of what Luke reports in Acts.[3] To what degree are the Roman governors and Roman-appointed kings like the Agrippas bound to respect decisions taken by the Sanhedrin? How much importance are the other Roman authorities likely to attach to speeches or other activities hostile to the Sanhedrin? To what degree do the other Roman authorities regard the enemies of the Sanhedrin as the enemies of the larger Roman system? These questions and others related to them bear upon the detailed analysis of the apostles' response to the Sanhedrin that will be made in the next section and it would be helpful to have answers for them at hand. Nevertheless, even without them, it is possible to grasp the basic thrust of what Luke portrays.

2. PETER AND JOHN BEFORE THE SANHEDRIN

In light of the foregoing considerations regarding the authority and role of the Sanhedrin, it is now appropriate to consider the instructions that Luke portrays the Sanhedrin giving to Peter and John at the conclusion of their trial:

So they called them and charged them not to speak or teach at all in the name of Jesus [4:18].

Unmistakably the sense of Luke's report here is that, in addition to the power of arrest and interrogation, the Sanhedrin also has the power for determining the types of public activity that are permissible within Jerusalem. Public speeches about Jesus are prohibited. And the prohibition seemingly extends beyond the temple precincts to the streets and synagogues of Jerusalem itself.

What response does Luke portray the two apostles making when they are faced with such an order? Luke reports the following brief, but extremely far-reaching, reply:

Whether it is right in the sight of God to listen to you rather than to God, you must judge: for we cannot but speak of what we have seen and heard [4:19–20].

The first point to be noted regarding their response is that the apostles explicitly refuse to follow the Sanhedrin's orders. They indicate that they cannot cease speaking of Jesus and they strongly imply that they will again do so if given the opportunity.

Interestingly, as Luke reports their response, the apostles do not question the Sanhedrin's authority for issuing such an order. The sense of their reply is not that the Sanhedrin has exceeded its authority in trying to forbid such activities. Rather, while seeming to recognize the existence of the order, they steadfastly refuse to obey it.

Just as significant as the apostles' refusal to obey is the principle on which they base their refusal. In the first part of their answer, they speak in terms of a conflict between what is regarded as right by the Sanhedrin and what is seen as right by God. Having adverted to the possibility of such a conflict, the apostles then turn the issue back upon the council members. If such a conflict does indeed exist, then what course of action do the Sanhedrin members think it is appropriate for the apostles to follow?

Implicit within their words are Peter and John's conviction that such a conflict does exist in the present situation and that they themselves know what course of action is required of them. They must proceed with what is right in the sight of God. They cannot desist from preaching and teaching about Jesus.

Such is the carefully nuanced position that Luke portrays Peter and John adopting with respect to the binding force of the Sanhedrin's decrees. It should also be observed that, as Luke has reported it, the apostles' reply suggests that the principle they are expressing could be extended to the decrees of other political authorities as well as to those of the Sanhedrin. In this instance the apostles are speaking directly to the Sanhedrin members when they ask whether it is right "to listen to *you*." However, inasmuch as the primary justification for their stance is that they are "listening to God," the apostles' position seems potentially open to application in other situations as well.[4]

3. THE APOSTLES' SUBSEQUENT CONFRONTATION WITH THE SANHEDRIN

When Peter and John are again on trial before the Sanhedrin in 5:17–32, the situation is altered in that the verbal defiance expressed at their first trial has now been expressed in practice. During the interim they and the other apostles have continued to preach and teach in the name of Jesus. Indeed, as the comments which Luke attributes to the high priest indicate, the apostles have done this throughout the entire city:

> And when they had brought them, they set them before the council. And the high priest questioned them, saying, "We strictly charged you not to teach in this name, yet here *you have filled Jerusalem* with your teaching and you intend to bring this man's blood upon us" [5:27–28; emphasis added].

Luke indicates that Peter and the others replied to this indictment in a way that was remarkably similar to the way in which Peter and John had responded at their first trial:

> But Peter and the apostles answered, "We must obey God rather than men. The God of our fathers raised Jesus whom you killed by hanging him on a tree. God exalted him at his right hand as Leader and Savior, to give repentance to Israel and forgiveness of sins. And we are witnesses to these things, and so is the Holy Spirit whom God has given to those who obey him" [5:29–32].

An initial consideration of the above passage reveals that the apostles did not avail themselves of two possible lines of defense in responding as they did to the Sanhedrin. In a way seemingly consistent with the approach followed by Peter and John earlier, the apostles did not question the validity of the Sanhedrin's issuance of an order prohibiting them from public speech. Secondly, the apostles also did not contest the accuracy of the high priest's accusations; in effect they admitted his charge that they had not ceased to proclaim Jesus and teach in his name.

In contrast with either of these possible types of defense, the apostles defended their conduct on the basis that it was justified by a higher authority, namely, the authority of God.

Because the principle which Luke shows the apostles enunciating in this passage is highly significant for an assessment of their overall political stance, it is desirable to analyze it carefully. In the original Greek, Luke reported their words as follows: "*peitharchein dei theō mallon ē anthrōpois*" (5:29). A close literal translation of this clause would render it as: "It is necessary to obey God rather than human beings."[5]

As given in the passage above, the RSV's translation is: "We must obey God rather than men." While this and other versions depart slightly from the literal sense of the Greek, the fundamental contrast given in the apostles' statement is still plainly apparent. For, unmistakably, Luke has indicated that the apostles referred to a potential conflict between the decrees of God and the decrees of human authority and stated that they themselves must first obey God.[6]

In comparison with the sentiments Luke attributed to Peter and John at their earlier trial, the sentiments here attributed to all of the apostles are more direct and confrontational. Previously the two apostles had expressed their own position by asking the Sanhedrin members whether it was right in the sight of God for the apostles to listen to them rather than to God. Here the apostles use extremely direct language in telling the Sanhedrin that they have chosen to obey God rather than the orders of the Sanhedrin.[7]

Not only is the apostles' reply sharper and more direct at this trial, the principle they enunciate is also more encompassing in its frame of reference.

In the analysis made of their response at the first trial, it was noted that the phrasing of Peter and John's reply allowed for the possibility that the apostles' position could be extended to other political institutions beyond the Sanhedrin. In the present passage the character of the apostles' words is such as to even more explicitly raise the possibility of a wider application. The apostles' words are still directed specifically to the Sanhedrin members. Nevertheless, the character of their statement is such that it more readily functions as a general principle applicable to specific circumstances. Luke seems to present the apostles stating that they are committed to giving obedience to God and only then to any human institution, including, in this instance, the Sanhedrin.[8]

It should also be noted that in the last verse of this passage, Peter and the others claim that the Holy Spirit is given to those who obey God. In the context that Luke describes, the implication is that the apostles have received the Holy Spirit (while the Sanhedrin members have not) because of their faithful obedience and witness. Inasmuch as there are numerous other passages testifying to the presence of the Holy Spirit within the developing Christian community, this claim linking the Holy Spirit's presence with faithful obedience to God is a claim of considerable importance.

4. THE APOSTLES' APPROACH IN COMPARISON
WITH THAT OF JESUS

When the political stance that Luke presents the apostles adopting in these passages is compared with the political stance that he shows Jesus adopting in the Gospel, it is clear that the two stances are in close correspondence.

Within the Gospel the central passage presenting Jesus' outlook on the relationship between human authority and God's authority is the tribute passage of 20:20–26. As indicated in chapter one of the present study and at greater length in *Jesus, Politics, and Society,* the response Luke portrays Jesus giving is essentially a call for evaluation. Before a sound judgment can be reached regarding the payment of Roman taxes, Luke's Jesus answers that it is first necessary to evaluate "the things of Caesar" in reference to "the things of God."

The response of the apostles in Acts corresponds to the response of Jesus within the Gospel in several important ways. The first is that both Jesus and the apostles give recognition to the role of human authority. In his answer Jesus does not counsel his hearers to refuse to pay Caesar's taxes and he does not deny that Caesar has responsibility for certain things. Similarly the apostles do not reject human authority in general and do not mount any criticism against the various types of authority exercised by the Sanhedrin.

Secondly, both Jesus and the apostles affirm that God's authority is of ultimate importance. As indicated in *Jesus, Politics, and Society,* Jesus' affirmation of God's sovereignty over all of creation and over all of human life constitutes the context against which his words in the tribute passage concerning the "things of God" are properly situated. Similarly, in both 4:19–20 and 5:29, Luke also shows the apostles acknowledging the priority of God's law. Clearly the apostles' fundamental concern is to adhere faithfully to God's word.

Thirdly, Luke indicates that both Jesus and the apostles recognized the possibility of situations arising in which simultaneous obedience to human authority could not be given. Within the tribute passage Jesus' call to evaluate the things of Caesar in light of the things of God implies that, in at least some of their aspects, Caesar's programs, Caesar's practices, Caesar's directives may not agree with those things that pertain to God's kingdom.

Within Acts the comparative note that is present in both of the apostles' statements is a sign of the possible conflict between the words of human authorities and the words of God. The Greek words *mallon ē* ("rather than") appear in both statements. Peter and John initially ask whether they should listen to the Sanhedrin "rather than to God." Peter and the entire group of apostles later state that they must obey God "rather than human beings."

Fourthly, both the Jesus of Luke's Gospel and the apostles of Acts adopt the stance of upholding human laws and human authority when they are not in conflict with the higher law of God but refusing to sanction them when a conflict does exist. The Gospel tribute passage itself does not indicate Jesus' refusal to support human authority when it is in conflict with divine authority, but such a stance is attested to by several other passages in the Gospel and is consistent with the teaching given in the tribute passage. Both of the Act passages attribute such a stance to the apostles as well. In the first passage, as noted above, Peter and John straightforwardly tell the Sanhedrin members that they cannot and will not stop speaking in Jesus' name. In different words, the apostles' second statement similarly testifies to their willingness to disobey human decrees if obedience to God requires it.

5. THE CHARACTERISTIC OF BOLDNESS

The preceding sections have analyzed the political implications of the apostles' unswerving allegiance to God. At this juncture, it is desirable to appreciate that Luke does not portray them as tentative or meek in their allegiance. In fact, just the opposite is true. According to Luke their allegiance to God and Christ is affirmed with great boldness and conviction.

It will be seen below that Luke describes a number of Paul's speeches in terms of the quality of boldness and also portrays Paul acting vigorously and boldly in a number of situations. In the present setting, the focus is upon the four instances within the early chapters of Acts in which boldness is in some way associated with the preaching and conduct of Peter and the other apostles.

As Luke describes it, Peter's speech on the day of Pentecost was an eloquent and bold proclamation. After first describing the large crowds that had assembled, Luke reports that Peter stood up and, with loud voice, embarked upon a solemn, formal address. Parts of this speech have already been adverted to above. An additional important feature is that, in attesting to Jesus' connection with David, Peter stated that he felt able to speak on that and other point(s) "confidently" or "boldly." The Greek word used here (2:29) is *parrēsia*, a term whose primary meaning is "boldness," especially boldness in political and ethical contexts.[9]

If Luke portrays Peter and the apostles speaking confidently and boldly before the receptive crowds gathered on Pentecost, this same characteristic is also a feature in his presentation of their conduct in the two hearings which took place before the Sanhedrin. In describing Peter and John's first appearance before the council, Luke uses the same word, *parrēsia*, in indicating that the council members were startled by the "boldness" that the two apostles displayed. He also states that the apostles' stance was all the more surprising to the Sanhedrin members because they knew Peter and John to be uneducated commoners.

Luke's account of the second Sanhedrin trial does not contain *parrēsia* or any other term that specifically indicates confident, bold speech or behavior, but the forthrightness of the apostles' stance still is unmistakably described.

Luke indicates that the high priests charged them with unrepentant, bold conduct: "We strictly charged you not to teach in this name, yet here you have filled Jerusalem with your teaching . . . " (5:28). And in portraying the apostles responding with the statement that they must obey God rather than human beings he provides his readers with a model of bold proclamation given in the face of great danger.

Within the early chapters of Acts the other instance in which Luke describes the apostles and disciples witnessing "boldly" to Jesus is an instance in which they are in a private, as opposed to a public, setting. Luke indicates that after Peter and John had been released from their first hearing before the Sanhedrin, they rejoined the other apostles and disciples at an unspecified place (4:23). At that point a prayerful outpouring took place and Luke specifically indicates that the assembly prayed for a strengthened witness in the face of the dangers facing them: "And now, Lord, look upon their threats, and grant to thy servants to speak thy word with all boldness . . . " (4:29).

The *threats* referred to in the above citation refer to the threats and warnings that Peter and John received from the Sanhedrin and it is significant that the boldness which Luke presents the disciples praying for is a boldness that will help them to withstand threats from the political authorities. It should also be noted that the disciples' precise prayer is to speak God's word with *all boldness*.[10] Luke's portrait is thus that of a community exuberant over an unexpected respite yet still under pressure and earnestly beseeching God for strength to witness with all possible conviction and confidence.

In the verses which follow this prayer, Luke indicates that God's presence became visibly manifest to those assembled. He relates that the room in which they were gathered was shaken and that they were all filled with the Holy Spirit, and that the disciples "spoke the word of God *with boldness*" (4:31, emphasis added). The sense of Luke's report here is that the disciples' prayer had been heard by God. They had asked for the gift to speak with all boldness and received the Holy Spirit's power for doing so.[11]

What emerges from a consideration of these passages in which the disciples' boldness and/or their prayers for boldness are prominent is the conclusion that, as Luke presents them, the apostles and other members of the Jerusalem community are convinced and dedicated witnesses to the risen Jesus and to God's word expressed through him. Peter has made a powerful proclamation before the crowds of Pentecost without hesitating or wavering. Nor was there any hesitance or wavering to be found in the witness Peter and John gave at the time of their first arrest. They testified with boldness and they then joined the assembled community in praying for still greater boldness. When they and the remaining apostles were again arrested by the chief priests, they continued to proclaim their allegiance to God in uncompromising terms. Before a Sanhedrin already hostile toward them, they proclaimed unflinchingly: "We must obey God rather than human beings." Such bold testimony so enraged that body that the majority of its members wanted to kill the apostles then and there.

6. HEROD AGRIPPA'S EXECUTION OF JAMES
AND HIS IMPRISONMENT OF PETER

Within the body of Acts, Luke does not mention the ascendance of Caligula in A.D. 37 or the fact that Caligula was friendly toward Agrippa I, the grandson of Herod the Great, and twice assigned significant territories, as well as the title of "king," to him. He is also silent regarding the assassination of Caligula, the intrigues which placed Claudius upon the throne in A.D. 41, and Claudius' decision to increase Agrippa's realm through the addition of the Judean territory previously ruled by the Roman governors who had succeeded Pilate.[12]

It may have been the case that Luke chose to assume his readers' knowledge of these imperial developments and the resultant rise to power of Agrippa I or perhaps he felt that it was uneconomical to provide background information for all of the Herods present within his two-volume narrative. In any case, in chapter twelve, when Luke relates Agrippa's persecution against members of the Jerusalem community, his readers have not previously been introduced to this Herodian king:

> About that time Herod the king laid violent hands upon some who belonged to the church. He killed James the brother of John with the sword; and when he saw that it pleased the Jews, he proceeded to arrest Peter also. This was during the days of Unleavened Bread. And when he had seized him, he put him in prison, and delivered him to four squads of soldiers to guard him, intending after the Passover to bring him out to the people [12:1–5].

Luke here identifies the James who is murdered by Herod only as "the brother of John." However, a look back to verse 5:10 of the Gospel reveals that both James and John were sons of Zebedee and fishing partners with Simon Peter. By reason of the calling that he received from Jesus, this James is one of the original twelve apostles. However, he should be distinguished from James, the son of Alphaeus, also one of the Twelve (Luke 6:15), and from the James who Luke subsequently portrays playing an extremely influential role within the life of the Jerusalem community (Acts 12:17; 15:13; 21:18).

What was Herod Agrippa's motive for proceeding against James in such a fashion? Luke's succinctly worded report[13] does not provide sufficient information to make possible a definitive response to this question. Nevertheless, by giving careful attention to the phrasing in this report as well as to elements that are present in other parts of the Acts narrative, an answer which possesses a high degree of probability can still be given.

Luke's note that Agrippa killed James "with the sword" may be intended to indicate that Herod moved against James on distinctly political grounds. Beheading with a sword seems to be the type of execution implied here; and there are a number of commentators who hold that, in contrast with stoning, this form of punishment was generally used in instances where the person was judged guilty of disloyal or treasonous conduct.[14] An analysis of the other instance in which beheading is referred to in the Lukan writings also affords support for such an interpretation. For in 9:9 of the Gospel Luke portrays Herod Antipas indicating that he "beheaded" (*apekephalisa*) John the Baptist; earlier Luke had stated that John's "misconduct" had been to reprove Antipas for taking his brother's wife and for "all the evil things that Herod had done" (3:19).

An additional element in Luke's report that also pertains to the subject of Agrippa's motive is contained in the statement: " . . . when he saw that it pleased the Jews, he proceeded to arrest Peter also." This statement implies that Herod had acted on his own initiative in proceeding against James. However, the positive response that he received from "the Jews" provided him with encouragement and reinforcement for moving in a similar fashion against Peter.

In light of the fact that Luke has previously portrayed the high priest and his Sanhedrin allies as extremely hostile to the apostles and disciples and actually desirous of their death, it is highly probable that, as used in this passage, the term "the Jews," refers to this group.[15] Within Acts Luke uses the term "the Jews," to designate a variety of Jewish groups who actively resist the Christian message. Here, however, the context suggests that it is the Sanhedrin authorities who are meant.

Such an understanding also illuminates the questions of *how* and *what* Herod Agrippa had learned about the activities of James and Peter. For, if "the Jews" is a cipher for the high priest and his allies, then Luke may well be implying that this group had already established a relationship with Agrippa. To be clear, what Luke expressly states is that King Agrippa executed James on his own initiative and, after the fact, received a positive response from "the Jews." However, to hold that Luke's full sense of the situation (only indirectly and implicitly indicated) includes prior contact between Herod Agrippa and the chief-priestly group does not run counter to the description that Luke has actually presented and, in fact, makes it more comprehensible.[16]

The argument for the interpretation that an understanding regarding prior contact between Herod Agrippa and the chief priests lies in the background of Luke's brief account of James' execution becomes still stronger when full attention is given to the last element that Luke includes in his report, namely, that Herod intended to bring Peter before "the people" when Passover is completed.

Up until this point in his narrative Luke has been careful to draw a contrast between the response that the high priests and their Sanhedrin allies give to the apostles and that given by "the people." For example, in 2:47 Luke describes the apostles as "having favor with all the people" and in 5:13 he reports that "the people held them in high honor."

Luke also reports that the high priest and those allied with him resented the apostles' activity among "the people" (4:1–2; 4:17; 5:17). And what is even more significant, he twice specifically indicates that the Sanhedrin leaders wanted to proceed vigorously against the apostles but could not do so because of the popular support they enjoyed:

> And when they had further threatened them, they let them go, finding no way to punish them, *because of the people* [4:21, emphasis added].

> Then the captain with the officers went and brought them, but without violence, *for they were afraid of being stoned by the people* [5:26, emphasis added].

In all of these instances the Greek words translated by "the people" are *ho laos* and in the early chapters of the Acts narrative, this group is always portrayed as being favorable to the activities of the apostles and disciples. It is only in chapter six, in reporting Stephen's case, that Luke first makes mention of any shift in attitude by the members of this group. While he states in 6:8 that Stephen "did great wonders and signs among the people," Luke indicates a few verses later that Stephen's opponents successfully "stirred up the people and the elders and the scribes" against him by secretly instigating witnesses to claim that Stephen had blasphemed (6:11–12). Luke subsequently presents the high priest and his allies taking control of the campaign against Stephen. He portrays them and not "the people" actually putting Stephen to death. However it is significant that in describing Stephen's stoning Luke makes no mention of any protest by "the people" against this action.

Between the death of Stephen and the execution of James the three instances in which the narrative makes reference to "the people" do not bear upon the response of this group to the apostles (10:2, 41, 42). It is thus the case that when Luke reports Herod's plan to bring Peter out "to the people," the careful reader recalls the patterns of Luke's previous reports and ponders the meaning of this new piece of information in light of them.

Luke's statement that Herod intended to bring Peter before "the people" implies that some type of public session was envisioned as a prelude to Peter's execution.[17] Luke does portray him proceeding cautiously. (He will wait until after Passover and, in the meantime, Peter is heavily guarded).[18] But the king is seemingly confident that he will be able to achieve a degree of popular support for Peter's death. He seems to anticipate that he will have the backing of "the people" or at least their acquiescence.

Again, Luke does not explicitly state that Herod Agrippa I acted in concert with the chief priests and their allies ("the Jews") in destroying James and in attempting to destroy Peter. Nor does he expressly state "the people" moved from their earlier positive estimation of the apostles to the point where they would acquiesce in Peter's execution. Nevertheless, when Luke's description of these events is read carefully and when it is read against the background of his earlier reports in Acts, there seems substantial grounds for holding that Luke himself possessed such an understanding in setting forth his report of these events.

Previously in his narrative Luke has indicated that Stephen was stoned to death by the Sanhedrin leaders (7:58–60) and that the apostles, presumably including James, were whipped by them (5:40). However, up until this point none of Jesus' apostles has died at the hands of the political authorities. James, brother of John, partner of Simon Peter, and son of Zebedee, is thus the first of Jesus' inner circle to experience this fate.

Also the significance of Luke's indication that James was executed by a king who was directly appointed by the emperor, by an imperial representative who enjoyed the confidence and even the friendship of two emperors, should not be overlooked. Just as Jesus himself had met death at the hands of an emperor-appointed "governor," so now does one of the apostles experience a comparable death at the hands of an emperor-appointed "king."

As argued in the preceding paragraphs, the sense of Luke's account is that the high priest and his allies had at least some degree of involvement in Agrippa's efforts against James and Peter. There is still one additional inference to be developed in connection with this line of analysis. This inference arises from reflection upon the stance which Luke has previously described Peter and all of the apostles adopting in their last appearance before the Sanhedrin. On that occasion they defended their activities by stating forthrightly: "We must obey God rather than men" (5:29).

Within the framework of his narrative in chapter twelve Luke does not report any comparable interaction between Herod Agrippa and James and Peter. Nevertheless, having indicated earlier that such was the apostles' response when faced with efforts by the authorities to halt their activities in Jesus' name, Luke may well expect discerning readers to bear this in mind when they now read his account of Agrippa's efforts against James and Peter.

To the degree that Luke's readers do recall these previous developments in reading the present passage, the news of James' execution is less surprising or "abrupt" for them. For while Luke does not in this instance provide any indication of James' or Peter's responses to Herod's moves against them, he has earlier indicated the position which these two men, and indeed all of the apostles, adopted when faced with comparable efforts against them by the Sanhedrin authorities.

4

The Social Stance of Paul

Within the narrative of Acts Paul[1] is mentioned for the first time at the end of chapter seven when Luke indicates that he was an accomplice to the execution of Stephen. He next appears at the beginning of chapter nine where he is portrayed undertaking a vigorous campaign of persecution against the disciples. Luke then recounts the Lord's powerful intervention while Paul was on the way to Damascus and the amazing conversion which Paul experienced. A substantial section of chapter nine then details Paul's activities in Damascus and Jerusalem prior to his return to Tarsus.

For a time the Acts narrative then concentrates upon Peter's activities, particularly Peter's role in preaching to the Gentile Cornelius and his household. Paul returns to the account at 11:25 when Luke reports that Barnabas went to Tarsus and brought Paul to Antioch. From that point forward, with only a few exceptions, Paul becomes the person around whom Luke's narrative centers. With well over half of Acts thus concerned with his activities, it is clear that any analysis of the social and political stance of Jesus' disciples must carefully investigate Luke's many reports concerning Paul's approach and the events which befell him.

1. THE SOVEREIGNTY OF GOD AND PRAYER

In terms of Paul's emergence as a leading disciple of Jesus and as the central figure in the spread of the gospel, the conversion that Luke portrays him undergoing is of unsurpassed importance. Prior to his conversion Paul was a leading antagonist of the Christian movement. Afterwards he became its leading exponent. Luke also indicates that the memory of his conversion was something that continued to guide and sustain Paul throughout his life.

In addition to the third-person description of Paul's conversion that he presents in chapter nine, Luke twice portrays Paul himself telling of the dramatic and powerful events he had experienced (22:3–16 and 26:4–18). Thus, there are three separate accounts of Paul's conversion within Acts. All of these descriptions highlight the same reality of the risen Jesus' personal intervention;

51

but each of them relates this event from a different perspective and each of them emphasizes particular details.

The power with which the risen Jesus intervened is a point of considerable importance in all three accounts. All three report that a light flashed from heaven, that Paul fell to the ground, that he heard the Lord speaking to him, and that he was without sight when the vision ended. In addition the first report adds that Paul did not eat or drink for three days and that his sight was not restored until the Lord sent him and Ananias corroborating visions and Ananias came to him.

A second important aspect of Paul's conversion was the fact that the Lord was assigning a particular role to him. All three accounts indicate that Paul was not only to stop persecuting Jesus. He was also being chosen to play a central role in the spread of the gospel. He was to undertake a mission that would also include Gentiles.

Luke relates that almost immediately after his conversion experience and his baptism by Ananias, Paul began to proclaim the risen Jesus by going to the synagogues of Damascus and stating: "He is the Son of God" (9:19–20). From this point forward, in a variety of ways, Luke's reports show that Paul remained totally dedicated in his allegiance to Jesus and was fully given over to accomplishing God's plan of salvation.

An important factor to be noted in regard to Paul's faithfulness is that his visions of the risen Lord did not cease with his conversion. As his narrative proceeds, Luke details two other appearances of the risen Jesus to Paul as well as several interventions by the Holy Spirit. As Luke describes them, both of these later visitations by Jesus accorded Paul guidance and encouragement. Concrete guidance for specific situations was also a characteristic of the Holy Spirit's interventions.[2]

In addition to being expressed through the visions entrusted to him, Luke also indicates that God's sovereign power was manifest in Paul's life and ministry through many miracles. Several of these miracles were directed to the cure of the sick or the infirm; two of them involved the expulsion of evil spirits; one of them involved the raising of a dead man to life.

Luke reports that, after setting out on their first journey, Paul and Barnabas reached Paphos on the island of Cyprus and encountered a certain magician and false prophet named Bar-Jesus. Recognizing that the Roman proconsul of the island wanted to hear more of Paul and Barnabas' message, this magician tried to prevent him from coming to the faith. However, Luke relates that, filled with the power of the Holy Spirit, Paul denounced the magician for his deceit and predicted that God would strike him blind for a time, an outcome that immediately occurred (13:6–11).

Luke indicates in passing that when Paul and Barnabas were in Iconium, the Lord granted "signs and wonders to be done by their hands" (14:3), but the next extended report that he gives concerning a miraculous healing comes in 14:6–10 when Paul and Barnabas have reached Lystra. Luke reports that when Paul was preaching there, he gazed upon a man listening to him, a man crippled from birth. Seeing that he had the faith necessary to be cured, Paul loudly bid him to stand upright and the man did so immediately and began walking.

With an angry response similar to the one that he had given to the magician, Bar-Jesus, Luke also portrays Paul challenging the spirit that was possessing and manipulating a young girl in the town of Philippi (16:16-18). The girl had been following Paul and the others in his party, harassing them in a loud voice. Finally Paul became angry and ordered the spirit to come out of her in the name of Jesus Christ. Much to the dismay of her owners, Paul's words immediately expelled this demon.[3]

What is perhaps Luke's most striking report of God's power made manifest through Paul occurs in 20:7-12, a passage describing the concluding events of Paul's stay at Troas. Members of the Christian community there were gathered in an upper room listening to Paul when one of them, a young man named Eutychus, fell from the third storey, mortally wounding himself. Luke relates, almost without special emphasis, that Paul descended, picked him up and embraced him, thereby bringing him back to life.[4] Paul stated: "Do not be alarmed, for his life is in him" (20:10b). Luke then concludes the episode by saying that those present took the lad away alive and were extremely comforted.

The final miraculous intervention to be treated in this section concerns the cure that Paul effected for the father of Publius, the chief official of the island of Malta. In 28:8 Luke reports that Publius treated Paul and those in his party hospitably and that Paul laid hands on Publius' father, curing him from fever and dysentery. After this had taken place Luke states that "the rest of the people on the island who had diseases also came and were cured" (28:9).

In the sequence of actions which Luke portrays Paul following to heal Publius' father, it is significant that Paul began with a prayer. Only after praying over him did Paul then lay his hands upon him and heal him.

In all there are seven instances within the narrative of Acts in which Luke portrays Paul at prayer. Along with the passages describing his visions and his miracles, these passages serve to depict Paul as a figure deeply immersed in an experience of God's sovereign power.

The passages describing Paul's practice of prayer testify to a regular pattern of ongoing communication with God. Two of them, 16:13 and 16:16, simply indicate that Paul was in the custom of going to a place of prayer on the Sabbath. These passages both pertain to Paul's stay at Philippi. Still a third reference to their prayer in that city is contained in 16:25 where Luke describes how Paul and Silas were given over to prayer and to the singing of hymns when they were imprisoned overnight.

Two other references to the place of prayer in Paul's life occur within the framework of his final journey to Jerusalem. Luke reports that the instances in which Paul took leave from his disciples and friends at Miletus and at Tyre (21:5) were special times for prayer. His description of the scene of Paul sharing prayers with the Ephesian elders at Miletus is particularly poignant:

And when he had spoken thus, he knelt down and prayed with them all. And they all wept and embraced Paul and kissed him, sorrowing most of all because of the word he had spoken, that they should see his face no more [20:36–38].

In terms of chronology, Luke's last note regarding Paul at prayer actually refers to the time when Paul was still very much under the influence of his initial conversion experience. In the speech that Luke portrays him making after being arrested in Jerusalem, Paul indicates that it was during his prayer at the Jerusalem temple that the risen Jesus had given him his mission to the Gentiles (22:17).

2. CONCERN FOR THE SICK AND THE POOR

With respect to Paul's ministry to the sick, the analysis made in the preceding section indicated that Paul dramatically healed a crippled man at Lystra and also the father of Publius and many others after being shipwrecked at Malta. These two instances, along with one other, represent the major passages in Acts in which Paul is presented exercising a concern for the sick and the infirm.

Luke's report in 19:11–12, a report which describes events that occurred when Paul was in Ephesus, could also have been treated in the preceding section. In a manner which recalls his report in Acts 5:14–16 describing Peter's miraculous healing of the sick, Luke here states the following regarding God's grace manifested through Paul:

And God did extraordinary miracles by the hands of Paul, so that handkerchiefs or aprons were carried away from his body to the sick, and diseases left them and the evil spirits came out of them [19:11–12].

On the subject of Paul's attitude toward the poor, it has already been noted that the principal term which Luke uses in the Gospel to designate the poor, *ptōchos*, does not appear in Acts. There is, however, one passage in which Luke portrays Paul indicating that he has been concerned to help "the weak" (*ton asthenounton*).[5]

This reference occurs in Paul's farewell address to the Ephesian elders gathered at Miletus, an instruction in which Paul also touches upon his own attitude toward material possessions. Luke indicates that Paul provided the elders with an additional perspective for his own stance by drawing their attention to a teaching that came from Jesus himself:

In all things I have shown you that by so toiling one must help the weak, remembering the words of the Lord Jesus, how he said, "It is more blessed to give than to receive" [20:35].

The words of Jesus cited here do not appear in any of the gospels and their exact meaning has sometimes been disputed. However, particularly given the context in which the citation occurs, an interpretation which views them as stressing that the sharing of one's resources with the weak is more blessed than accumulating additional wealth seems secure.[6]

Whether "the weak" mentioned here should be understood restrictively as referring to the weaker members of the church at Ephesus or whether this term also takes in the weak members of the larger community is also an issue that merits attention. Seemingly, the more restrictive frame of reference is to be understood. In the preceding verses Luke has portrayed Paul making an overall assessment of the situation facing the church at Ephesus. Paul has reviewed his efforts to build up that community, including the stance that he personally adopted regarding the acquisition and disposal of material possessions (to be considered in the following section). Viewed against this context, the present verse suggests that he has done so to help the weak of *that* community. Paul is thus now encouraging the elders not to neglect the care of the weak in their ministry for the community.

3. THE USE OF MATERIAL POSSESSIONS

The verse analyzed at the end of the preceding section is the last verse of Paul's address at Miletus. The immediately preceding verses, verses pertaining to Paul's personal stance regarding material possessions, were alluded to above. It is now appropriate to cite them in full:

And now I commend you to God and to the word of his grace, which is able to build you up and give you the inheritance among all those who are sanctified. I coveted no one's silver or gold or apparel. You yourselves know that these hands ministered to my necessities, and to those who were with me [20:32–34].

As Luke reports his words in this passage, Paul describes himself as someone who makes adequate provision for his "necessities" (*chreiais*[7]), but does not seek to acquire luxuries such as gold or silver or fine clothing. Further he indicates that he provides for his necessities through his own labor.

In terms of the present analysis there are thus two significant elements in the summary of his practice that Paul has given. The first is the reminder that Paul lived simply during the time of his ministry at Ephesus and did not devote any of his time or energy to the acquisition of luxuries. The second important element is that Paul was self-supporting with respect to his own needs and also helped to provide for the needs of those who were with him.

In his earlier descriptions of the economic practices of the apostles and the Jerusalem community, Luke described the spirit of sharing which prevailed and indicated the manner in which distribution was made to the members of the community who were in need. However, he did not include any indication as to whether the twelve and the seven were engaged in economic pursuits in addition to their ministerial activities within the community. Luke's report of Paul's statement that he worked with his own hands thus represents a new note in his overall portrayal of Jesus' leading disciples.

On the subject of Paul's attitude toward material possessions, there is one other passage which deserves attention. In Acts 11:29–30 the practice which Luke describes being followed with respect to material possessions is not solely Paul's undertaking. Rather Luke indicates that Paul was one of the members of the Antioch community when that community decided to send famine relief to the disciples in Judea. This undertaking has already been analyzed in chapter two. What it is appropriate to note in the present context is that, when the Antiochian disciples determined to send relief, each did so according to his or her ability (11:29).

From Luke's notice that Paul and Barnabas were entrusted to take the relief monies to Jerusalem, it is easy to infer that he understands Paul to be included among those contributing to the needs of the Judean disciples out of their own resources. There is thus a seeming correspondence between Luke's report of Paul's practice at Antioch and his subsequent descriptions of Paul's conduct at Ephesus. In both instances Paul is portrayed using his resources, at Ephesus the fruits of his own labor, in attempting to provide for those not able to fulfill their needs.

Related to the subject of Paul's personal stance regarding material possessions is the issue of the impact that Paul's preaching made upon the economic patterns and practices in the localities to which his journeys brought him.

The narrative of Acts makes little mention of the economic activities and the patterns of trade and commerce that prevailed in the world around Paul and, as a general rule, Paul's teachings do not address issues of economic practice. Nevertheless in his overall portrayal of Paul's activities, Luke does report three instances in which Paul's message resulted in conflict with the economic-related practices of some of those around him.

In this context it is appropriate to return to one of the exorcism passages analyzed in an earlier section of this chapter. The passage in question, in which Paul expels a clairvoyant spirit from a possessed girl and then is subsequently imprisoned, appears at 16:16–40 of Luke's account. The treatment that Paul receives upon his arrest and the role of his Roman citizenship will be discussed in a subsequent chapter. Presently, the spotlight is upon the economic consequences of Paul's intervention.

In verse 16 Luke states that the girl[8] brought her masters much gain as a result of her uncanny ability to tell fortunes. In verse 19, Luke reports the fury of the girl's owners over the fact that her ability to generate revenue was ended abruptly as a result of Paul's exorcism. Although the girl's masters succeed in having him and Silas thrown in prison, Luke does not portray Paul as being in any way intimidated by this ominous turn of events. Rather the sense of Luke's report is that Paul is a disciple powerful in the Lord who did what had to be done to advance the Lord's way—even if he himself were forced to pay a price because of his stand.

Luke's second and third reports concerning some of the economic consequences of Paul's ministry come in chapter nineteen when he is describing Paul's activities at Ephesus.

In the first instance Luke does not show Paul as directly responsible for the events which occurred as he does in the second. Luke reports that, after large numbers of the sick were healed through contact with Paul, some itinerant exorcists tried to imitate Paul's ministry with disastrous consequences. Luke then relates the following:

> And a number of those who practiced magic arts brought their books together and burned them in the sight of all; and they counted the value of them and found it came to fifty thousand pieces of silver [19:19].

In describing this outcome Luke does not state that Paul himself had inveighed against these magical practices. Nevertheless, the reported sequence of events does make clear that Paul's ministry had resulted in a new consciousness among the populace: the consciousness that magic was obsolete in light of the word of God.[9]

As Luke's account of Paul's activities at Ephesus continues, it also becomes apparent that Paul's preaching undermined the economically significant practice of idolatry. Indeed the charge of Demetrius against Paul is as follows:

> Men, you know that from this business we have our wealth. And you see and hear that not only at Ephesus but almost throughout all Asia this Paul has persuaded and turned away a considerable company of people, saying that gods made with hands are not gods. And there is danger not only that this trade of ours may come into disrepute but also that the temple of the great goddess Artemis may count for nothing, and that she may even be deposed from her magnificence, she whom all Asia and the world worship [19:25–27].

Luke's reports of how the Asiarchs of Ephesus and the town clerk responded to the popular uproar that these charges engendered will be analyzed more fully in a subsequent chapter. Here it is sufficient simply to note that Demetrius' speech indicates that Paul's preaching was having a considerable impact. Seemingly Paul was accomplishing such a shift in popular attitudes that the continued viability of an entire industry was being called into question.

4. AFFIRMATION FOR OTHER LESS REGARDED GROUPS: WOMEN

As indicated above in chapter two, Luke does not make reference to tax collectors and sinners anywhere in Acts; it therefore follows that Paul is never portrayed addressing these groups or responding to them. Samaritans, too, are nearly absent from Paul's travels and activities. Luke only portrays Paul having contact with them when he and Barnabas were passing through Samaria on their way to Jerusalem. At that time Paul and Barnabas reported to the Samaritan disciples the conversion of the Gentiles, a report which generated considerable joy (15:3).

In contrast with Luke's silence regarding the place of tax collectors and sinners in Paul's ministry and his near silence regarding the place of Samaritans, Acts contains a number of references to Paul's contacts with women and many references to his encounters with Gentiles.

Luke's first and principal description of the converted Paul's contact with women comes in his account of Paul's sojourn at Philippi. Because of what it reveals about Paul's attitude toward women as potential (and actual) disciples, it is a description that deserves to be cited in full:

> And on the sabbath day we went outside the gate to the riverside, where we supposed there was a place of prayer; and we sat down and spoke to the women who had come together. One who heard us was a woman named Lydia, from the city of Thyatira, a seller of purple goods, who was a worshiper of God. The Lord opened her heart to give heed to what was said by Paul. And when she was baptized, with her household, she besought us, saying, "If you have judged me to be faithful to the Lord, come to my house and stay." And she prevailed upon us [16:13–15].

Luke's narrative at this point is given in the first person.[10] As it is phrased, his description suggests that circumstances prevented Paul from finding a synagogue for the usual sabbath services. However, Paul does not hesitate to take advantage of the opportunity to discourse with the women who had gathered. Luke indicates that the combination of Paul's preaching and the Lord's grace resulted in Lydia and her household receiving baptism. Paul subsequently affirmed her faith by agreeing to accept her offer of hospitality.

It is worth dwelling a moment on the last element included in Luke's portrayal. There is an assertive note to the invitation he portrays Lydia extending to Paul; seemingly she wishes to challenge him regarding the implications that conversion carried for relationships between and among Christ's disciples. Significantly, Luke portrays Paul accepting Lydia's invitation and, by implication, her challenge to a relationship involving mutuality.

The dynamic interchange which Luke has detailed in this passage takes on additional importance, and its richness of detail becomes increasingly apparent, when two of Luke's other descriptions of Paul's interactions with women are placed alongside it. In his report of Paul's preaching at Thessalonica, Luke simply indicates that "not a few of the leading women" were among those who heard Paul's preaching and joined him (17:4). Similarly, in describing the effect of Paul's efforts at Beroea, Luke succinctly states: "Many of them therefore believed, with not a few Greek women of high standing as well as men" (17:12).

In detailing Paul's subsequent activity in Greece, Luke indicates that a woman named Damaris was among those who responded positively to Paul's preaching at Athens (17:34). He also indicates that, at Corinth, Paul came into contact with a couple, Aquila and Priscilla, who were already disciples, staying with them (18:3), and ultimately sailing for Syria with them (18:18).[11]

The sense of mutuality that Luke conveyed in his earlier description of the exchange between Lydia and Paul is also conveyed by his descriptions of Paul's interactions with Priscilla and Aquila. That Paul remains the leading figure in the ministry at Corinth is without question. Nevertheless, Luke clearly does convey the sense of a shared endeavor and portrays Priscilla as having a definite personal standing in the circle around Paul.[12]

Luke provides an additional indication of Priscilla's prominent role in a subsequent passage. Apollos, another disciple, had been speaking boldly in the synagogue, but he had only received the baptism of John. As a consequence, "when Priscilla and Aquila heard him, they took him and expounded to him the way of God more accurately" (18:26). Significantly Luke names Priscilla first in ascribing to her and to Aquila this important work of instructing another leading disciple.

5. AFFIRMATION FOR OTHER LESS REGARDED GROUPS: GENTILES

Virtually from the time of his conversion onwards, the narrative of Acts provides abundant documentation of the outreach that Paul made to the Gentiles of the Mediterranean world. Paul was not the first disciple to undertake such a ministry. Nor does Luke portray him emphasizing his mission to the Gentiles to the extent that he neglects to evangelize the Jews of the Diaspora. Nevertheless, bearing these two qualifications in mind, the account of Paul's experiences and activities in chapters thirteen through twenty-eight of Acts is more than sufficient to merit for him the title, "The Great Missionary to the Gentiles."[13]

At the time of Paul's conversion, Luke indicates that the Lord adverted to Paul's future role among the Gentiles in instructing Ananias to go to Paul: "Go, for he is a chosen instrument of mine to carry my name before the Gentiles and kings and the sons of Israel" (9:15). And later in the narrative, when Paul is relating a vision he received in Jerusalem just after his conversion, he states that the Lord spoke quite emphatically regarding a mission to the Gentiles: "Depart [from Jerusalem]; for I will send you far away to the Gentiles" (22:21).[14]

In reference to the verse just cited, it is significant that Luke portrays the risen Jesus not only giving a (major) authorization for a mission to the Gentiles but also the specific (minor) instruction that Paul should now leave Jerusalem. This directive is only the first of many similar divine directives that Luke portrays Paul receiving at various places and stages of his journey. For the reader of Acts the net impact of these various visions and directives concerning the regions to which Paul should travel,[15] how long he should stay in a given place,[16] the sufferings he should expect upon his final return to Jerusalem,[17] and the necessity of his witness in Rome,[18] is the definite impression that Paul was closely guided by God throughout his journey.

After describing the circumstances under which Paul departed Antioch, Luke portrays him undertaking extensive journeys in the provinces and cities of Cyprus, Asia Minor, and Greece. Luke indicates that he frequently began his ministry in a new town or region by preaching in the local synagogue.[19] In most cases Paul received an initially favorable response from at least some of the Jews and "worshipers of God"[20] who were present.[21] However, Luke also indicates that his message frequently resulted in such controversy and opposition that he was forced to leave the synagogue and even the town itself.[22]

It has sometimes been asserted that Luke portrays Paul as having held the conviction that he was not free to preach to the Gentiles until he had exhausted his possibilities for successful preaching among the Jews of the Diaspora. While there are individual passages in Acts which provide some basis for such an interpretation, there are two principal reasons why this is not the sense of Luke's account considered as a whole. The first factor is that within Acts, Paul never exhausts his possibilities for preaching to receptive Jews.[23] Secondly, within Acts there are also several instances in which Luke portrays Paul preaching directly to the Gentiles of a locality without having first experienced rejection from any Jews of that place.[24] Also, in at least one case, Luke implies that Paul's approach was to alternate his preaching between the synagogues and public places of the city.[25]

Luke thus portrays Paul evangelizing among the Gentiles even as he continued to evangelize among the Jews of the Diaspora. While indicating that setbacks of various kinds occurred, Luke's various reports cumulatively indicate that Paul's preaching was effective among both groups, among Gentiles as well as among Jews.

In addition to having been entrusted by the Lord himself with a mission that included the Gentiles and in addition to having carried out this mission by preaching effectively to Gentiles in a variety of settings, Luke's Paul also merits the title "The Great Missionary to the Gentiles" for two other reasons.

The first reason is that Paul engaged in vigorous efforts to prevent the mission to the Gentiles from being jeopardized by the imposition of the full Jewish law upon new Gentile converts. The second is that, as a consequence of his various endeavors on behalf of the Gentiles, Paul experienced controversy and suffering. Inasmuch as these factors are both important to an assessment of the outcome of Paul's personal journey, they will receive extended consideration in a subsequent chapter devoted to an analysis of Luke's reports concerning Paul's non-Roman opponents.

6. SERVICE AND HUMILITY

Within Acts the most central passage for an assessment of Paul's approach regarding service and humility falls within the setting of his address to the

Ephesian elders at Miletus. There, in what can be considered a classical conjoining of these two elements, Paul states: "You yourselves know how I lived among you all the time from the first day that I set foot in Asia, *serving the Lord with all humility* and with tears and with trials which befell me through the plots of the Jews" (20:18–19; emphasis added).[26]

In addition to thus portraying Paul claiming these qualities as hallmarks of his ministry, Luke also reports two other instances in which Paul's words indicate that his approach is characterized by these attributes. Previous to the passage just cited, Luke reports Paul expressing similar sentiments at Lystra; later, a sentence from his address before Festus and Agrippa also reflects them.

In describing how Paul miraculously cured the man who had been crippled from birth, Luke indicates that the crowds of people who were present were awestruck by the power that Paul had manifested. Indeed, they thought that Paul and Barnabas were gods who had come down to them in the likeness of human beings (14:8–12). Luke reports, however, that Paul and Barnabas would have nothing of such misplaced popular acclaim. Instead, they stated emphatically that they too were created beings and then humbly directed attention to the greatness of God, the creator of heaven and earth and every good thing (14:15–17).

In his speech before Festus and Agrippa II, Luke portrays Paul as being extremely concerned to present a clear explanation of his own history and activity. In the course of his explanation Paul acknowledged that it had been because of God's help that he had been able to persevere in his witness: an acknowledgment testifying to his humility. He also indicated that he had consciously directed his ministry to the small as well as to the mighty: an indication of a spirit of service without concern for prestige. Remarkably both of these claims occur within the space of one sentence: "To this day I have had the help that comes from God, and so I stand here testifying both to small and great . . . " (26:22).

One final feature of Paul's spirit of service and humility within Acts is indicated by two passages which show him willing to accept humiliation and suffering for the sake of his mission. One reference to this aspect of his service is present in the "serving the Lord" passage just analyzed (20:18–19); there Paul also referred to the "tears and trials" that attended his service. A similar reference is also to be found at 14:22–23 where Luke reports Paul's statement that "through many tribulations we must enter the kingdom of God."

7. OPPOSITION TO INJUSTICE AND CORRUPTION

In section six of chapter two, it was pointed out that the injustice most frequently and explicitly addressed by Peter and the other apostles and by Stephen was that perpetrated in Jesus' execution. Jesus' death was mentioned a total of five times, and in Peter's later speeches and particularly in Stephen's speech the chief priests and other Sanhedrin members were charged with having had the primary responsibility for Jesus' demise. However, while leveling reproaches concerning Jesus' death, these early speeches of Acts contained almost no reference to the charge that Luke had portrayed Jesus himself pressing in the Gospel: the charge that the chief priests were corrupt in their administration of the temple and were in effect "wicked tenants."

It is significant that both of these elements are present in Luke's description of Paul's social stance. The former, Jesus' unwarranted death, is an issue that Paul explicitly adverts to in his speech at Pisidian Antioch and one that he seemingly mentions implicitly when he is before the Sanhedrin in Jerusalem. The latter, the corruption of the chief priests (actually the high priest), figures prominently in his trial speech before the Sanhedrin.

The section of Paul's speech at Pisidian Antioch in which he refers to the circumstances of Jesus' death reads as follows:

> For those who live in Jerusalem and their rulers, because they did not recognize him nor understand the utterances of the prophets which are read every sabbath, fulfilled these by condemning him. Though they could charge him with nothing deserving death, yet they asked Pilate to have him killed. And when they had fulfilled all that was written of him, they took him down from the tree, and laid him in a tomb [13:27–29].

Although Paul clearly emphasizes that justice was lacking in the procedures against Jesus ("though they could charge him with nothing deserving death, yet they asked Pilate to have him killed") his speech also contains exonerating notes ("because they did not recognize him nor understand the utterances of the prophets"). It should also be noted that Luke portrays Paul using the more general term, "rulers" (*archontes*), in referring to the chief priests and the other Sanhedrin leaders. And Paul does not portray this group acting independently but rather in concert with those who live in Jerusalem.

As just indicated, the high priest's corrupt conduct is the issue of justice that is prominently portrayed in Paul's speech before the Jerusalem Sanhedrin. Nevertheless, according to the interpretation that is proposed below for verse 23:1, the issue of Jesus' unjust death may also have been implicitly present in Paul's charges.

In approaching this passage it is well to bear in mind that there is no other section within Acts in which so many forceful responses occur with such little elaboration. For this reason, arriving at a satisfactory interpretation requires a careful attention to each element of the situation that Luke describes and a careful effort to assess the contribution that each element makes to the picture that gradually emerges.

In light of these preliminary comments Luke's entire account of Paul's trial before the Sanhedrin is now appropriately considered:

> And Paul, looking intently at the council, said, "Brethren, I have lived before God in all good conscience up to this day." And the high priest Ananias commanded those who stood by him to strike him on the mouth. Then Paul said to him, "God shall strike you, you whitewashed wall! Are

you sitting to judge me according to the law, and yet contrary to the law you order me to be struck?" Those who stood by said, "Would you revile God's high priest?" And Paul said, "I did not know, brethren, that he was the high priest; for it is written, 'You shall not speak evil of a ruler of your people.' "

But when Paul perceived that one part were Sadducees and the other Pharisees, he cried out in the council, "Brethren, I am a Pharisee, a son of Pharisees; with respect to the hope and the resurrection of the dead I am on trial." And when he had said this, a dissension arose between the Pharisees and the Sadducees; and the assembly was divided. For the Sadducees say that there is no resurrection, nor angel, nor spirit; but the Pharisees acknowledge them all. Then a great clamor arose; and some of the scribes of the Pharisees' party stood up and contended, "We find nothing wrong in this man. What if a spirit or an angel spoke to him?" And when the dissension became violent, the tribune, afraid that Paul would be torn in pieces by them, commanded the soldiers to go down and take him by force from among them and bring him into the barracks [23:1-10].

Given the complex character of this passage, a step-by-step analysis of five important elements contained in it may well be the most satisfactory way of proceeding. Accordingly, the analysis which follows will treat: (1) Paul's opening comments; (2) the high priest's sharp reaction; (3) Paul's cursing indictment of the high priest; (4) Paul's second comment regarding the high priest; and (5) subsequent developments at the trial. By carefully reflecting upon Luke's wording concerning each of these elements and by bearing in mind what Luke has portrayed in other previous situations involving the Sanhedrin, the full dimensions of meaning that are present in this passage gradually emerge. In essence Luke is portraying Paul affirming the rightness of his own conduct and charging the high priest with corrupt and illegitimate behavior.

(1) By indicating that Paul looked "intently" (*atenisas*) at the Sanhedrin members before beginning, Luke conveys the impression that what Paul is about to say is well considered. Before being quashed by the high priest, Paul speaks only one sentence, however. Yet because of its scope and its summary character, this single sentence makes all of Paul's past activities subject matter for the present hearing and, by implication, also reopens the case of Jesus of Nazareth.

"I have lived before God in all good conscience up to this day" is the exact statement that Luke portrays Paul making and there are two particular factors to be noted in it. The first is a value factor: Paul assesses his conduct to be in accord with the laws of God. The second is a temporal factor: Paul claims to have been in good conscience in former times and claims to be in good conscience *at the present time.*

Given the fact that Luke has previously shown the high priest and the Sanhedrin members to be well familiar with Paul's former position[27] and the turn that he had taken as a result of his conversion, it seems evident that the high priest would understand Paul's present claim as having consequences for the high priest himself and his allies. For if Paul has followed the path of good conscience in changing from a persecutor to a proclaimer of Jesus, then the integrity and good conscience of those who have remained opponents and persecutors is called into question. Analyzed from such a perspective, it seems clear that the sense of Luke's portrayal is that Paul has implicitly challenged the Sanhedrin members regarding their integrity and the state of their own consciences. This implicit challenge regards their continued persecution of Jesus' disciples and, ultimately, regards the state of their consciences regarding their involvement in Jesus' death.

(2) Confirmation for the interpretation just proposed is given by Luke's description of the sharp response that Paul's statement elicits from the high priest. Paul is ordered struck on the mouth so that he will speak no further of such things.

The angry reaction that Luke attributes to the high priest here is reminiscent of the responses he has previously attributed to Sanhedrin officials when they were faced with comparable statements by Peter and the apostles (5:33) and by Stephen (7:54). Throughout Acts Luke's portrayals make it clear that talk before the chief priests and their allies on the Sanhedrin about Jesus or the circumstances of his death involves considerable risks. In this instance Luke portrays the high priest physically compelling Paul to desist from such talk.

(3) Luke next reports that Paul immediately responded angrily to the high priest, actually cursing him. A close analysis of this reply and the context in which it is given suggests that Luke may have wished to indicate that Paul's outburst challenged the high priest in two ways.

Clearly Paul charges the high priest with having caused him to be illegally struck,[28] emphasizing that such conduct renders the high priest's interrogation of him a sham. This charge in itself represents a serious indictment. In addition Luke also portrays Paul reviling the high priest with the epithet: "you white-washed wall!" This term seemingly recalls the unsteady wall that was daubed with whitewash by false prophets and Ezekiel's bitter prophecy that the whitewash could not prevent the corrupted wall from crashing under the impact of the storm sure to come.[29] If this is the case, then Paul's words may have also hurled a broader indictment: that the high priest was generally corrupt.

The abrupt severity of Paul's reply sometimes catches Luke's readers by surprise. Luke does indeed show Paul responding almost reflexively and with great sharpness. However, it should also be noted that Luke's earlier descriptions of the apostles, and particularly of Stephen, when they were arraigned before the Sanhedrin serves to prepare the reader for the stinging reply that he now attributes to Paul. In many respects the explosive indictment that Stephen delivered at the conclusion of his speech serves as the literary analogue for Paul's response here.

(4) If verse 23:5 is taken at face value, then Luke is indicating that Paul (for unspecified reasons) did not realize that it was the high priest who ordered

him slapped and, as a consequence of learning this, apologized for his angry outburst. However, partially on the grounds that a failure on Paul's part to recognize the high priest seems to clash with other elements in the scene that Luke has just described and partially because the image of Paul embarking upon a sudden apology does not cohere well with Luke's subsequent descriptions, it seems preferable to adopt a version of the so-called "ironic" interpretation that various commentators have put forward.[30]

The interpretation to be proposed is as follows: Paul's words do not represent an apology but rather a sarcastic rejoinder. Paul is actually indicating that it is hard to recognize this priest as God's chosen high priest because of his conduct. For, if he truly were God's high priest, then he would not be acting in such a manner.[31] And if he truly were God's high priest, he would have nothing to fear from Paul, for Paul respects the traditional teaching (Exod. 22:28) prohibiting the cursing of God's appointed leaders.

If this interpretation is accepted, then Luke has, in effect, painted the portrait of a Paul who argues for the rightness of his own conscience and severely castigates the high priest for his own misconduct. Luke's Paul states at the outset that he is in good conscience about what he has been doing. He then angrily rebukes the high priest for having him struck, likening him to a whitewashed wall that is rotting. He then sarcastically retorts that the high priest's behavior is such that he can hardly be recognized as God's appointed officer.

(5) There is comparatively less difficulty involved in interpreting the verses which follow next. Luke shows Paul retaining the initiative and seemingly returning to the line of "testimony" given in his opening comment.[32] Inferring that he hoped to build rapport with the Pharisees present, Luke portrays Paul explaining that he continues to be a Pharisee in good standing and that his present circumstances are related to his faith in Jesus' resurrection.[33]

Luke reports that when Paul expressed these sentiments, great dissension broke out among the Sadducees and Pharisees on the council, and that the Roman tribune eventually intervened. In terms of the present analysis, what is particularly significant is the precise motive for which the tribune acted. According to 23:10 he intervened because he was afraid that Paul would be "torn in pieces by them."

The importance of this report lies with what it implicitly reveals concerning the attitude of the high priest and his Sadducean allies toward Paul. For clearly some of those present want Paul "torn in pieces" (and were actually about to do so!). And, given Luke's previous reports and his present indication that scribes of the Pharisees had spoken in Paul's defense, the unavoidable conclusion is that such sentiments now reside with the high priest and those aligned with him.[34]

8. REJECTION OF VIOLENCE AGAINST PERSONS

Before describing the appearances of the risen Lord to him and his resulting conversion, Luke indicates that Paul was involved in a violent persecution of the Jerusalem church. In 7:58 Luke states that Paul was an approving by-stander at Stephen's execution and in 8:3 he reports Paul's subsequent destructive activity by stating: "But Saul *was ravaging*[35] the church and entering house after house, he dragged off men and women and committed them to prison" (emphasis added).

Later Luke also portrays Paul himself adverting to his violent efforts against the disciples in Jerusalem and Damascus. In addressing the populace of Jerusalem (22:3–21) Paul twice refers to his efforts to combat and destroy those proclaiming Christ. In verses 4–5 he states: "I persecuted this Way to the death,[36] binding and delivering to prison both men and women . . . [bringing] them in bonds to Jerusalem to be punished." Then in verses 19–20 he recounts what he had stated in conversation with the risen Jesus: " . . . in every synagogue I imprisoned and beat those who believed in thee. And when the blood of Stephen thy witness was shed, I also was standing by and approving, and keeping the garments of those who killed him."

His earlier hate-filled persecution of the disciples is also a subject that Luke portrays Paul referring to in his speeches to Festus and Agrippa. Using language that emphasizes the intense anger he had felt toward the disciples, Paul states: "And I not only shut up many of the saints in prison . . . but when they were put to death I cast my vote against them. And I punished them often in all the synagogues and tried to make them blaspheme; and *in raging fury against them,* I persecuted them even to foreign cities" (26:10–11; emphasis added).[37]

Given these passages and the absence of any descriptions to the contrary, the violent impulses and behavior of the pre-conversion Paul toward those he considered his enemies, specifically the disciples of Jesus, is exceedingly well established within Acts. But what of the behavior of Paul after his conversion? Does Luke present a portrait of a Paul who retains his former inclinations to deal harshly and violently with those who refused to accept his message and those who actually persecute him (!) because of it?

Inasmuch as Paul's angry outburst against the high priest was just adverted to in the preceding section, it is clear that Luke's post-conversion portrayal of Paul carries forward at least some features from his earlier depiction of Paul as an outspoken, angry persecutor. In addition, a review of the account of Paul's harsh words against the magician, Bar-Jesus, and his curse of blindness upon him in 13:10–11 also confirms this impression.

Thirdly, any analysis of angry or harsh behavior by the converted Paul should also give attention to Luke's report regarding the serious disagreement that occurred between Paul and Barnabas. As Luke reports in chapter fifteen, this disagreement arose over the issue of whether John Mark should have a place with them on their second journey.

And Barnabas wanted to take with them John called Mark. But Paul thought best not to take with them one who had withdrawn from them in Pamphylia, and had not gone with them to the work. And there arose a sharp contention, so that they separated from each other. Barnabas took

Mark with him and sailed away to Cyprus, but Paul chose Silas and departed . . . [15:37–40].

Since this report of the parting of the ways comes after Luke's previous descriptions highlighting Barnabas' exemplary conduct and, in particular, his crucial support for Paul, it is a report that is all the more disturbing to readers of Acts. While Luke does not indicate that the dispute was beclouded by harshness on the part of Barnabas or Paul, he clearly does portray it as a "sharp contention" (*paroxusmos*) rooted in their differing estimations of John Mark's viability. Inasmuch as the narrative of Acts reports no further contact between these two leading disciples, Luke's readers are left only with sobering reflections over the meaning of the unreconciled situation that he has portrayed.[38]

This much having been said in recognition of those instances in Acts in which the behavior of the converted Paul is less than serene, it is now appropriate to analyze those passages in which Paul's behavior is portrayed in different terms. For, notwithstanding the passages in which Paul's anger is detailed, and notwithstanding the fact that Luke never explicitly utilizes such terms as "love of enemies" or "forgiveness" in referring to Paul or his activities,[39] Luke's portrait of the converted Paul does admit of new irenic elements. These new elements have the effect of depicting Paul as a figure whose way of engaging in controversy is less violent and whose behavior in one case provides a paradigmatic illustration of what it means to reconcile lovingly with one's opponents.

To begin with, the converted Paul no longer seeks to deal with his opponents through physical coercion. He no longer attempts to beat or flog any of those with whom he engages in controversy.

Secondly, the converted Paul is, to a remarkable degree, ready to accept violent treatment at the hands of his enemies without seeking to retaliate against them. The various forms of violence and persecution which Paul suffers will be explored in greater detail in coming chapters. However, for purposes of illustration, Luke's report of Paul's response to what befell him at Lystra is appropriately considered here.

In 14:19 Luke succinctly relates that Paul's opponents stoned him and dragged him outside of the city, leaving him for dead. Just as succinctly Luke then relates in the following verse that "when the disciples gathered about him, he rose up and entered the city; and on the next day he went on with Barnabas to Derbe" (14:20). Efforts to seek retribution, vengeful anger, lingering hostility: these sentiments and other comparable attitudes are *absent* from the portrayal of Paul's response here and consistently absent from his response in similar circumstances at other points on his journey. Indeed, within Acts, the general response of the post-conversion Paul to opposition of various kinds is not any kind of retaliation or vengefulness but rather to continue his journey, to take his preaching of the risen Jesus to another city or region.

In addition to instances in which Paul accepts persecution and violence without responding in kind, there is also one passage in Acts in which Luke portrays Paul actually achieving a remarkable reconciliation with someone whose position placed him in opposition to Paul. What is more, this reconciliation results in, and to a degree is bound up with, the conversion of this erstwhile opponent. The person with whom this reconciliation takes place is Paul's jailer at Philippi.

Luke's account of the events which occurred after the Philippian magistrates had had Paul and Silas thrown into prison is so highly telescoped that the full meaning of various events in the sequence is not always immediately clear. Nevertheless, careful reflection upon the particular details of the account Luke supplies (16:23–39) can lead to an integrated understanding of the interactions which Luke describes as having taken place between Paul and his unnamed jailer.

At the outset of the passage Luke portrays the jailer responsibly carrying out the orders he has received from the magistrates by jailing Paul and Silas in the inner prison and fastening their feet in stocks (16:24). At this point Luke reports no personal conversation or interaction and gives no indication that the jailer took any particular interest in the identity of his new charges.

Paul and Silas were not, however, ordinary prisoners. For Luke describes them praying and singing hymns to God well into the night, and he also reports that the other prisoners were listening attentively to them (16:25).

It was while Paul and Silas were praying that an earthquake occurred, shaking the foundations of the prison and causing all of the doors to open and all of the prisoners' chains to become unfastened (16:26). Luke does not explicitly state that Paul and Silas or the other prisoners had the possibility of escaping, but this is the sense of his subsequent report that the jailer prepared to kill himself, thinking that the prisoners had escaped (16:27). It is at this point that Luke portrays Paul explicitly intervening for the purpose of preventing the suicide: "Do not harm yourself," Paul shouts, "for we are all here" (16:28).

Luke does not indicate the specific grounds on which Paul gave the assurance contained in the second part of his shouted plea to the jailer, but it is appropriate to assess this cry in the light of the brief description that Luke has already given regarding Paul's relationship with the other prisoners. Although it was scarcely more than a passing reference, Luke did indicate three verses previously that the other prisoners were listening attentively to Paul's prayer. In doing so he intimated that Paul and Silas had come to a position of some influence with those in the surrounding cells even though they had only been in jail for some hours.

There is, then, at least the hint of a suggestion in Luke's account that Paul could assure the jailer that no prisoners had escaped because of the fact that Paul himself had a certain amount of moral pre-eminence in the situation. This line of inference receives additional support from Luke's subsequent report that the jailer then rushed in and threw himself at the feet of Paul and Silas, pleading for instruction as to what he should do to be saved (16:29–30).

Clearly, Luke's description of the jailer's extraordinary gesture toward Paul takes his readers somewhat by surprise. Yet, in the interpretation being proposed, the jailer is actually indebted to Paul on two counts. First, Paul did not take advantage of the earthquake to escape and may have had an influence upon the other prisoners as well. Secondly, he assertively intervened to bring this information to the jailer's attention and to prevent his suicide.

Because the first factor is not as well established in the text, less weight should be attached to it in seeking to analyze Luke's understanding of the jailer's motivation for casting himself at Paul's feet. Nevertheless, the second factor alone establishes Paul's concern for the jailer's well-being and supplies a plausible basis for the extraordinary affirmation of Paul and his message that Luke subsequently portrays the jailer making.

The specifics of the changed relationship and ultimately of the jailer's full Christian conversion are detailed in the verses which follow. Luke reports (1) that Paul instructed the jailer in the faith (16:32), (2) that the jailer washed the wounds of the two disciples (16:33), (3) that he and all his family were baptized (16:33), and (4) that he then brought Paul and Barnabas up into his house for a meal and much rejoicing (16:34).

There are still further aspects of Luke's account to be analyzed (for Paul will not leave Philippi until he has invoked his Roman citizenship and received redress for the mistreatment he suffered) but what has just been considered stands as a remarkable illustration of reconciliation between persons on opposing sides of a specific situation. Instead of treating him with hostility or indifference, Luke has portrayed Paul exercising a loving concern for the well-being of his jailer. This concern has resulted in a new relationship characterized by shared faith, by joy, and by peace.[40]

5

The Non-Roman Opponents of Paul

According to Luke's reports in Acts, Paul faced opposition from members of the Christian community who were dedicated to the full observance of the Jewish law. He also faced life-threatening opposition from Gentiles who were threatened by the implications of his message, from Jews of the Diaspora and Jews in Jerusalem who refused to believe in his message, and from the chief priests and their Sanhedrin allies.

The purpose of the present chapter is to place fuller light upon Paul's interactions with these five groups and the kind of opposition that he received from each. Paul was also obstructed and opposed by several Roman officials. However, an analysis of Luke's reports regarding the exact attitude of the Roman authorities toward Paul and his toward them will be deferred for study in the following chapters.

1. OPPOSITION FROM "JEWISH-LAW" CHRISTIANS

It has been previously noted that certain members of the Jerusalem community criticised Peter for his initiative in visiting Cornelius and mandating his baptism and that of his household. "Why did you go to uncircumcised men and eat with them?" Such was the challenge that Luke portrays members of "the circumcision party" presenting to Peter in 11:3.

Peter's explanation that he had not undertaken such a venture on his own authority but rather on God's and his description of the Holy Spirit's confirming intervention had the effect of placating his critics. Luke reports that, as a consequence, those present glorified God and said: "Then to the Gentiles also God has granted repentance unto life" (11:18). However, at this point in his narrative, Luke does not indicate that Peter or any of the others at Jerusalem addressed the issue of whether Cornelius and other Gentile converts should be expected to undergo circumcision and undertake the full observance of the Jewish law.

It is this very issue that comes to the fore several chapters later when Luke relates that "some men . . . from Judea" had arrived at Antioch and began to teach: "Unless you are circumcised according to the custom of Moses, you cannot be saved" (15:1). Seemingly, the implication of this report is that Gentile converts at Antioch had been received into the Christian community without accepting circumcision or a commitment to the other practices specified by Jewish law.

As indicated, Luke does not here refer to those presenting this teaching as "members of the circumcision party" but as "some men . . . from Judea." Nevertheless he seems to imply that the concerns of the two groups are similar in character. In addition, a few verses later, in describing those who challenge Paul on this point in Jerusalem, he identifies them as "some believers who belonged to the party of the Pharisees" (15:5a).

As a means of facilitating reference to all those within Acts who hold the position that Gentile converts should undergo circumcision and adhere to the other provisions of the Jewish law, the term, "Jewish-law" Christians, will henceforward be utilized. This term should be understood to encompass the three groups identified in the preceding paragraph as well as those who subsequently appear in Luke's narrative expressing similar concerns.

Luke does not state that those "Jewish-law" Christians who came to Antioch preaching the need for circumcision singled out Paul as being particularly responsible for the situation which they deplored in that community. However, it is Paul himself, along with Barnabas, that Luke portrays stepping forward to defend vigorously the practice which had been followed at Antioch and, seemingly, the practice which Paul had followed in his own missionary travels up until this point.[1]

As a result of the controversy and the debate which took place, Luke reports that Paul, Barnabas, and some others were appointed to go up to Jerusalem for deliberation with the apostles and elders about this question (15:2). Upon arriving in Jerusalem they were cordially welcomed and afforded an opportunity to recount the success that God had achieved through them (15:4). Then, however, they faced the following situation:

> But some believers who belonged to the party of the Pharisees rose up, and said, "It is necessary to circumcise them, and to charge them to keep the law of Moses" [15:5].

According to Luke's portrayal of the subsequent deliberations, Peter played a crucial role in them. In his intervention Peter first recalled that God had originally used him as the means by which the Gentiles heard the word of the gospel and came to faith. He then took the position that it would "make trial of God" (15:10) if those gathered decided to place the obligations of the Jewish law upon Gentile converts (15:7–11).

As a result of Peter's speech, the assembly kept silence for a time and then heard again from Barnabas and Paul about the wonders God had accomplished through them among the Gentiles (15:12). As a part of a more extended speech, Luke then portrays James making the following definitive intervention:

Therefore my judgment is that we should not trouble those of the Gentiles who turn to God, but should write to them to abstain from the pollutions of idols and from unchastity and from what is strangled and from blood [15:19–20].

According to Luke's report, "the apostles and the elders, with the whole church" (15:22) concurred with James' assessment and decided to send representatives with an official letter back to Antioch communicating their decision. In this instance, Paul thus received an extremely high degree of support for the approach that he had supported. His position was upheld by those assembled at Jerusalem with only minor modifications. Indeed, as is evident from Luke's description of their letter to Antioch, the Jerusalem leaders also delivered an explicit reprimand to Paul's "Jewish-law" opponents:

The brethren, both the apostles and the elders, to the brethren who are of the Gentiles in Antioch and Syria and Cilicia, greeting. Since we have heard that some persons from us have troubled you with words, unsettling your minds, although we gave them no instructions, it has seemed good to us in assembly to choose men and send them to you with our beloved Barnabas and Paul, men who have risked their lives for the sake of our Lord Jesus Christ. We have therefore sent Judas and Silas, who themselves will tell you the same things by word of mouth. For it has seemed good to the Holy Spirit and to us to lay upon you no greater burden than these necessary things: that you abstain from what has been sacrificed to idols and from blood and from what is strangled and from unchastity. If you keep yourselves from these, you will do well. Farewell [15:23–29].

In later summarizing Paul's ministry among the Gentiles in the aftermath of the decision reached at Jerusalem and communicated in the letter to Antioch, Luke portrays him operating faithfully in terms of what had been decided: "As they went on their way through the cities, they delivered to them for observance the decisions which had been reached by the apostles and elders who were at Jerusalem" (16:4).[2]

This summary verse, read in light of what has preceded, might well incline readers of Acts to conclude that chapter sixteen marks the end of Luke's descriptions of Paul's controversy with his "Jewish-law" Christian opponents. However, inasmuch as Luke presents another report bearing upon this controversy five chapters later, such a conclusion would be premature.

The setting for the last episode of this particular controversy is Paul's conference with James and the elders upon his final return to Jerusalem. The sense of his account is that James and the others do not give credence to the report that Paul's opponents have spread about him, but Luke does portray them telling Paul the following:

You see, brother, how many thousands there are among the Jews of those who have believed; they are all zealous for the law, and they have been told about you that you teach all the Jews who are among the Gentiles to forsake Moses, telling them not to circumcise their children or observe the customs [21:20b–21].

Careful attention to the way in which the criticism regarding Paul is phrased in this passage indicates that Luke now shows Paul's opponents having broadened their charges against him. Previously Luke has portrayed them alleging that Paul was lax for not insisting that *Gentile* converts keep the Jewish law. Now the allegation is that he had indicated to *Jewish* converts to the Christian movement that they themselves no longer need to keep the law or bother to have their children circumcised.

In their speech James and the elders do not indicate the precise identity of the group that has been spreading these new charges against Paul. However, the overall sense of what Luke reports is that those doing so are Christians who have a special concern that especially *Jewish* members of the Christian community observe the Jewish law faithfully. As such, they thus stand in close proximity with, and Luke may understand them to be identical to, the "Jewish-law" Christians whom he has portrayed previously opposing Paul.

It is significant that, by Luke's account, James and the elders are enough concerned about the situation to instruct Paul as to the steps he should take to alleviate the suspicions raised by these reports. Their speech to him continues on in the following vein:

What then is to be done? They will certainly hear that you have come. Do therefore what we tell you. We have four men who are under a vow; take these men and purify yourself along with them and pay their expenses, so that they may shave their heads. Thus all will know that there is nothing in what they have been told about you but that you yourself live in observance of the law [21:22–24].

Luke portrays Paul faithfully embarking upon the course of action prescribed for him by James and the elders (21:26–27a).[3] However, as a result of an uproar generated against him by some "Asian Jews," he was not able to complete the ritual (21:27b–30). From this point forward in Acts, he must deal with the threat posed by this and other hostile Jewish groups, two of whom threaten him even while he is a prisoner of the Romans. Consequently, nothing further is heard regarding the activities of those who have opposed him from within the Christian community up until this time.

It is thus the case that Luke portrays "Jewish-law" Christians opposing Paul at various stages of his ministry, indeed even after concord was supposedly reached at the council of Jerusalem. While Luke portrays their opposition as a significant factor with which Paul had to contend, it is noteworthy that they alone among all of his other opponents are never portrayed desiring his death or physically threatening him. Such is not the case with the Asian Jews just mentioned; nor is it the case with the various Gentile groups whose opposition will be considered next.

2. GENTILES IN ASIA MINOR AND GREECE

In describing Paul's journeys during the middle chapters of Acts, Luke indicates that Paul twice experienced significant opposition from Gentiles whose economic livelihood was undermined by his teaching and activity. (Both of these episodes were treated in section three of chapter four.) In the first, at Philippi, Paul expelled a divining spirit from a servant girl and thus deprived her masters of the source of their income. Luke reports that their response was to drag Paul into the marketplace and denounce them before the city's magistrates (16:16–19).

Remarkably, the charges which the girl's masters made against Paul and Silas went far beyond the deed of exorcism. Luke relates that they specifically denounced the two disciples for being Jews and for being disturbers of the public order: "These men are Jews and they are disturbing our city. They advocate customs which it is not lawful for us Romans to accept or practice" (16:20–21).

As a result of this public denunciation, other Gentiles joined the girl's masters in their attack upon Paul and so too did the magistrates. Luke indicates that, as a consequence Paul and Silas were severely beaten and thrown into prison (16:22–23).

As a result of his rejection of idols, Paul also experienced serious opposition from Gentile opponents at Ephesus. Luke portrays Demetrius raising a public outcry against Paul and engendering much confusion and indignation among the populace of the city (19:24–29). Although his report is not totally clear in this regard, Luke seems to indicate that some Jews of the city were also on the verge of being attacked by the crowd which gathered.[4]

Following counsel from his own disciples and some of the Asiarchs, Paul did not enter the town theater and was not a part of the tumultuous events that took place there. As Luke describes the situation, the town clerk played a decisive role in alleviating the crowd's concerns and reassuring them regarding the vitality of the Artemis cult. As a result, no personal harm came to any of those who were present, nor did any harm subsequently come to Paul himself (19:35–41).[5]

In chapter fourteen Luke records two other instances in which Gentiles were involved in efforts against Paul. In both of these cases, however, Paul's initial adversaries were unbelieving Jews. Rejecting Paul's message themselves, they conspired among the Gentiles and (in one case) among the rulers so that Paul himself might be destroyed.

Luke first reports that the unbelieving Jews at Iconium so poisoned the minds of the Gentiles against Paul that the city became divided with some of the populace opposing Paul and Barnabas and some supporting them (14:2–4). He then relates that " . . . an attempt was made by both Gentiles and Jews, with their rulers, to molest them and to stone them . . . " (14:5).[6]

In comparison, when he describes the situation that developed later at

Lystra, Luke indicates that Gentiles were less centrally involved in the action against Paul although the action itself inflicted greater harm upon him. According to 14:19–20, unbelieving Jews from Pisidian Antioch and Iconium came to Lystra and stoned Paul so severely that they left him for dead. Inasmuch as Luke states that they attacked Paul after "having persuaded the people" (14:19), he also seemingly indicates that the (Gentile) townspeople of Lystra had at least some level of involvement in this attempted assassination.[7]

3. THE "UNBELIEVING" JEWS OF THE DIASPORA

As indicated in chapter four, Luke does portray Paul achieving considerable success in preaching among the Jews who were dispersed in various cities and locations outside of Jerusalem and Judea. Nevertheless, along with the converts that he made in the Jewish communities he visited, Luke also reports that Paul frequently encountered serious opposition.

Luke only once explicitly uses the term "unbelieving" as an adjective characterizing those Jews who rejected Paul's message.[8] However, the understanding that those who oppose Paul do so because they are unbelieving with respect to his message is implicit in virtually all of the other passages in which Luke portrays Paul experiencing hostility from Jews. And for this reason, as well as for the consideration that Christian interpreters need be scrupulously careful in differentiating between the various kinds of "Jewish" responses that Luke portrays,[9] this adjective will be consistently used to describe Paul's opponents within the Diaspora and (apart from the special case of the high priest and the Sanhedrin officials) also within Jerusalem itself.

In all there are fully twelve instances in which Luke portrays Paul experiencing hostility from Jewish groups of the Diaspora. In five of these instances the unbelieving Jews of the particular place actually seek to kill Paul.[10] In four other instances they oppose him so strongly that he is forced to leave town.[11] In addition, Luke also describes two cases in which the opposition manifested does not greatly influence Paul[12] and one case (the Jewish magician, Bar-Jesus on Cyprus) in which Paul actually overcomes the unbelieving Jew who opposes him.

Describing events that occurred right after Paul's conversion, Luke reports that the Jews who lived in Damascus reacted to Paul's demonstration that Jesus was the Christ by plotting to kill him. Indeed, Paul was only able to escape their hands by having his disciples lower him over the city wall in a basket by night (9:23–24).

Similarly, after Paul returned to Jerusalem, his bold preaching and his disputes with "the Hellenists" resulted in the members of this group wanting to kill him (9:28–29). Luke does not indicate precisely who comprised this latter group but various factors suggest that he understood it to be composed of Greek-speaking Jews, formerly resident in the Diaspora, but now living in Jerusalem.[13] Luke states that the Jerusalem disciples took the Hellenists' machinations so seriously that they brought Paul out of Jerusalem to Caesarea and sent him on a ship to Tarsus (9:30).

Later on, at Cyprus, Paul did not receive opposition from Jews in any of the synagogues that he visited but the Jewish false prophet, Bar-Jesus, did seek to obstruct his preaching to Sergius Paulus, the proconsul (13:6–8).

At Pisidian Antioch, jealous of his initial success among the Jewish community there, some Jews rejected Paul's message and began to oppose and revile him (13:45). They eventually organized "devout women of high standing and the leading men of the city"[14] to drive Paul and Barnabas out of the district. The two disciples left, shaking the dust from their feet in protest (13:50–51).

According to Luke's narrative the coalition organized by the unbelieving Jews of Iconium was, if anything, even more formidable than that at Antioch. A "great company" of Jews accepted Paul's message; but, as noted in the preceding section, those that did not stirred up the Gentiles of the city and succeeded in dividing the public opinion regarding Paul. Eventually the unbelieving Jews, along with the Gentiles they had influenced and their rulers, made plans to stone Paul and Barnabas. However, upon learning of this, the two missionaries fled the city (14:5–6).

It was following this at Lystra that Paul came closest to death at the hands of his opponents. Initially he received much support from the populace. However, as noted previously, Luke then indicates that some of the unbelieving Jews from Pisidian Antioch as well as Iconium arrived on the scene and turned the situation against Paul. Luke provides only the sparsest description of what occurred at this point: " . . . and having persuaded the people, they stoned Paul and dragged him out of the city, supposing that he was dead" (14:19). Paul was not dead, however. He was eventually able to walk back into the city and the next day left with Barnabas for Derbe (14:20).

Later in his narrative Luke portrays unbelieving Jews from Thessalonica opposing Paul with almost as much diligence as those from Pisidian Antioch and Iconium. In their own city these Jews, jealous of Paul, manipulated some local troublemakers, gathered a crowd, and set the city in an uproar (17:5). These same Jews then followed Paul to Beroea and incited the crowds against him to such a degree that he was eventually obliged to sail for Athens (17:13–15).

Later, at Corinth, Paul once again encountered intense hostility from those Jews who rejected his message. Luke portrays him shaking out his garments against them and moving the base of his activities to a neighboring house that was owned by a receptive "God-worshiper" (18:6–7). Luke also reports that Paul's Jewish opponents made a united attack upon him a year and a half later, bringing him before the Roman proconsul. However, the proconsul refused to take action against him, and in this instance Paul came to no harm (18:12–18).

At the end of chapter eighteen, Luke reports that Paul stopped for a period at Ephesus and "argued with the Jews" there (18:19). Later, within the context of Paul's return to that city, Luke indicates more explicitly that some members of Paul's Jewish audience "were stubborn and disbelieved, speaking evil of the

Way before the congregation . . . " (19:9). Luke reports that Paul deemed it advisable to withdraw from the synagogue to a neighboring lecture hall in the light of this opposition.

Prior to his last journey to Jerusalem, the final passage in which Luke portrays unbelieving Jews opposing Paul's efforts comes at 20:2-3 when Paul is in Greece. Luke relates that a group of unbelieving Jews plotted against Paul just as he was about to set sail for Syria. As a consequence he was forced to alter his plans and went to Troas by a land journey through Macedonia (20:4-5).

In the opening section of this chapter, mention was made concerning the activities of certain "Asian Jews" against Paul in Jerusalem. Since Luke literally describes this group as "the Jews from Asia" (21:27), it is a matter of speculation whether he understood these Jews to be Paul's opponents from the recent or distant past.[15] What is clear from his account at this point is that these Jews remember and recognize Paul when they see him in Jerusalem. In fact, in attempting to rally the populace of Jerusalem against Paul, they infer that they themselves have personal knowledge of Paul's subversive activities:[16]

Men of Israel, help! This is the man who is teaching men everywhere against the people and the law and this place; moreover he also brought Greeks into the temple, and he has defiled this holy place [21:28].

The next verse in Luke's account indicates that the spark which fired their outburst against Paul was actually a fiction of their own imaginations: they had seen Trophimus the Ephesian with Paul in the city and had leapt to the conclusion that Paul must have brought him into the temple as well. Nevertheless, their anger against Paul is such that they want to kill him then and there. Luke's description at this point depicts a scene of great chaos. Having taken hold of Paul (21:27), the Asian Jews succeed in arousing a large crowd of people. Paul is dragged out into the city proper and the gates of the temple are quickly shut. A riotous uproar ensues (21:30-31).[17]

Luke next reports that the Roman tribune, Lysias, responding to the threat of a riot, extricates Paul from his attackers (21:31-36). From this point forward in the narrative, Paul remains in Roman custody. This does not mean, however, that he is free from further attacks by unbelieving Jews. While nothing more is heard regarding machinations against him by unbelieving Jews from the territory of Asia or elsewhere in the Diaspora,[18] Paul must still face great threats from the unbelieving Jews of Jerusalem and particularly from the high priest and those associated with him on the Sanhedrin.

4. THE "UNBELIEVING" JEWS OF JERUSALEM

In describing the response which followed their outcry, Luke indicates that the Asian Jews struck a responsive chord with the larger Jewish populace. Then "all the city was aroused, and the people ran together; they seized Paul and dragged him out of the temple, and at once the gates were shut" (21:30) is how he describes the resulting scene.

Initially it is not clear whether those joining against Paul are doing so because they accepted the report that he had profaned the temple, because they gave credence to the charge that he had been teaching everywhere "against the people and the law and this place," or for a combination of these factors. Whatever their exact concerns, the crowd which gathered manifested a furious violence against Paul:

> And when he came to the steps, he was actually carried by the soldiers because of the violence of the crowd; for the mob of the people followed, crying, "Away with him!" [21:35–36].

Subsequently, by virtue of the fact that he began to address them in Hebrew, Paul succeeded in temporarily pacifying the mob (22:2). However, Luke indicates that a highly controversial item in Paul's address rekindled all of their hostility toward him. When Paul quoted the Lord's instruction to him concerning his mission to the Gentiles, the crowd reacted in the following manner:

> Up to this word they listened to him; then they lifted up their voices and said, "Away with such a fellow from the earth! For he ought not to live." And . . . they cried out and waved their garments and threw dust into the air [22:22–23].

Clearly the sense of Luke's account is that the gathered crowd would not accept any words of Jesus as justification for a mission among the Gentiles. Luke's description does not precisely indicate whether the crowd's outrage flowed exclusively from Paul's advertence to the mission he had undertaken among the Gentiles or whether their fury should also be understood as having arisen from other factors as well. Luke may mean to indicate that the crowd now believed all of the charges against Paul and considered him not only an apostate Jew but also a positive threat to Judaism's central institutions.[19]

As a consequence of the Roman tribune's intervention to quell the disturbance and extract Paul from the clutches of the mob, Paul became a Roman prisoner, a status that his adversaries among the Jerusalem populace had to reckon with in making one final attempt to destroy him. Luke reports that after his hearing before the Sanhedrin, the tribune ordered Paul brought back to the Roman barracks (23:10). As a consequence, when more than forty of Paul's opponents bound themselves by an oath not to eat or drink until they had killed him (23:14), they first had to find a way of gaining access to him.

According to Luke's account, the plan which they developed involved getting Paul out of the barracks and into the city proper; there an ambush would take place. Accordingly, the conspirators went to the chief priest and elders and asked them to request that Paul be brought to the Sanhedrin for another hearing on his case (23:14–15).

It is at this point in his narrative that Luke presents a certain "fusion" between two groups of Paul's opponents in their efforts against him. It has been established in the preceding paragraphs that unbelieving Jews from among the population of Jerusalem were formidable opponents of Paul. And, as was indicated above in the section of chapter four dealing with Paul's Sanhedrin hearing, Luke has also portrayed the high priest and his allies as intent upon Paul's demise. Now Luke reports that both of these groups cooperated in a mutual effort to destroy him.

In the following passage, excerpted from the report of their conspiracy that Paul's nephew gave to the tribune, Luke indicates that "the Jews" agreed to ask the tribune to bring Paul to a meeting of the Sanhedrin on the following day. Given the context that Luke's other reports have established, and the wording of the passage itself, "the Jews" presumably refers to all of the unbelieving Jews (the priestly group as well as those who formulated the plot) who are now allied against Paul:

> And he said, "The Jews have agreed to ask you to bring Paul down to the council tomorrow, as though they were going to inquire somewhat more closely about him. But do not yield to them; for more than forty of their men lie in ambush for him, having bound themselves by an oath neither to eat nor drink till they have killed him; and now they are ready, waiting for the promise from you" [23:20–21].

5. THE CHIEF PRIESTS AND THEIR SANHEDRIN ALLIES

Before examining the range of measures which Luke now portrays the chief priests and their Sanhedrin allies undertaking against Paul, it is well to review the record of their contacts with him up until this point in the narrative. At the outset it should be noted that, previous to the time of Paul's sharp controversy with the high priest during his Sanhedrin hearing, Luke has portrayed Paul standing in alliance *with* the chief priests *against* the disciples of Jesus.

The first passage in Acts which depicts Paul standing together with the chief priests and other members of the Sanhedrin is that in which the circumstances of Stephen's execution are detailed. There, Luke not only reports that Saul took care of the garments of those who stoned Stephen (7:58), he also states: "And Saul was consenting to his death" (8:1a). The significance of this latter note concerning Paul's attitude should not be underestimated. By it, Luke portrays Paul agreeing with the Sanhedrin members that Stephen's activities and words could not be tolerated and agreeing with them that death by stoning was the way to put an end to them.

In the second set of reports which bear upon his prior relationship with the chief priests and their associates, Paul is portrayed in still closer relationship with them. In 8:1b Luke implies that those who murdered Stephen were then responsible for a more general persecution against the Jerusalem church, and in 8:3 he portrays Saul participating in this persecution and actually playing a central role in it. Then in 9:1 Luke indicates that Paul himself thought of extending the persecution to disciples in Damascus and went to the high priest for letters authorizing him to do so. Within Luke's portrait of his activities, the fact that Paul received approval for this initiative implies that he had emerged as a dedicated and trusted ally of the chief priests and was no longer to be regarded merely as the young custodian of their cloaks.

It is against this background of Paul's previous association with the chief priests that Luke portrays him addressing the angry Jerusalem crowd. Although a considerable amount of time has elapsed between the time of Paul's mission to Damascus in chapter nine and his presence before the mob in Jerusalem in chapter twenty-two, Paul still presumes to tell the crowd that "the high priest and the whole council of elders"[20] will bear witness to him. Paul describes his previous collaboration with them ("From them I received letters . . . ") and seems to suggest to the crowd that the chief priests' prior knowledge of Paul will give them a basis for speaking on his behalf (22:5).

Luke's description of the attitude with which Paul approached his initial hearing before the Sanhedrin shows him proceeding in a similarly positive manner. Luke does not portray him as in any way reluctant to appear before that body.[21] And, once there, Paul begins straightforwardly to explain that he has operated in good conscience in all that he has done, past and present alike. Seemingly, Paul expects to be able to persuade the Sanhedrin members concerning the validity of the path he has followed since the time of his conversion.

Just how mistaken Paul was in thinking that he could now receive a favorable hearing from his former allies is clearly revealed by the slap on the mouth that Luke describes him receiving at the high priest's instruction. An analysis has already been made of this incident and Paul's subsequent angry reply in chapter four. Luke then describes a situation which deteriorates so rapidly that the Roman tribune's intervention is necessary to prevent Paul from being torn limb from limb (23:2–10).

From this point forward Luke portrays the high priest and his allies using a variety of strategies in trying to achieve Paul's death. Initially, they willingly abet the plot of "the forty" to ambush Paul (23:15, 20). That plot being foiled by the tribune's quick action, they then seek to have Paul condemned to death by the Roman governor.

At the beginning of chapter twenty-four, Luke describes how the high priest, Ananias, and a number of elders traveled to Caesarea to press the case against Paul. An additional note in Luke's narrative at this point is that Ananias and the elders brought along an orator named Tertullus to serve as their official speaker in denouncing Paul to the governor (24:1).

The precise nature of the charges presented by Tertullus as well as Paul's defense against them will be analyzed in a subsequent chapter. Here it is sufficient to note that, according to Luke's report, the pressure generated by Ananias/Tertullus was intense enough to persuade Felix to keep Paul in custody and to keep him from being released two years later when Felix's time in office ended. Luke indicates both of these points as follows: "But when two years had elapsed, Felix was succeeded by Porcius Festus; and desiring to do the Jews a favor, Felix left Paul in prison" (24:27).[22]

Luke next shows that once the new governor, Festus, had arrived, the chief priests and their allies wasted no time in moving forward against Paul. At the time of the governor's first visit to Jerusalem, they immediately presented their charges against Paul and asked that he be remanded to Jerusalem. Luke does not report that they took this step out of any desire to bring Paul before the Sanhedrin; again he does not portray them as having any interest in judicial proceedings at this point. Rather he portrays them as "planning an ambush to kill him on the way" (25:3).

What was previously not completely explicit from Luke's earlier reports concerning the character of the chief priests' opposition to Paul is now manifestly clear: they so desire Paul's death that they are prepared to intervene against him themselves.

Prevented from carrying out their plan by Festus' reply that he would conduct an investigation into Paul's case in Caesarea (25:4), the chief priests then revert back to their plan for having Paul executed by judicial verdict. Luke first portrays Festus extending an invitation: "So . . . let the men of authority among you go down with me, and if there is anything wrong about the man, let them accuse him" (25:5). Luke then reports the following regarding developments at Caesarea: " . . . the Jews who had gone down from Jerusalem stood about him [Paul], bringing against him many serious charges which they could not prove" (25:7).

Luke next portrays Paul making a direct denial of the charges against him (25:8) and Festus rather quickly bringing forward a proposal of his own. The proposal, inimical to Paul, was that the trial now be shifted back to Jerusalem (25:9). Using words similar to those he used in describing Felix's motivation for leaving Paul in prison, Luke reports that Festus' reason for wanting to shift Paul's trial back to Jerusalem was that he wished "to do the Jews a favor" (25:9). By the use of this phrase, Luke indicates that the chief priests and their allies had ultimately been successful in influencing Festus to adopt their point of view.

Having delivered this final attack against Paul, and having forced him into a risk-filled appeal to Caesar, the chief priests and their allies then depart from Luke's stage. Paul was once their trusted ally. As a consequence of his conversion, they came to view him as a dangerous enemy. They themselves were not able to destroy Paul, however, by reason of their influence with Festus, they succeeded in leaving him a legacy of continued imprisonment and perhaps ultimately of death.

Such is the portrait which Luke has given of Paul's last explicitly delineated enemies. By recounting his strong adversion to falling into the chief priests' hands through a Jerusalem trial, Luke implies that Paul had come to appreciate the depth of their hostility toward him. The other side of Paul's strategy for avoiding their clutches, and what Luke reports regarding the conditions and consequences of Paul's appeal to Caesar, still remain to be examined.

EASTERN PROVINCES
OF THE ROMAN EMPIRE

BLACK SEA

MOESIA

THRACIA

DALMATIA

MACEDONIA
• Philippi
Thessalonica •
Beroea •

ADRIATIC SEA

ITALIA
• ROME

SICILIA

MALTA •

PONTUS

BITHYNIA

GALATIA

CAPPADOCIA

KINGDOM OF ANTIOCH

CILICIA
Tarsus •

• Antioch

SYRIA
Damascus •

JUDEA
Caesarea •
Jerusalem •

ASIA
Colossae •
Ephesus •
Miletus •

Iconium •
Antioch •
Lystra •
Derbe •

PAMPHYLIA

LYCIA

Troas •

CYPRUS

EGYPT

ACHAIA
Corinth •
Athens •

CRETE

MEDITERRANEAN SEA

CYRENAICA

6

Paul and the Roman Authorities in Greece and Asia Minor

In chapters sixteen through nineteen of Acts, Luke portrays Paul carrying his message regarding Jesus to four well-known Greek cities and also returning for a second time to Ephesus in Asia Minor. In three of the Greek cities, Philippi, Thessalonica, and Corinth, Luke portrays Paul coming into contact with the political authorities as a result of charges brought against him by others. He also portrays Paul and his companions undergoing a similar experience in Ephesus.

Inasmuch as several of the political offices and procedures which Luke refers to in this section have not previously been encountered either in the Gospel or up until this point in Acts, it is well to place them in context through a brief overview of the Roman provincial system. Such background will be provided in the section which immediately follows and then a detailed examination will be made of Paul's activities in each of the four cities listed above.[1]

1. THE ROMAN PROVINCIAL SYSTEM IN GREECE, ASIA MINOR, AND JUDEA

Senatorial provinces, imperial provinces, territories administered by Roman client-kings, and so-called "free" cities were all, in different ways, significant elements in the system of rule that the Romans evolved for the conquered territories that came to comprise the Roman empire. To different degrees, all four of these administrative entities are in evidence in the narrative of Luke-Acts.

For instance, Judea under Pontius Pilate and the later governors, Antonius Felix and Porcius Festus, stands in the category of an imperial province. Governors of such provinces were directly appointed to their offices by the emperor and had imperial troops at their disposal for securing the public order within the province and responding to threats (and opportunities) from the other side of the empire's boundaries. Depending on such factors as the effectiveness of their service and the emperor's disposition toward them, imperial governors might well enjoy extended years in office. Directly appointed by the emperor, they shared in his sovereign power and served at his pleasure.

In contrast Macedonia, Achaia, and Asia, the provinces that are of particular importance for chapters sixteen through nineteen of Acts, were senatorial provinces at the time when Luke portrays Paul visiting them. The governors who administered them were selected by the Roman senate and were themselves members of the senate. Many of these men had already served in Rome as consuls; they would normally at least have held the office of praetor.

Since the power these governors exercised in the provinces was comparable to that of a consul in Rome, they were titled *proconsuls.*[2] Their authority was supreme within the province's boundaries. However, in practice two factors significantly influenced their exercise of this authority. First, their term of office was only for one year. Secondly, another point of contrast with the governors of imperial provinces, they usually did not have a significant number of Roman troops or a large administrative staff directly under their control. As a general rule senatorial provinces were more "pacified" in character and thus less in need of large complements of Roman forces and personnel.

Philippi and Thessalonica, the first two cities which Luke portrays Paul stopping at in Europe proper, were both located within the province of Macedonia. Thessalonica, originally so named by one of Alexander the Great's generals in honor of his wife (Alexander's half sister) was actually the capital of this province and the center from which the Roman proconsuls conducted their administration. In addition to serving as the capital of the province, Thessalonica, along with many other Greek cities, also had its own semi-autonomous standing as a "free" city. As such it appears to have had an elected city council that, in turn, elected administrative magistrates to supervise the governance of the city.

It appears that the elected magistrates of Thessalonica were known as *politarchs*. If their responsibilities were along the same lines as those of magistrates in other free cities, these politarchs would have been responsible for virtually all aspects of city life. They would have supervised a wide range of civic activities including the construction and operation of public facilities. Nevertheless, in certain judicial and other matters, particularly those involving Roman citizens, the politarchs were ultimately subject to the jurisdiction and the influence of the proconsul. While the Romans did indeed make significant concessions on behalf of local autonomy, the exercise of such autonomy would not run contrary to established Roman procedures and objectives.

With respect to Philippi (given its name by Philip II, the father of Alexander the Great, when he conquered and then strengthened it in 356 B.C.), arrangements roughly comparable to those for Thessalonica were seemingly in effect at the time of Paul's visit. The standing of Philippi as a city enjoying local autonomy was enhanced by reason of the fact that the emperor Augustus established a Roman colony there in the wake of the great victory that he and

Mark Antony had won there against Brutus and Cassius in 42 B.C.

Various Roman leaders established such colonies to reward retiring Roman soldiers for their service, to compensate displaced Italian nationals, and to provide pockets of "Roman stability" within conquered provinces. While the cities chosen as colonies also contained native and other population groups (including Jews), an important feature of the administrative arrangements was that the Roman colonists themselves exercised control over the city government.[3]

Accordingly, the magistrates of Philippi were inhabitants of that city who had been elected to office by their peers. Like the politarchs of Thessalonica, they presumably exercised control over a wide range of social and economic activities at the city level but were, in ultimate cases, subject to the jurisdiction of the provincial proconsul. In the Roman system, the power of the provincial governor was always a force to be reckoned with. Within the province he alone possessed *imperium*, the supreme power.[4]

Corinth, the third Greek city in which Paul had significant contact with the established political authorities,[5] had had a long and distinguished history before it warred with Rome and was completely destroyed in 146 B.C. The city lay desolate for one hundred years. However, in 44 B.C. it was re-founded as a Roman colony by Julius Caesar and soon prospered to such a degree that it subsequently became a commercial center and the capital of the Roman province of Achaia.

As a Roman colony, Corinth possessed magistrates for social and economic matters comparable to those who held office in Philippi.[6] However, as the capital of a senatorial province, it was also the seat of the proconsul and it was one of these proconsuls, Gallio, who is highlighted in Luke's account of Paul's experiences there. In fact, Luke makes no mention of any local magistrates or city council at Corinth.

The history of Ephesus, the last city in which Paul had contact with the political authorities prior to his arrival in Jerusalem, was influenced greatly by its location on the west coast of the land mass that is frequently referred to as Asia Minor. Because Asia Minor is contiguous with Asia proper, the region's early history was influenced by political kingdoms in the east. However, as the "westward projection" of Asia,[7] separated from Europe proper by only a narrow strait, Asia Minor was also proximate to the political currents of the Aegean and Mediterranean worlds.

Over time, the Romans had gradually extended their control throughout this region and by the time of Paul's visits there, all of Asia Minor had been subdivided into Roman provinces. The westernmost of these provinces was simply called *Asia*.[8] It was bordered by the Aegean Sea on the west and northwest, by the province of Bithynia on the northeast, by the province of Galatia to the east, and by the province of Lycia and the Mediterranean Sea to the south. Ephesus was its capital city.

In several respects the Roman administrative arrangements for Ephesus were comparable to those in effect for Thessalonica and Corinth. The senate-appointed proconsul exercised his authority over the province as a whole from his seat at Ephesus. However, the city itself possessed a significant degree of autonomy and by means of a city council and annually elected magistrates exercised a considerable control in social and economic matters.

An added element in the administrative structure of various cities in Asia Minor was the office of city clerk. At Ephesus, this official acted as a kind of city manager, initially functioning in partnership with the magistrates, seemingly superseding them in authority with the passage of time.[9] Also present in Ephesus as well as in other cities of the region were a group of officials known as "Asiarchs." Various explanations have been put forward to explain the civic and/or religious standing of these officials. However, other than a consensus that they were wealthy and respected members of their communities, there is little agreement as to their precise civic responsibilities.[10]

Although the rule of Herod Agrippa I over Judea and Galilee and other adjacent territories has already been adverted to in a preceding chapter, reference here to his position as a Roman client-king helps to complete the present analysis of key elements in the Roman administration of provincial territories. For, as the cases of Agrippa I and his more famous grandfather, Herod the Great, both illustrate, it was sometimes feasible for the Romans to appoint indigenous leaders to administer territories or regions that would normally be administered through a provincial governor.

Under Roman auspices, Herod the Great ruled over the principal territories of Palestine for over thirty years and three of his sons ruled as his successors over parts of his kingdom, each for a different length of time. However, in the years from A.D. 6 to 41, no member of the Herod family was highly enough regarded to be given responsibility for Judea. Instead a series of seven imperial governors was appointed by Augustus and by his successors, Pontius Pilate being the fifth in this series.

Then, as has been previously noted, the emperor Gaius appointed Agrippa I as king over Judea in A.D. 41. Both Gaius and Claudius then subsequently augmented the lands under Agrippa to the point where his kingdom encompassed virtually all of the territory that his grandfather had ruled.

Upon Agrippa's death the pattern of imperial governors resumed with Antonius Felix and Porcius Festus, the two governors before whom Paul appeared, as the fourth and fifth to be appointed to this office.[11]

A point which is obvious from a consideration of the status of Agrippa I and the other Herodian rulers in Palestine also has relevance for an understanding of the status of magistrates who exercised a governing role in the free cities within other provinces of the empire. While the reality of Roman rule might not be as immediately visible when it was partially masked by the physical presence of intermediary rulers like the Herods, in the end these men owed their titles and appointments to the emperor and ruled according to Roman procedures for Roman objectives. Agrippa I, or any other client ruler, might effect "kingly" ways and even be regarded as a king by significant segments of the populace. Nevertheless, in the end he was but a representative of the

Romans; and the people over whom he "ruled" were not his subjects but theirs.

Although appropriate qualifications need to be introduced to cover their particular circumstances, the same basic considerations also hold in respect to the status and standing of the magistrates and other public officeholders in free cities. While these officials frequently came to their offices through election or through forms of appointment that were nominally independent of the Roman governors, in practice they were obligated to conduct their affairs in a manner which was consistent with the Roman objectives for that particular province.

If Roman taxes were expected from that city, then the magistrates had to play at least a passive role in their collection. Similarly if Roman troops were to be raised or deployed in that city or region, a degree of cooperation on their part was presumed. And, in addition to furthering Roman rule in such specific matters, the magistrates possessed an abiding responsibility for the general public order of their cities. If a situation developed in which the public order might be threatened the magistrates were to have immediate recourse to the provincial governor.

Local magistrates might or might not be as personally loyal to the Roman cause as were the Herods or other client rulers whose loyalty brought them great personal gain. Nevertheless, by reason of the Roman framework within which they came to office, they were ultimately faced with accountability to the provincial governor and beyond him to Rome itself.[12] To some degree at least, their acceptance of public office in a situation in which Roman power was paramount required them to be at least tacit supporters of Roman objectives. And to this degree they were in some sense *Roman* officials.

2. PAUL'S ENCOUNTER WITH THE AUTHORITIES AT PHILIPPI

In previous chapters Luke's reports concerning various occurrences at Philippi have been analyzed: Paul's encounter with Lydia, his expulsion of the spirit possessing the clairvoyant girl, his conversion of the town jailer. It is now appropriate to consider what Luke has also reported regarding Paul's dealings with the political authorities there.

At the outset it should be noted that the very terms which Luke employs in describing the Philippian situation tend to highlight the Roman presence there. In 16:12 Luke indicates to his readers that Philippi is actually a Roman colony,[13] and his subsequent portrayal of the authorities who hear Paul's case, the charges against him, and the punishments inflicted all describe a situation in which Roman procedures and prerogatives are in place.

The story of Paul's travail begins when the owners of the formerly possessed girl denounce him and Silas to officials who are first referred to as "rulers" (*archontas*, in 16:19) and then more precisely as "magistrates" (*stratēgoi*, in 16:20).[14] Luke describes the owners' denunciation in the following terms:

These men are Jews and they are disturbing our city. They advocate customs which it is not lawful for us Romans to accept or practice [16:20–21].

Luke's readers are already aware of the exploitative behavior of the possessed girl's owners. Nevertheless, the phrasing of these charges provides a further indication of their malevolence. They are now misrepresenting the character of Paul's ministry and attempting to manipulate anti-Semitic feelings in their efforts to undermine him.

It is worth taking a moment to reflect over the craftiness with which Luke portrays Paul's opponents proceeding here. Their fundamental allegation against Paul—that he is purposefully engaging in anti-Roman activity—is false. However, they have phrased their denunciation in such a way that certain aspects of Paul's activities (as they have heretofore been presented in the Acts narrative) seem to validate their charges.

Are Paul and Silas Jews? By everything that is known about them, of course they are Jews. Are they disturbing the city? Luke's account reveals that Paul has not deliberately sought to create disorder, yet disturbances have frequently been created by others in reaction to him. Is Paul advocating customs which it is unlawful for Roman citizens to accept or practice? The sense of Luke's account is that Paul has not advocated *illegal* customs and practices, yet it is also the sense of his account that Paul has advocated *new* customs.

While it is clearly Luke's understanding that their charges against Paul were made in bad faith, Luke also communicates that Paul's opponents hit upon a way of proceeding that enabled them to direct attention to certain things about him that were true. Luke's readers know at this point that Paul has not been seeking to undermine the Roman social order but they are also in a position to appreciate that his opponents have laced their false charges with enough truth to make it difficult for someone not familiar with Paul to make an accurate determination of his position.

Thus the reflective reader is not totally taken aback by Luke's next report that the magistrates themselves as well as a crowd which has collected actually believe the charges against him (16:22). However, what *is* surprising is that the magistrates begin to act on the charges without making any attempt to learn Paul's response to them or to carry out any serious investigation about the matter. As Luke portrays the scene (16:22-23), the magistrates themselves tear the garments off Paul and Silas, order them severely beaten, and then throw them into prison—all without as much as a single question to Paul or Silas or to anyone else about them.

Luke's depiction of these magistrates as derelict in their responsibilities is partially softened as a consequence of the exchange regarding Paul's Roman citizenship that he portrays taking place the next morning. Luke shows the magistrates sending "the police" (the term "lictor," referring to the official attendants of Roman magistrates, would be a better translation of the Greek here[15]) to the jail with the order that Paul and Silas should be freed. Paul, however, makes the surprising[16] declaration that he is a Roman citizen and refuses to be released. He maintains that the magistrates are in the wrong for having had him beaten and imprisoned without a proper investigation;[17] and he demands that the magistrates should now come personally to the jail and release them (16:37).

Luke portrays the magistrates responding to Paul's declaration with a considerable amount of trepidation. He indicates that they were shaken when their lictors told them of it and that they immediately acceded to Paul's demand that they come personally to the jail and release them (16:38–39).

Nevertheless, attention to Luke's entire description of the incident makes clear that the magistrates' repentance did not result in a complete vindication for Paul. The magistrates do come and "conciliate"[18] with him; however, nothing is said to indicate that the magistrates acknowledged that the charges against Paul were misrepresentations. Indeed, the outcome is that the magistrates still want Paul and Silas to leave the city (16:39).

With a final report that the two missionaries acceded to the magistrates' request that they depart, Luke then brings to a close his exceedingly rich narrative of Paul's experiences in Philippi. The two disciples leave according to their own timetable, however. Before departing, they first stop to visit Lydia and to encourage her and the other members of the new Christian community now present at Philippi (16:40).

3. PAUL'S ENCOUNTER WITH THE AUTHORITIES AT THESSALONICA

According to Luke's report, Paul spent only approximately three weeks in Thessalonica. Nevertheless, within that period a series of events occurred which are extremely important for any assessment of Paul's social and political stance.

The jealousy and the hostile actions of the unbelieving Jews of Thessalonica have previously been noted. However, what has not been heretofore examined is Luke's narrative of how this group attempted to have the politarchs intervene against Paul. Actually it was Jason, Paul's host, and others of his household, that these unbelieving Jews ended up bringing before the authorities; during the uproar they instigated, they were not able to lay their hands directly upon Paul.[19]

After they had arraigned Jason and some others before the politarchs, these jealous opponents proceeded to denounce Paul's activities and to implicate Jason (whom they know by name) for harboring and abetting the likes of Paul. It is well to consider their complaints as a unit before analyzing the individual nuances of each charge:

These men who have turned the world upside down have come here also, and Jason has received them; and they are all acting against the decrees of Caesar, saying that there is another king, Jesus [17:6–7].

In the original Greek the first charge against Paul and Silas is considerably stronger than is indicated in the RSV translation above. The RSV renders *tēn oikumenēn anastatōsantes* as "[they] have turned the world upside down." However, a more accurate translation would be: "they have stirred up revolution throughout the world"[20] or "they have caused trouble everywhere."[21]

Whatever the precise translation, the sense of what Paul's adversaries are relating to the politarchs is that Paul and Silas will generate turbulence at Thessalonica, just as they have in other provinces, unless the politarchs take action against them.

The second charge alleges that what Paul and his supporters have been doing is a direct violation of "the decrees of Caesar." Just what decrees are being referred to here cannot be established from Luke's account.[22] However, Paul's opponents are seemingly emphasizing that the type of conduct Paul has engaged in is covered by specific imperial edicts. It is not just that Paul and his friends threaten the public order. The politarchs and the citizens of Thessalonica must know that their activities are expressly prohibited by the emperor's decrees.

The third charge alleges that, as a means of justifying their behavior, Paul and his companions have put forward a claim that is itself highly subversive. Paul holds that his conduct is justified, so this accusation runs, because he believes that "there is another king, Jesus."[23]

Paul's opponents do not indicate to the politarchs Jesus' precise identity; however the phrasing of their charge implies that, in Paul's mind at least, this Jesus has a standing rivaling that of the Roman emperor. The Greek word *heteron* emphasizes that Jesus is *another* king, someone whose authority and prerogatives are comparable to those of Caesar.

Seen from this standpoint there is an inner logic and power to the charges that Luke presents Paul's opponents making against him. They denounce Paul's activities as subversive and then argue that he acts so lawlessly precisely because he believes that there is another king whose order and decrees have priority over the order and decrees of the emperor.[24] Luke does not expressly indicate the conclusion that Paul's opponents would have the politarchs draw as a result of this denunciation. Nevertheless the course of action they desire is clearly implied: the politarchs must take Paul's subversive activity seriously and deal with him resolutely.

Given the context which Luke has described, charges such as these represented a grave danger not only for Paul and Silas but also for Jason and the others. Luke makes it clear to his readers that this indictment was given out of jealousy and made in bad faith (17:5). Nevertheless, in light of what Luke has elsewhere portrayed regarding Paul's activities and his claims for Jesus, his readers can also see that the opponents' charges also contain "the color of truth."[25] As will be argued in greater detail below, Luke's overall presentation of Paul does not depict him seeking to supplant the Roman emperor or the Roman order. However, inasmuch as Luke does portray him giving his unqualified allegiance to Jesus and as willing to undertake controversial missions for the sake of Jesus, it cannot be said that Luke understands the bad faith charges of Paul's opponents to be totally fabricated.

What response does Luke describe the politarchs giving to those explosive allegations? In the verses which follow Luke portrays the politarchs taking the allegations seriously. In verse 17:8, he indicates that they, as well as the crowd which had gathered, "were disturbed"[26] (*etaraxan*) over what they had heard. He then reports that their course of action was to take security from Jason and those with him as a condition for releasing them.

In light of contemporary procedures regarding the giving of security, the meaning of Luke's phrase "take security" (*labontes to hikanon*) in verse 17:9 is probably that Jason and the others had to post a bond that would be forfeited if any activities resembling those specified in the charges were henceforth to take place in Thessalonica.[27] The politarchs were seemingly concerned to head off the possibility of any future disruptive activity either by Paul himself or by Jason and his household.

It is an interesting feature of Luke's report at this point that Paul is portrayed as willing to abide by the arrangements that the politarchs have determined. Luke states that, right after they had been released, "the brethren [presumably including Jason] immediately sent Paul and Silas away by night to Beroea . . ."(17:10). At this juncture, then, Paul makes no effort to controvert the charges that have been made against him nor does he choose to risk violating the terms of the bond by any additional preaching or activity in Thessalonica.

4. PAUL AND THE AUTHORITIES AT CORINTH

According to Luke's account Paul was not denounced to any of the lower authorities at Corinth, but rather to the Roman proconsul himself. Luke simply introduces this figure, known from other sources to be Lucius Junius Gallio Annaeus[28] by stating, "But when Gallio was proconsul of Achaia . . . " (18:12).

As at Thessalonica, Paul's enemies are unbelieving Jews. The course of action which Luke portrays them following is also similar to that of Paul's opponents at Thessalonica (as well as that of his enemies at Philippi): they denounce him before the official in charge as one disturbing the community's peace and order. Luke indicates that the following was their specific charge:

This man is persuading men to worship God contrary to the law [18:13].

Because Luke subsequently portrays Gallio giving a response to this charge that, *at face value*, seems to reduce the matter to a dispute about the Jewish law, the charge can be interpreted as nothing more than an attempt by Paul's opponents to have the civil authorities intervene in a dispute internal to Judaism. However, the matter is more complicated than it first appears. And, upon reflection, it seems evident from the presence of the Greek word *anthropous* (rendered in the above verse as "men" but more accurately rendered as "people") that the charge actually alleges that Paul is inciting behavior that runs contrary to Roman law.[29] What Paul is doing, so his opponents state, is inducing[30] the people of Corinth (not merely the Jewish inhabitants) to worship God in ways prohibited by Roman law.

The sense of Luke's narrative is that Paul's enemies expected the proconsul to act decisively against anyone who was contravening the law and disturbing the public order in such a fashion. However, carefully assessed, the response Luke portrays Gallio giving actually reveals the proconsul's prejudice against Paul's opponents:

> But when Paul was about to open his mouth, Gallio said to the Jews, "If it were a matter of wrongdoing or vicious crime, I should have reason to bear with you, O Jews; but since it is a matter of questions about words and names and your own law, see to it yourselves; I refuse to be a judge of these things" [18:14–15].

As stated above, it is possible to interpret this reply at face value as indicating that Gallio considers it outside of his responsibilities as proconsul to accept such a complaint.[31] However, several related elements of Luke's account, one present within the citation just made and others contained in the verses which follow, suggest that Luke is actually portraying Gallio not simply as misunderstanding the character of the charge but rather as *choosing to disregard it*, as willfully misrepresenting it as a charge not worthy of his attention.

Read carefully, Luke's report of Gallio's reply to Paul's accusers actually represents the Roman proconsul as having harbored anti–Jewish sentiments. The term "O Jews" reflects disdain; and the phrasing of the rest of Gallio's reply suggests a certain exasperation on the proconsul's part that he must be bothered by the likes of such a group. This impression is confirmed and strengthened by what Luke subsequently reports concerning Gallio's behavior.

Luke relates that, after telling Paul's accusers that he would not involve himself in the matter, Gallio then "drove them from the tribunal" (18:16). The sense of Luke's phrasing here is that the proconsul peremptorily ordered them out of his presence and perhaps even had his lictors physically assist them in their departure.[32] Luke then describes an unusual development. For reasons that are not clear, some of those who were present seized Sosthenes,[33] the new ruler of the synagogue, and pummeled him right in front of Gallio's tribunal (18:17). However, by Luke's report, Gallio took no account of this action even though he was still present.[34]

When these latter two aspects of Gallio's behavior are considered alongside of his "O Jews" epithet, it seems clear that Luke has actually portrayed Gallio disregarding the allegation against Paul because of his prejudice against Paul's accusers. Although Paul's enemies presented a charge that was relevant for a proconsul to consider, Gallio took no serious account of it because he disdained Jews and would not be bothered about a situation in which one group of Jews was denouncing another.

The fact that Luke does not portray Gallio making any effort to investigate the charges against Paul must also be noted in any assessment of what Acts relates concerning the episode at Corinth. Gallio does not ask, or allow, Paul's opponents to clarify their charges against him and he even prevents testimony from Paul.

When these latter considerations regarding Gallio's behavior are added to those previously mentioned, the result is a portrait of the proconsul that is far from flattering. In Luke's description Gallio has a charge presented to him regarding activities that contravene Roman law. However, because of his prejudice against Jews, he makes no effort whatsoever to investigate the situation. Instead he cavalierly dismisses the charge as lacking in substance and drives those making it away from his tribunal. In the process, a conflict breaks out, and the president of the local synagogue is beaten before his eyes. Gallio, however, looks the other way at this breach of the very public order that he as proconsul is supposed to maintain.

As a concluding consideration it should be mentioned that it is far from the sense of Luke's account to say that Paul was "acquitted" or "exonerated" as a result of Gallio's response to his case.[35] On the contrary, what a close assessment of the episode reveals is that Paul benefited from a combination of the proconsul's anti–Semitism and his lack of regard for established Roman procedure. For, according to Luke's report, Paul was not exonerated by the considered judgment of a responsible Roman official. Rather, Paul survived this attack because of the manifest bias of his judge, a bias against Paul's accusers which prevented the judge from taking any interest in Paul or in the contents of his preaching.

5. PAUL AND THE AUTHORITIES AT EPHESUS

The impact of Paul's preaching upon the idol industry located at Ephesus has already been analyzed in chapter four. Attention is now appropriately given to the events which ensued after Demetrius raised his outcry against Paul.

Luke reports that, upon hearing Demetrius' speech, the idol workers began to chant, "Great is Artemis of the Ephesians," and soon generated widespread confusion causing a large crowd to gather in the theater of the city (19:28–29a). Gaius and Aristarchus, Paul's companions from Macedonia, were dragged into the theater and Paul himself wished to go among the crowd[36] but was dissuaded from doing so by the disciples and some of the Asiarchs (19:29b–31).[37]

In his description of the events which subsequently took place in the theater, Luke depicts the city clerk (*ho grammateus*) playing a decisive role. By a skillful speech he quiets the crowd and then proceeds to address various aspects of the situation in an extremely orderly fashion.

The clerk first assesses the case against Gaius and Aristarchus. Luke portrays him interpreting the complaint against Paul's companions as having to do with sacrilegious and blasphemous behavior regarding the cult of Artemis.[38]

Seemingly on his own authority, the clerk states that the two Macedonians are not guilty of such conduct (19:37).

Subsequently, in a comment that sheds light upon the administrative structure which Luke understood to be operative at Ephesus, the clerk reminds Demetrius and his co-workers (and the crowd as a whole) about the procedures that are available to them for resolving disputes of this sort. One possibility would be for the matter to be taken to the courts for a hearing by the proconsuls (19:38).[39] Another option would be for the complaint to be settled at a meeting of the regular assembly (l9:39).[40]

The final matter which Luke portrays the city clerk taking up is the matter of the riotous events which had now occurred. The clerk expresses his concern that no adequate explanation could be given for the "commotion" (*sustrophēs*) which had taken place and he stated that all of them, himself included, were in danger of being charged with "rioting" (*staseōs*[41]) (19:40). Although no particular official is mentioned at this point, the implication is that those assembled know very well that higher authorities possess the power for bringing such a charge and that it is desirable to avoid such a development. Having delivered this sobering warning to them the clerk then dismisses the crowd and thus brings a tumultuous situation to a peaceful end (19:40–41).

While Paul himself was not personally present at the proceedings, it is the sense of Luke's account that he too was exonerated by the city clerk's statement decreeing that Gaius and Aristarchus were not guilty of sacrilegious or blasphemous activity against the cult of the goddess Artemis. Indeed such an exoneration fits well with what Luke has previously reported of Paul's activities. For at no time in his description of events at Ephesus did Luke ever portray Paul directly attacking the cult of Artemis.

Nevertheless, as has been noted above in chapter four, Luke's readers know that Paul's preaching actually did represent a threat to the worship and construction of idols. And with this knowledge in their minds, they can hardly fail to appreciate that the course of action taken by the city clerk resulted in an amazingly benign outcome for Paul and his friends. Given the level of outrage that Luke has here described Demetrius generating, and given what he has earlier indicated regarding Paul's unswerving allegiance to Jesus, Luke's readers can only wonder at the orderly and gracious way in which the city clerk diffused an electric situation without allowing any spark to fall upon Paul or his co-workers.

As a conceptual resource for shedding additional light upon the relatively complex character of Luke's descriptions of Paul's activities at Ephesus and the city clerk's response to them, it is appropriate at this point to introduce a series of considerations regarding "the Way." This is an expression that Luke himself employs in his description of the events at Ephesus. And utilizing this expression even before its meaning has been fully explained, it can now be stated that Luke presents the city clerk reaching his decisions about Gaius and Aristarchus (and Paul) without fully adverting to the social and economic consequences of "the Way."

Luke first uses this term in the ninth chapter of Acts when he states that Paul undertook a trip to Damascus "so that if he found any belonging to the Way, men or women, he might bring them bound to Jerusalem" (9:2). An acknowledgment of his prior persecution of the Way is also an element in the speech that Luke portrays Paul later making before a hostile crowd in Jerusalem: "I persecuted this Way to the death, binding and delivering to prison both men and women" (22:4).

In his description of the situation at Ephesus, Luke twice utilizes this same term. In the first instance he reports that some members of the synagogue there were rejecting Paul's preaching and "speaking evil of the Way" (19:9). Then, in introducing the controversy raised by Demetrius, he states: "About that time there arose no little stir[42] concerning the Way" (19:23).

An important conclusion emerges from a consideration of these four occurrences of the term as well as from the two instances in which it appears in Paul's subsequent trial[43] before Antonius Felix: within Acts, "the Way" identifies the disciples as constituting a socially cohesive movement, a movement arising out of and grounded in their shared faith in the risen Jesus.[44] What is more, especially in light of the use of the term in 19:23, it is also clear that this movement actually impacted, and had the potential for impacting, social and economic practices that were in effect within the Roman province of Asia and beyond.

As previously determined, Luke never indicates that Paul ever directly attacked the cult of Artemis. Yet knowing what they already do about Paul, Luke's readers still easily understand that there is a certain validity to the complaint against Paul that Demetrius voiced:

And you see and hear that not only at Ephesus but almost throughout all Asia this Paul has persuaded and turned away a considerable company of people, saying that gods made with hands are not gods [19:26].

For Paul had indeed been *almost throughout all Asia.* And it is indeed an aspect of his message that *gods made with hands are not gods.* And, by Luke's account, Paul is highly *persuasive,* persuasive with Jew and Gentile alike, and highly capable of *turning* (into new patterns of behavior and conduct) those who accept his message about the risen Jesus.

Against such a background it is clear that Luke's city clerk treats the Christian missionaries very lightly indeed. For Luke does not portray him interrogating them (at that time or on any other occasion) concerning the substantive criticisms raised about the nature of their allegiance to Jesus or their membership in "the Way." Not a question is put to them concerning the social and economic consequences of their faith. Instead the city clerk of Ephesus graciously and benignly clears them of a "non-accusation," the non-accusation that they have committed blasphemy and sacrilege against the cult of Artemis.

7

Paul and the Roman Authorities
in Jerusalem and Caesarea

Prior to describing the uprising which Demetrius generated against Paul and his companions at Ephesus, Luke had already indicated to his readers that Paul had "resolved in the Spirit" to pass once more through the provinces of Macedonia and Achaia, to go again to Jerusalem, and afterwards to travel to Rome (19:21). The subsequent chapters of Acts narrate the various journeys that Paul undertook to accomplish this plan and describe in great detail the events and the circumstances which finally did lead him to "see" Rome.

The efforts of the chief priests and their allies to destroy Paul in Jerusalem have previously been analyzed in chapter five of this study. It is now appropriate to consider the responses of four Roman officials to the charges and the other stratagems that Paul's enemies used against him. In order of their appearance in Luke's narrative these four officials are (1) Claudius Lysias, the tribune in charge of the Roman garrison in Jerusalem, (2) Antonius Felix, the fourth governor to serve in Judea after the death of Herod Agrippa I, (3) Porcius Festus, the fifth governor, and (4) Herod Agrippa II, a son of Herod Agrippa I whom the Romans appointed "king" over some of the Palestinian territory adjacent to Judea.

In the course of investigating the treatment that these four officials accorded Paul, it will also be appropriate to consider what Luke relates concerning Paul's attitude toward his Roman citizenship and the circumstances of his appeal to Caesar.

1. PAUL IN THE CUSTODY OF CLAUDIUS LYSIAS

When news of the public outcry which Paul's enemies had generated reached him, Luke describes the Roman tribune[1] of Jerusalem gathering his centurions and soldiers and moving vigorously to intervene. Noting that the tribune's name (Claudius Lysias) is given later in the narrative, it is desirable to consider in full Luke's description of his response:

And as they were trying to kill him, word came to the tribune of the cohort that all Jerusalem was in confusion. He at once took soldiers and centurions, and ran down to them; and when they saw the tribune and the soldiers, they stopped beating Paul. Then the tribune came up and arrested him, and ordered him to be bound with two chains. He inquired who he was and what he had done. Some in the crowd shouted one thing, some another; and as he could not learn the facts because of the uproar, he ordered him to be brought into the barracks. And when he came to the steps, he was actually carried by the soldiers because of the violence of the crowd; for the mob of the people followed, crying, "Away with him!" [21:31–36].

While the report which Luke provides in this passage is, on the whole, easily comprehended, two aspects of it deserve further analysis because of their importance in an assessment of the outlook of Roman officials concerning Paul's case. The first aspect concerns the motive for Lysias' intervention. The second regards the step he took in chaining Paul.

Contrary to the view which has sometimes been advanced, it is not the sense of Luke's account here that Lysias intervened in the situation for the purpose of *rescuing* Paul.[2] That Paul is brought into the precarious "safety" of Roman custody is actually a by-product of the tribune's intervention. As Luke portrays the situation the tribune is primarily concerned with maintaining the public order. He arrived on the scene with the intention of preventing a full-scale riot from breaking out and, determining that Paul was the principal cause of the trouble, he had him arrested.[3] He then tried to find out more precisely what Paul had done;[4] but, as a result of the tumult which again ensued, he was not able to do so and so had Paul removed for further questioning.

That, according to Luke's portrayal, Lysias was initially of the opinion that Paul was the cause of the furor is confirmed by the question which he asks Paul on the steps to the barracks after he learns that Paul speaks Greek: "Are you not the Egyptian, then, who recently stirred up a revolt and led the four thousand men of the Assassins out into the wilderness?" (21:38). Since, at this stage of the proceedings, Lysias has not yet learned the nature of Paul's opponents' charges against him, it must be presumed that Luke understands his identification of Paul as an Egyptian revolutionary to be based on reports he had received from other (unspecified) sources.[5] In arresting him Lysias was thus acting as a responsible Roman official concerned to maintain the Roman order and to prevent a disturbance from developing into a full-scale uprising.

A second noteworthy feature of the passage just cited is that it indicates the point at which Paul's long period of imprisonment and chaining began. While a consideration of Paul's chaining requires considering several passages of Luke's narrative out of sequence, the subject is important enough to justify a brief excursus, two paragraphs in length.

In reporting that the tribune ordered him to be bound with two chains, it is probably Luke's meaning that Paul was handcuffed to a soldier on each side of him.[6] (It should be recalled that in 12:6 Luke described Peter being similarly bound under the order of Herod Agrippa I.) As just explained Lysias took this step because he initially believed that Paul was an Egyptian revolutionary and the cause of the disturbance. However, even after Paul succeeded in convincing the tribune that he was not this person, he still remained in chains. And indeed it is a significant feature of Luke's account that, in the years that followed, Paul was never again at liberty and very probably never again really free from physical chains.

Luke does indicate that Lysias temporarily removed Paul's chains so that he could address the Sanhedrin (22:30). However, when that session also ended in an uproar, Lysias ordered his soldiers to the floor to extricate Paul from the melee and bring him back to the barracks (23:10). From the larger context of the Acts narrative, it seems clear that Luke understands Paul to have been re-chained at this point. For it is as a prisoner that he is sent to the governor Felix (23:35); and some years later when Paul, still a prisoner, is given the opportunity to address Herod Agrippa II and Festus, he makes reference to the fact that he is bound with chains (26:29).[7] In addition, when Luke later describes his circumstances in Rome, Paul is still guarded by a soldier (28:16) and Luke also portrays Paul stating: " . . . it is because of the hope of Israel that I am bound with this chain" (28:20).

As Luke narrates Lysias' actions chronologically from the point of Paul's arrest, he portrays the tribune responding in an orderly and careful manner to the situation that developed.[8] First, seemingly reassured by Paul's answer that he was not an Egyptian seditionist but actually a Jew and a citizen of Tarsus, the tribune agreed to Paul's request that he be allowed to speak to the mob (21:39–40).

As has been previously indicated, Paul's address was received well enough by the crowd until he came to the point where he recounted instructions from the risen Jesus to depart Jerusalem and go among the Gentiles. At those words those present cried out vehemently against him and began to wave their garments and throw dust in the air (22:22–23).[9]

Luke indicates that the tribune did not understand why the crowd had reacted so violently toward Paul and resolved to interrogate Paul directly and severely to get to the bottom of the matter. The sense of the account is that, while Lysias knew that Paul was not the Egyptian who had led the earlier uprising, he could not make sense of Paul's standing vis-à-vis the Jews of Jerusalem and wanted to force Paul to explain what he had done to generate such controversy. Accordingly, he ordered that Paul be interrogated by means of a whipping (22:24).[10]

It is at this juncture of his narrative that Luke portrays Paul adverting to his Roman citizenship and indicating to the centurion in charge of the whipping that it would be illegal to scourge a Roman citizen who had not first been found guilty of some offense (22:25). More will be said about Paul's attitude to his citizenship below. Here it suffices to note that Paul's mention of his rights as a citizen[11] was sufficient to bring the tribune quickly to the scene, and to cause him to void the order for Paul's scourging (22:26–29).

Despite this unexpected turn of events, Luke portrays Lysias continuing his efforts to determine exactly why Paul was a focus of so much controversy and whether he had done anything that was illegal. It was for this reason that he convened a meeting of the Sanhedrin (22:30). However, as has already been indicated in chapter five as well as in the preceding paragraphs, this meeting ended in a great uproar and Lysias had to send his troops on to the floor in order to prevent Paul from nearly being killed.

Faced with this additional setback, how does Luke portray the tribune proceeding? Lysias still seemed to think that Paul should be kept under arrest. Luke states that he had his soldiers bring Paul back to the barracks and house him there overnight. He did not indicate to Paul that he had gained any insight from the Sanhedrin hearing or that he had any plans for releasing him.

However, at this point Luke relates that Lysias faced yet another unexpected development: the plot by more than forty of Paul's enemies including the chief priests and the elders to ambush and kill him. Luke portrays the tribune responding vigorously when Paul's nephew brings him news of this conspiracy. Verses 23:23–24 show him dispatching a large force of two hundred soldiers, two hundred spearcarriers, and seventy cavalry in order to insure Paul's safe conduct to the governor's residence in Caesarea. What follows next in Luke's account is the text of the letter that Lysias sent to the governor to explain his handling of Paul's case.

> Claudius Lysias to his Excellency the governor Felix, greeting. This man was seized by the Jews, and was about to be killed by them, when I came upon them with the soldiers and rescued him, having learned that he was a Roman citizen. And desiring to know the charge on which they accused him, I brought him down to their council. I found that he was accused about questions of their law, but charged with nothing deserving death or imprisonment. And when it was disclosed to me that there would be a plot against the man, I sent him to you at once, ordering his accusers also to state before you what they have against him [23:26–30].

Read against the light of what has preceded in Luke's account, Lysias' letter can only be regarded as a creative interweaving of fiction and fact. The tribune purports to provide his superior with a succinct account of what has transpired in Paul's case. Yet, read closely in the light of what Luke has previously narrated, his letter contains a significant number of inaccuracies and distortions.

In verse 23:27 Lysias informs the governor that he rescued[12] Paul from the crowd because he had learned that Paul was a Roman citizen. However, from his earlier narrative, Luke's readers already know that Lysias did not learn that Paul was a Roman citizen until considerably later and that Lysias' primary intention was not so much to rescue Paul as it was to arrest the person who appeared responsible for the disturbance. In addition the attentive reader cannot fail to notice that Lysias' letter does not mention that Lysias had taken steps to have Paul scourged and would have completed the process if Paul had not spoken up.

The net impact of this crucial omission and the two preceding distortions is to present Lysias' handling of Paul's case in a decidedly favorable light. Indeed, the sense of Luke's account is that the governor would scarcely have reason to fault Lysias' handling of the matter if he were to form his opinion based upon Lysias' own report. Quite the contrary, the tribune's letter portrays his own conduct as careful, thorough, and responsible.

It is of more than passing interest to note that Lysias' letter summarizes the matter in a way that is also slanted in Paul's favor! For Luke shows Lysias stating to the governor that he had determined that Paul was *"charged* with nothing deserving death or imprisonment" (23:29; emphasis added) and his formulation conflicts with Luke's other reports in two minor, but still significant ways.

First, Luke has not presented Lysias previously indicating (to Paul or to anyone else) that he had reached any conclusion regarding Paul's innocence. Secondly, the way in which Lysias phrases his conclusion seems perhaps *too exonerating* of Paul. Lysias reports not that he considers Paul to be innocent of the charges against him but that *no* substantive charges have been preferred against him. Such a professed interpretation conflicts, at least implicitly, with Luke's other reports about the substantive charges of the Asian Jews and the substantive charges preferred by Ananias/Tertullus.

In light of these considerations, may it not actually be the case that Luke understands Lysias to have attempted to "cover" himself with Paul at the same time that he sought to "cover" himself with Felix. In this reading, Luke understands Lysias' letter to be an adroitly political move: Lysias is sending the governor a prisoner who is not only a Roman citizen, but a highly articulate one; and, to the degree possible, he wishes the "prisoner" as well as the governor to have a positive estimation of the way he has handled the matter.

2. PAUL'S ATTITUDE TOWARD HIS ROMAN CITIZENSHIP

As observed in chapter six of this study, Luke introduced the topic of Paul's Roman citizenship when he cited Paul's reproach to his jailer at Philippi. As noted in the preceding section, this issue again emerged when Paul confronted Lysias' soldiers with his citizenship as they were about to scourge him. A comprehensive assessment of exactly what Luke presents on this subject requires an analysis of the conditions and circumstances in which Paul makes each of these references to his Roman status and also necessitates a consideration of other passages in which Luke included material on various aspects of Paul's identity.

As Luke portrays the circumstances at both Philippi and Jerusalem, Paul's announcements of his citizenship can easily be criticized *from a Roman point of view* as having been irresponsibly tardy. It has been previously observed that Luke does not portray the magistrates at Philippi providing Paul and Silas with any opportunity to explain their conduct. Rather they summarily ordered the beating of the two disciples and then had them thrown into prison (16:22–23). Nevertheless, Luke does not depict Paul trying to speak any word of protest at the time of this beating and he indicates that Paul and Silas spent the entire night in prison without making any mention to the jailer that such treatment violated their rights as citizens. (It will be recalled that this was an extremely remarkable night.) In fact Luke reports that Paul only made his identity known when he learned that the magistrates intended to compound the mistreatment which had already occurred by trying to release them "secretly" (*lathra*). Luke indicates that Paul was outraged by such a proposal and that it galvanized him into declaring emphatically: " . . . and do they now cast us out secretly? No!" (16:37).[13]

If reflective readers of Luke's account of Paul's sanctions at Philippi became puzzled over the somewhat unusual way in which Paul's citizenship came to the fore, their sense of puzzlement would only be heightened in reading Luke's description of Paul's approach during his encounter with Claudius Lysias. Once again, from a Roman point of view, Paul's advertance to his citizenship came unseemly late in the proceedings.

As noted previously Lysias had already bound Paul with two chains and was having his soldiers bring him into the barracks when Paul asked to speak with him. Lysias, surprised to learn that Paul spoke Greek, responded that Paul must not be the Egyptian who had led four thousand Assassins into the wilderness. Given that Paul's standing as a Roman citizen would have supreme significance for the tribune and given that virtually no other piece of information could be so helpful to Paul's cause at this point, readers of Acts can only be astounded by Luke's report that Paul said nothing about his Roman citizenship at this juncture but emphasized instead his pride at being a citizen of Tarsus![14]

Later when Paul is on the verge of being whipped, Luke portrays him suddenly and abruptly decrying such a violation of his citizen's rights. However, this declaration seemingly only adds to the difficulty of interpreting Paul's attitude toward his citizenship. If Paul was reluctant to claim Roman status at the outset, why does he claim it now? Does Luke intend to suggest that it was out of a desire to avoid being whipped? Yet, at Philippi Paul accepted a beating without shouting out that it violated his Roman rights. These and other related questions all arise as the reader initially puzzles over the sense of Luke's reports.

In contrast with the discrepancies that initially seem to be present in Paul's approach to his citizenship, Luke portrays Lysias as being unambiguously convinced as to the value of citizenship. Learning of Paul's status, Lysias himself states: "I bought this citizenship for a large sum" (22:28a). However, to this disclosure Paul simply replies, "But I was born a citizen" (22:28b).

What is the meaning of Paul's reply at this juncture? Various commentators have interpreted Paul's words as indicating his claim to a higher standing than that of the tribune.[15] In this interpretation Paul's answer draws attention to the fact that he himself possessed citizenship before Lysias and that his father had been a citizen before him.[16]

Such an interpretation may possibly express Luke's understanding of the matter, but it may also be the sense of the passage that Paul does *not* take any special pride at having been born a citizen. Rather, Paul's announcement may be either a) a simple explanation of how he, a person of no great means has come to citizen status or b) affirmation by Paul that he himself never sought citizenship but rather received it as a consequence of his birth.

Favoring the latter interpretation is the fact that, elsewhere in Acts, Paul never refers to this aspect of his background. Seemingly, the overall sense of Luke's narrative is that Paul was a Roman citizen by birth but did not attach great importance to this status and did not advert to it in presenting himself to various audiences. Also to be considered in this regard are the numerous situations and settings in which Paul preached, the great variety of individuals and groups with whom he interacted and from whom he frequently suffered adverse responses. Except for the two instances just mentioned, Luke never portrays him making reference to his citizenship in any of these encounters.

Once observed, this pattern encourages the attentive reader of Acts to return to the two passages in which Paul does mention his citizenship and assess them more carefully. Upon such review these passages can be seen to have several elements in common, elements which shed additional light on some of the subtler lines within Luke's portrait of Paul.

First it should be noted that, in both cases, Paul only draws his citizenship to the attention of Roman officials and those working under them. In neither case does he bring his Roman status forward when non-Romans are present. At Philippi Paul's mistreatment took place in the market place and presumably in a setting where non-Romans and Romans were present (16:19). However, Luke portrays him making no mention of his citizenship in this "mixed" setting. Only later through a statement to his jailer and through him to the Roman magistrates does Paul indicate his standing (16:37).

Similarly Luke does not portray Paul adverting to his citizenship when he speaks to the Jerusalem crowd or when he speaks to Lysias in front of the crowd (21:39). Rather, it is only afterward, in the relative seclusion of the barracks, that he indicates his status to the centurion and through him to the tribune (22:25–26).

Second, in both cases Paul's announcement of his citizenship is made for the purpose of influencing the conduct of his fellow Roman citizens. He brings it to the fore only as a means of forcing his fellow citizens into altering their plans for treating him improperly. At Philippi Luke implies that Paul was particularly offended when he learned of the Roman magistrates' plan to have him and Silas released secretly and presumably, dishonorably (16:37). And clearly, at Jerusalem Paul was provoked by Lysias' decision to examine him by whipping (22:24–25).

Perhaps the most appropriate generalization in light of all of these various elements is to state that the Acts narrative does not portray Paul attaching particular importance to his Roman citizenship.[17] Luke never shows Paul publicizing his citizenship before any of the non-Roman groups or individuals whom he addresses and, even before Roman officials it is not something to which Paul immediately adverts. However, in two special cases, instances in which Paul could not abide the course of action proposed by the respective Roman officials, he did confront them with his status and thereby caused them to alter their plans for dealing with him.

3. PAUL TRIED BY AND IN THE CUSTODY OF ANTONIUS FELIX

Luke's description of the interactions between Paul and Felix can be analyzed in terms of three headings: (1) the initial interrogation, (2) the formal hearing, and (3) the extended imprisonment.

In reporting the initial steps which Antonius Felix[18] took regarding Paul's case, Luke shows the governor proceeding in an orderly fashion. According to 23:34, the first thing that Felix did when Lysias' soldiers brought Paul before him in Caesarea was to ascertain the Roman province to which Paul belonged. Learning that Paul was from the province of Cilicia,[19] he then told him, "I will hear you when your accusers arrive," and gave instructions that, in the meantime, Paul should be guarded in Herod's praetorium (23:35).[20]

Luke indicates that a formal hearing took place five days later when a delegation arrived from Jerusalem to press charges against Paul. As analyzed in chapter five above, Luke portrays the high priest and his allies proceeding to seek Paul's death through judicial channels undeterred by the failure of their conspiracy to ambush him. Luke also explains that they brought with them an orator named Tertullus; he would serve as their representative and actually prefer their charges against Paul.

As Luke recounts his speech, Tertullus began with a compliment, a *captatio benevolentiae,*[21] to the governor for the benefits of Roman rule in Judea and then proceeded to charge Paul with being an enemy of that rule. The text of his remarks is as follows:

> Since through you we enjoy much peace, and since by your provision, most excellent Felix, reforms are introduced on behalf of this nation, in every way and everywhere we accept this with all gratitude. But, to detain you no further, I beg you in your kindness to hear us briefly. For we have found this man a pestilent fellow, an agitator among all the Jews throughout the world, and a ringleader of the sect of the Nazarenes. He even tried to profane the temple, but we seized him. By examining him yourself you will be able to learn from him about everything of which we accuse him [24:2-8].

As just indicated the charges that Ananias/Tertullus presented were designed to persuade the governor that Paul was dangerous to Roman rule and must be dealt with severely. Either of the offenses specified—the more general charge that Paul was agitating against the Roman order and the specific claim that he attempted to desecrate the temple precincts—could provide Felix with grounds for ordering Paul's execution. And, in the light of what Luke has previously presented, such an outcome is clearly what Ananias and his allies desired.

Luke's readers already know of the chief priests' intense bias against Paul and recognize that their charges are not put forward in good faith. However, while Luke consistently provides signs of their malevolence, he never portrays the priestly group as being inept. Indeed the care with which their first charge is formulated testifies again to the priests' intelligence about claims that cry out for a Roman governor's attention.[22]

The RSV translation, " . . . we have found this man a pestilent fellow, an agitator among all the Jews throughout the world, and a ringleader of the sect of the Nazarenes," conveys the general thrust of Ananias' first charge.[23] However, a careful review of the underlying Greek suggests that his indictment of Paul was actually even more devastating. Indeed, insofar as the translation, " pestilent fellow," suggests that Paul was being characterized as merely quaint or eccentric, it does not well reflect the richer meaning of the Greek.

"This man is a plague (or a virus) and is transmitting revolution among Jews throughout the world" would seemingly be more reflective of what the Greek indicates regarding Tertullus' charge.[24] In effect, Tertullus and Ananias are arguing that Paul poses a threat akin to that of a contagious disease and urging that Felix proceed against him vigorously.

The second specific allegation that Luke portrays Tertullus making, that Paul had attempted to profane the temple,[25] should also probably be understood as an effort to provide additional grounds for a capital sentence. Nevertheless, the testimony of the Asian Jews would be necessary to establish this charge and since they were not among the delegation that had come from Jerusalem (24:1), it can be inferred that Luke understands Ananias/Tertullus to have placed less emphasis upon this charge. (Indeed, as will be indicated below, Paul highlights the absence of the Asian Jews when he makes his defense.)[26]

In contrast with the irregular actions he earlier attributed to the Roman magistrates at Philippi, Luke here portrays Felix granting Paul the right to make a formal defense against his opponents' charges. Like Tertullus, Paul also begins with a *captatio benevolentiae,* but it should be noted that it is shorter and more restrained even though Paul does describe his own outlook as cheerful: "Realizing that for many years you have been judge over the nation, I cheerfully make my defense" (24:10).

As the narrative continues, Paul then enters upon an extended defense of his conduct. His basic response is that his adversaries cannot prove their charges against him.[27] Without addressing the issue of his activities in other provinces of the Roman world, he denies stirring up any unrest in Jerusalem and states that his exemplary conduct in the temple has been misrepresented by the absent Asian Jews. Characteristically, he also makes reference to his allegiance to Jesus and his confidence in the resurrection. It will be seen in the full text given below that Paul also briefly took the offensive in drawing Felix's attention to a part of what had taken place when Lysias brought him before the Sanhedrin:

> As you may ascertain, it is not more than twelve days since I went up to worship at Jerusalem; and they did not find me disputing with any one or stirring up a crowd, either in the temple or in the synagogues, or in the city. Neither can they prove to you what they now bring up against me. But this I admit to you, that according to the Way, which they call a sect, I worship the God of our fathers, believing everything laid down by the law or written in the prophets, having a hope in God which these themselves accept, that there will be a resurrection of both the just and the unjust. So I always take pains to have a clear conscience toward God and toward men. Now after some years I came to bring to my nation alms and offerings. As I was doing this, they found me purified in the temple, without any crowd or tumult. But some Jews from Asia—they ought to be here before you and to make an accusation, if they have anything against me. Or else let these men themselves say what wrongdoing they found when I stood before the council, except this one thing which I cried out while standing among them, "With respect to the resurrection of the dead I am on trial before you this day" [24:11–21].

Luke indicates that, after he had heard Tertullus' charges and Paul's response to them, Felix's decision was to defer his judgment until Lysias could come down from Jerusalem, presumably to provide further information (24:22). Felix also instructed his centurion that Paul "should be kept in custody but should have some liberty, and that none of his friends should be prevented from attending to his needs" (24:23).

At this stage, the outcome of the hearing before Felix seems to be more favorable to Paul than what eventually proves to be the case as Luke's narrative moves forward. While the hearing has ended in a standoff, the tide seems to have turned in Paul's direction. He still must remain in prison, but the conditions of his imprisonment are alleviated slightly. And, significantly, after he reports Felix's initial decision in the matter, Luke then remarks that the governor possessed "a rather accurate knowledge of the Way" (24:22).

The reader's tendency to assume that the matter is going to be resolved in Paul's favor is further strengthened by Luke's report that "after some days Felix came with his wife Drusilla, who was a Jewess;[28] and he sent for Paul and heard him speak upon faith in Christ Jesus" (24:24).

However, it is at this point that Luke's portrayal of Felix, hitherto largely positive, begins to shift in the opposite direction. Within the space of just three verses, Luke now provides his readers with the following three adverse statements concerning Felix's character and his conduct:

(1) And as he (Paul) argued about justice and self-control and future judgment, Felix was alarmed and said, "Go away for the present; when I have an opportunity I will summon you" (24:25).
(2) At the same time he hoped that money would be given him by Paul. So he sent for him often and conversed with him (24:26).
(3) But when two years had elapsed, Felix was succeeded by Porcius Festus; and desiring to do the Jews a favor, Felix left Paul in prison (24:27).

In addition to what it expressly states regarding Felix's reaction, what the first reports implicitly indicates concerning Paul's boldness should also be noted. Indeed, Luke here describes an almost classic case of role reversal. Paul, the prisoner (presumably, still physically chained!) proceeds to lecture his judge, the Roman governor of Judea, on the meaning of an upright and ethical life.

Faith in Christ Jesus brings with it a responsibility for righteousness and self-control, standards of conduct that will be upheld in a future judgment: this is the thrust of what Luke portrays Paul preaching here, and seemingly it was precisely his emphasis upon this connection which caused Felix to become alarmed. Although Luke portrays Felix allowing for the possibility of future dialogue with him, Paul's proclamation has clearly made the governor uneasy.

Luke's second report concerning Felix's hope to receive a bribe presents the governor in an unflattering light. Luke's readers presumably know that over and above being antithetical to the gospel, such conduct was also specifically and explicitly prohibited by Roman law. The juxtaposition of this report with the preceding one also tends to provide a certain confirmation for the appropriateness of Paul's emphasis upon righteousness and self-control in his dialogue with the governor. Luke now shows Felix to be very much in need of such instruction!

Finally, the third report of this sequence also serves to impugn Felix's conduct of his office. Two years have now elapsed and Felix's originally stated plan to hear Lysias' testimony and then to proceed has not materialized. Meanwhile Paul has been kept chained and restricted for the duration of this period.[29] Such is the initial indictment carried by the report.

In addition, the report also indicates that Felix decided to leave Paul in prison when he was succeeded by Porcius Festus. Luke implies that Felix could have easily released Paul at this juncture but decided against doing so. Moreover Luke tells the reason for the governor's decision: to extend a "favor" to Ananias and his allies.

Such a report clearly does not portray an impartial Roman governor, but rather one in collusion with Paul's enemies. Coming as it does in the wake of Luke's earlier statement that Felix was interested in receiving a bribe, the new mention of a prejudiced granting of "favors" can only contribute to Luke's reader's disillusionment with this now departing Roman governor and his handling of Paul's case.[30]

4. PAUL ON TRIAL BEFORE PORCIUS FESTUS

Luke's reports regarding the efforts that the chief priests and their allies made against Paul when Porcius Festus became governor of Judea[31] have already been analyzed in chapter five. In the present section Festus' response to their efforts and Paul's reaction to Festus' proposal will be spotlighted.

Luke uses the word "favor" (*charis*) in a significant pattern when he describes the way in which both Felix and Festus handled Paul's case. As noted in the preceding section, it was because Felix desired to do Paul's opponents a *favor* (24:27) that he left Paul in prison. Luke now uses the same term in describing the chief priests' new plan for ambushing Paul:

> Now when Festus had come into his province, after three days he went up to Jerusalem from Caesarea. And the chief priests and the principal men of the Jews informed him against Paul; and they urged him, asking as a *favor* to have the man sent to Jerusalem, planning an ambush to kill him on the way [25:1–3; emphasis added].

At first Luke describes Festus acting independently and refusing to grant this request for transferring the case. Festus told Paul's enemies something that they knew quite well—that Paul was being held in Caesarea—and indicated that they could accompany him (Festus) there if they so desired (25:4-5). Indeed, the direct quotation which Luke attributes to Festus is not prejudicial to Paul and seems to envision the possibility that he might be exonerated:

> So . . . let the men of authority among you go down with me, and *if there is anything wrong about the man,* let them accuse him [25:5; emphasis added].

In reporting the trial at Caesarea, Luke does not indicate the specific allegations which the priests' group put forward but rather confines himself to relating that they made "many serious charges" (25:7). Presumably Luke understands these allegations to have been along the lines of those which Tertullus presented to Felix, i.e., that Paul was contravening Roman rule by inciting the Jews of the Diaspora to riot and that he had attempted to profane the Jerusalem temple. In his own comment upon the validity of Paul's opponents' charges (whatever their exact formulation) Luke simply states that they were charges "which they could not prove" (25:7).

Paul's defense speech is also reported in an economical fashion, indeed within a single verse. Luke portrays him following his earlier approach of arguing that there was no evidence for the charges. Paul insists that he has not profaned the temple or violated any other aspect of the Jewish law. He also denies that he has offended against Caesar in any fashion. (It should be noted that previously, in his defense speech before Felix, Paul did not explicitly deny such a charge or refer directly to the emperor. Luke will also portray him using this term "Caesar" several verses later when he directs his appeal to Caesar.) The exact phrasing of this brief defense speech is as follows:

> Neither against the law of the Jews, nor against the temple, nor against Caesar have I offended at all [25:8].

It is at this point in the narrative that Festus makes such an about-face as to leave Luke's readers in a state of amazement. Instead of some comment upon the charges against Paul or some reaction to Paul's defense, something that the reader is expecting at this point, Luke portrays Festus actually making the startling proposal that Paul's trial be shifted back to Jerusalem!

Even though this proposal is phrased mildly as a question ("Do you wish to go up to Jerusalem, and there be tried on these charges before me?"[25:9b]), Luke clearly understands it as a threatening and ominous initiative. He has already reported to his readers that Festus rejected this same proposal eight days earlier. And although he does not state that Festus knows anything about the plan for ambushing and killing Paul, Luke himself as well as his readers knows that such a plan is a part of the Jerusalem landscape.

These considerations would be sufficient in themselves to establish the negative character of Festus' proposal. However, Luke provides his readers with even more explicit ground for decrying the governor's proposed course of action. In 25:9a Luke states that Festus made his proposal "wishing to do the Jews a *favor*." He thereby indicates, in the plainest possible terms, that Festus has ceased to function impartially and uprightly. Once again a Roman governor has decided to do Paul's enemies a *favor.* Festus is now overtly acting in collusion with the chief priests!

The response that Luke describes Paul himself making to Festus' proposal consists of two parts. Initially Paul expresses his intense displeasure over what Festus has suggested. He then proceeds to counter Festus' move with a surprising maneuver of his own. What follows is Luke's report describing the first part of Paul's response:

> But Paul said, "I am standing before Caesar's tribunal, where I ought to be tried; to the Jews I have done no wrong, as you know very well. If then I am a wrongdoer, and have committed anything for which I deserve to die, I do not seek to escape death; but if there is nothing in their charges against me, no one can give me up to them" [25:10–11].

Seemingly a quality akin to outrage pervades this reply. Paul insists that there is no reason to shift his trial because it is already being held at the correct spot. He will have nothing to do with any argument that an offense against the Jewish law is more appropriately tried in Jerusalem; indeed, he remains convinced that he has not offended against Jewish law.[32]

It is worth reflecting upon the assertiveness that Luke shows Paul displaying in making such an indignant response. Still a Roman prisoner and still presumably chained to one or more soldiers, Paul nevertheless admonishes the governor hearing his case for proposing to depart from correct procedure and charges him (Festus) with failing to respect what he knows to be the truth of the matter. Paul's words, "as you well know," are clearly to be regarded as a direct rebuke to the governor. His statement, "no one can give me up to them," expresses similar extraordinarily defiant sentiments.[33]

The second part of Paul's response is, as Luke portrays it, a declaration of just four words: "I appeal to Caesar." By these words Luke shows Paul translating the sentiments he has just expressed to Festus into an action step. His appeal to Ceasar[34] also simultaneously constitutes a further rebuke to Festus. For, by claiming his right to be heard by Caesar, Paul is indicating his conviction that Festus is no longer capable of handling his case impartially.[35] He does not want the trial to continue under Festus' jurisdiction even at Caesarea.[36]

It is the sense of Luke's account that Paul did not lightly or cavalierly exercise his right of appealing to Caesar. Similar to the two earlier instances in which he claimed his rights of citizenship, Luke again here depicts Paul asserting his right of appeal before a small, predominantly Roman, group and only at a point in the proceedings when he could no longer tolerate a course of action being proposed by a Roman official. Indeed, what is implicit in the present narrative, that Paul exercised his right of appeal only under considerable pressure, is explicitly confirmed later. In the final chapter of Acts Luke portrays Paul stating to the members of the Jewish community at Rome: "But when the Jews objected, I *was compelled* to appeal to Caesar—though I had no charge to bring against my nation" (28:19; emphasis added).[37]

Luke closes his description of these proceedings with the report that Festus first conferred with his counselors and then responded to Paul that he would indeed be sent to Caesar (25:12). However, according to the narrative which follows, Paul's case was still to receive two additional assessments before he would depart for Rome.

5. THE NEW ASSESSMENT OF PAUL'S CASE BY FESTUS AND AGRIPPA II

Luke takes fully a chapter and a half of his narrative (25:13–26:32) in order to describe the events which occurred at Caesarea once Herod Agrippa II arrived on the scene. The interactions which Luke describes taking place are indeed complex and are perhaps best considered as a sequence of scenes which illumine different aspects of a connecting idea: Festus' desire to have his handling of Paul's case viewed in the best possible light now that Paul has appealed to Caesar.

In terms of the space Luke allots to it, Paul's own defense speech is manifestly the longest of these scenes. It is preceded by a scene in which Festus explains to Agrippa his handling of Paul's case and another in which Festus summarizes his conduct before an assembly he has convened. In the scene which follows Paul's speech, Agrippa expresses his own perspective concerning Paul's situation.

Luke indicates that some days after Paul's trial and his appeal to Caesar, Herod Agrippa II and Bernice, two children of Herod Agrippa I, arrived in Caesarea to welcome Festus (25:13). According to Josephus, the emperor[38] Claudius had considered Herod Agrippa II as a possible successor to his father in the rule of Judea and the other territories of Palestine. However, Claudius' advisors counselled against this on the grounds that a boy of seventeen would not be able to deal with the complexities of Roman rule in Judea.

As a result Roman governors were again appointed for Judea, and Agrippa II remained in Rome as a part of the emperor's court. However, some years later he was assigned to rule over the small kingdom of Chalcis and subsequently he was given responsibility for a larger territory including Ituraea, Trachonitis, and Abilene. Still later the emperor Nero added a number of cities and villages around the Sea of Galilee to these territories, and in gratitude Agrippa changed the name of the capital of his kingdom from Caesarea Philippi to Neronias.

Without indicating how much Festus knew concerning Agrippa's background or exactly what estimation the governor had of this neighboring king, Luke simply reports that Festus took advantage of the opportunity presented by Agrippa's visit to acquaint him with the particulars of Paul's case. The account of events which Luke portrays Festus giving Agrippa initially accords well with what Luke himself has previously narrated:

> Festus laid Paul's case before the king, saying, "There is a man left prisoner by Felix; and when I was at Jerusalem, the chief priests and the elders of the Jews gave information about him, asking for sentence against him. I answered them that it was not the custom of the Romans to give up any one before the accused met the accusers face to face, and had opportunity to make his defense concerning the charge laid against him. When therefore they came together here, I made no delay, but on the next day took my seat on the tribunal and ordered the man to be brought in" [25:14b–17].

Similarly, although some of the information that the governor communicates in the next verses is new to Luke's readers, it still fits well with the general picture of events that they have previously received. Indeed, in light of what has occurred in the previous scenes before Claudius Lysias and Antonius Felix, Luke's readers are not surprised by Festus' statement that the status of Jesus was a factor in the hearing he had conducted:

> When the accusers stood up, they brought no charge in his case of such evils as I supposed; but they had certain points of dispute with him about

their own superstition and about one Jesus, who was dead, but whom Paul asserted to be alive [25:18–19].

The same judgment may not be given, however, for the third part of Festus' speech. For here, by virtue of a crucial omission and a serious misrepresentation, Festus is unmistakably portrayed presenting a summary that is decidedly biased in his own self-interest:

Being at a loss how to investigate these questions, I asked whether he wished to go to Jerusalem and be tried there regarding them. But when Paul had appealed to be kept in custody for the decision of the emperor, I commanded him to be held until I could send him to Caesar [25:20–21].

The omission just referred to is Festus' failure to mention that his real motive for wanting to shift the trial was to do the chief priests and their allies a favor. Clearly this omission biases the report and results in Agrippa receiving a distorted picture of the circumstances under which Paul made his appeal to Caesar.

The misrepresentation alluded to is present in Festus' statement that Paul *had appealed to be kept in custody* for the decision of the emperor. Paul, according to Luke's reports, had never expressed such a desire. In fact the contrary would be true: according to Luke, Paul had always desired to be released.[39]

In addition to the presence of these two major distortions in the final section of Festus' remarks, it should now also be noticed that Luke has also portrayed the governor highlighting the brighter side of his own conduct in the earlier sections of his speech. Thus, looking back to verse 14, Festus had mentioned that it was from Felix that he inherited Paul's case. And in verse 17 he pointed out that he himself "made no delay" in handling the matter, implicitly contrasting his own approach with that followed by Felix. Also in verse 16 he portrayed himself as a responsible Roman administrator: "It was not the custom of the Romans to give up any one before the accused met the accusers face to face." Finally, in verse 20 Festus' words to Agrippa that it was not an easy matter to know how to proceed, can also be seen as an indirect plea for sympathy. The report which Luke describes Festus making to Agrippa II is thus laced through with elements which tend to protect the governor from criticism and enable him to project the image of a responsible and careful Roman administrator.

Comparable self-serving elements are also to be seen in the speech which Luke reports Festus making the next day. Luke relates that Agrippa agreed to assess Paul's case (25:22) and that Festus convened a large assembly the following day and had Paul brought before this gathering. After indicating the grandness of the setting (25:23) Luke then reports Festus' opening speech as follows:

And Festus said, "King Agrippa and all who are present with us, you see this man about whom the whole Jewish people petitioned me, both at

Jerusalem and here, shouting that he ought not to live any longer. But I found that he had done nothing deserving death; and as he himself appealed to the emperor, I decided to send him. But I have nothing definite to write to my lord about him. Therefore I have brought him before you, and, especially before you, King Agrippa, that, after we have examined him, I may have something to write. For it seems to me unreasonable, in sending a prisoner, not to indicate the charges against him" [25:24–27].

What are the significant "understandings" that Festus would have his audience gain as a consequence of this speech?

First, Festus advises his hearers concerning the volatile situation he had encountered:"The *whole* Jewish people petitioned me . . . *shouting* that he [Paul] ought not to live any longer" (emphasis added). On this point it should be noted that Festus' audience for this report consisted of Roman officials, Roman officers, and the presumably pro-Roman "prominent men of the city,"[40] an audience that would presumably be receptive and sympathetic to a report from the governor that he had faced a turbulent crowd in Jerusalem.

Secondly, Festus reports that he himself had determined (contrary to the assertions of Paul's enemies) that there was no reason for Paul's death. This is a claim that clashes resoundingly with what Luke has previously reported to his readers. In addition, Luke's readers are sensitive to the fact that Festus once again omits any mention of his own attempt to cooperate with Paul's enemies.

Thirdly, Festus suggests that, were it not for Paul's appeal to the emperor, the matter would have been resolved to Paul's satisfaction. The governor here implies that Paul was somewhat precipitous in making such an appeal. Again Luke's readers already know the true facts of the matter: Paul was *compelled* to make his appeal because he could no longer rely on Festus' impartiality.

Festus would thus have his audience adopt the view that he, as governor, had proceeded responsibly in the face of a difficult situation. And he would also have them believe that he was still proceeding to conduct the case in a responsible manner. He has decided to honor Paul's request to be sent to Rome, but he is in need of his hearers' help (especially Agrippa's) in order to be able to send appropriate charges to "my lord."[41]

If Luke here shows Festus indicating to the other high Roman officials of the province that his conduct of Paul's case is beyond reproach, it should not be overlooked that this same speech also enables the governor to assuage the indignation and the anger that Luke has previously portrayed Paul expressing. The inaccuracies and the distortions present in Festus' speech have just been alluded to. However, it should be noted that Paul's innocence is also clearly affirmed in the governor's remarks. Festus now indicates that Paul's enemies were incorrect in petitioning against him[42] and in shouting that he did not deserve to live any longer: "I found that he had done nothing deserving death."

Inasmuch as Acts has often previously portrayed Paul himself insisting on such an assessment, Luke's readers might conceivably expect Luke next to report that Paul affirmed and applauded this surprising assessment. However, in his subsequent speech Paul does not directly comment upon Festus' central statement about him, nor does he seek to counter any of the governor's aforementioned distortions. Rather, Luke presents Paul making a speech that is, to all intents and purposes, primarily oriented to the conversion of King Agrippa!

In the opening lines of his speech Paul refers to his desire to defend himself "against all the accusations of the Jews." Nevertheless, in a speech twenty-two verses long (26:2–23), only the last five verses constitute anything close to an explicit defense and even these latter verses stand more as a general statement concerning Paul's uprightness than they do as a specific refutation of the charges that have previously been made against him. Paul's speech is thus more appropriately regarded as a wide-ranging description of his own conversion, a description given for the purpose of justifying faith in Jesus to his hearers and particularly to Agrippa II. Only in the sense that it might persuade an audience that the person making it was not dangerous can such a speech be considered "defensive."

Luke portrays Paul beginning with an extended compliment to Agrippa, praising him as being well familiar with Jewish traditions and entreating him for an extended hearing:

> I think myself fortunate that it is before you, King Agrippa, I am to make my defense today against all the accusations of the Jews, because you are especially familiar with all customs and controversies of the Jews; therefore I beg you to listen to me patiently [26:2–3].

As the speech proceeds, Paul rehearses his Jewish background (26:4–8), his persecution of the disciples (26:9–11), his conversion on the way to Damascus (26:12–16), and his mission among the Gentiles (26:17–18). As indicated, it is at 26:19–23 that Paul comes closest to a defense statement.[43] In verses 20 and 21 he explains that it was because of his mission among the Gentiles that the unbelieving Jews seized him in the temple and tried to kill him. He then concludes with a vibrant affirmation regarding God's enduring help for the witness that he continues to give to Jesus.

Other elements beside his opening *captatio benevolentiae* contribute to the impression that Paul seeks to engage Agrippa personally with his speech. Paul frequently punctuates his statements with the appellative "O king." Such a personalizing form of address occurs at verses 7, 13, and 19. And at verse 8 Luke portrays Paul engaging Agrippa with the summoning personal question: "Why is it thought incredible by any of you that God raises the dead?"[44]

Luke reports that Festus interjected a comment at the end of Paul's speech and shows Paul responding to it. The character of this exchange will be treated below. However, in terms of a thematic development, attention is first appropriately given to the way in which Luke continues to portray Paul attempting to engage Herod Agrippa. Luke describes him again complimenting Agrippa for his knowledge and his acuity and then dramatically inviting him to a profession of faith:

> For the king knows about these things, and to him I speak freely; for I am persuaded that none of these things has escaped his notice, for this was not done in a corner. King Agrippa, do you believe the prophets? I know that you believe [26:26–27].

The interpretation that Paul has been boldly[45] seeking Agrippa's conversion is confirmed by the response that Luke now portrays the king giving (26:28): "In a short time you think to make me a Christian!" Paul admits as much in his own subsequent reply, also making reference to his situation as a prisoner:

> And Paul said, "Whether short or long, I would to God that not only you but also all who hear me this day might become such as I am—except for these chains" [26:29].

Luke portrays the hearing ending on this vivid note. Agrippa stood as did Festus, Bernice, and the others who had been sitting with them (26:30). As they withdrew, Luke reports them speaking in the following terms concerning Paul's case:

> This man is doing nothing to deserve death or imprisonment [26:31b].

Then in the next verse Luke shows Agrippa giving Festus the following assessment regarding Paul's case:

> This man could have been set free if he had not appealed to Caesar [26:32b].

In reporting these two assessments, Luke indicates that, even though Paul's speech did not explicitly address the charges against him, it still had the effect of convincing Agrippa that he was not the type of dangerous individual that the Romans were accustomed to punish through chains[46] or through death. Indeed the thrust of the first assessment is such as to call into question, at least implicitly, Felix's conduct in keeping Paul in prison for two years.[47] On another level of the narrative, however, those giving such an assessment are themselves judged by it. For when Paul departs from the view of Festus and Agrippa and those with them, Luke shows him still a prisoner and still presumably in chains.[48]

While Agrippa's involvement in Paul's case must be regarded as positive in terms of Festus' own objectives, there are subleties to Luke's presentation that should not be overlooked. Agrippa voices no direct criticism of Festus' conduct and his comment in 26:32b does have the effect of aligning him with Festus' decision to send Paul to Rome. However, on the other hand, Luke does not depict Agrippa offering to help Festus formulate any charges against Paul.[49] And it should also be noted that the first part of the king's comment serves to put a certain distance between himself and the governor. In stating "this man could have been set free," the king expresses an opinion which at least implicitly criticizes the course that Festus has followed. For, according to Luke's earlier reports, Festus had not come to the conclusion that Paul should be set free. Indeed, his specific proposal for transferring his case to Jerusalem was more oriented to Paul's death than to his liberty.

Comparable subleties must also be adverted to regarding Luke's reports with a view to determining the consequences that Agrippa's involvement had for Paul. As mentioned, Agrippa effectively concurs with Festus' judgment that Paul should be sent to Rome as a prisoner. However, Paul himself is shown to have a significant regard for the king's grasp of Jewish affairs and a regard for Agrippa's personal capacity to recognize Jesus as the fulfillment of God's promises. Agrippa's statment, "This man could have been set free if he had not appealed to Caesar," is also as straightforwardly favorable an assessment as Paul ever receives from a Roman official in Acts. In giving it Agrippa provides support for Paul's own longstanding contention that he has done nothing that would justify Roman chains much less a Roman capital sentence.

What then of Porcius Festus and Luke's description of his efforts to have his own conduct favorably regarded? The passages previously considered as well as the passage deferred for consideration until this point indicate that Festus succeeded reasonably well in this attempt—reasonably well with Agrippa and the other assembled personages and reasonably well with Paul himself.

As has been previously demonstrated, Festus took advantage of Agrippa's visit to place his handling of Paul's case in a positive light and to ask Agrippa's support in the formulation of the charges. In the actual event the governor did succeed in gaining at least partial support from Agrippa. Luke shows that the king became personally involved in the proceedings and made an assessment which supported the Festus' decision to send Paul to Rome.

In evaluating Festus' success in conciliating with Paul, it should be borne in mind that Luke had previously indicated Paul's outrage over the governor's proposal to transfer his trial to Jerusalem. However, in testifying before Agrippa and the entire assembly, Paul made no mention of any previous mistreatment except for his concluding comments that he desired to be free of his chains.

In addition, in the passage deferred for treatment until now, Luke actually shows Festus and Paul taking part in a positive exchange. This exchange begins when Festus breaks into Paul's speech in such a way that he effectively compliments Paul:

> Festus said with a loud voice, "Paul, you are mad; your great learning is turning you mad!" (26:24).

Luke shows Paul responding congenially to Festus' interruption. Paul addresses the governor courteously ("most excellent Festus"[50]) and explains that he is not out of his mind in speaking boldly about such matters. For, Paul continues, King Agrippa already possesses information about them (26:25-26). Paul then resumes his personal appeal to Agrippa in the manner indicated above, displaying no umbrage at all regarding Festus' "interruption."

Luke has thus depicted Festus proceeding to cover three of his principal bases prior to sending Paul off to Rome. Herod Agrippa II, himself a well-connected Roman official, has been schooled in the governor's own story regarding his handling of Paul's case. Similarly the lesser Roman officials and officers present at the assembly have also had an opportunity to hear the governor's "new" perspective on Paul's case. Paul himself, formerly portrayed as critical of the governor, is now no longer voicing such criticism and has actually been presented responding cordially and deferentially to the governor during the course of a public hearing.

The chief priests and their allies are the only group that Luke does not mention in his reports concerning Festus' final maneuvers. Festus had proposed to do them a "favor" by shifting Paul's case. However Luke does not show the governor making them a party to the events which subsequently occur. They have not been present to hear Festus tell the assembly that they were without grounds in their denunciations of Paul. And from this point forward nothing more is heard from them in the story of Acts.

Having completed his description of what can only be described as a highly complex and nuanced series of interactions, Luke then reports that Paul, along with some other prisoners, was delivered to the care of a centurion of the Augustan Cohort named Julius. Then began a long and arduous sea journey to Rome, the consequence of Paul's appeal to Caesar and the fulfillment of the risen Lord's words to him.

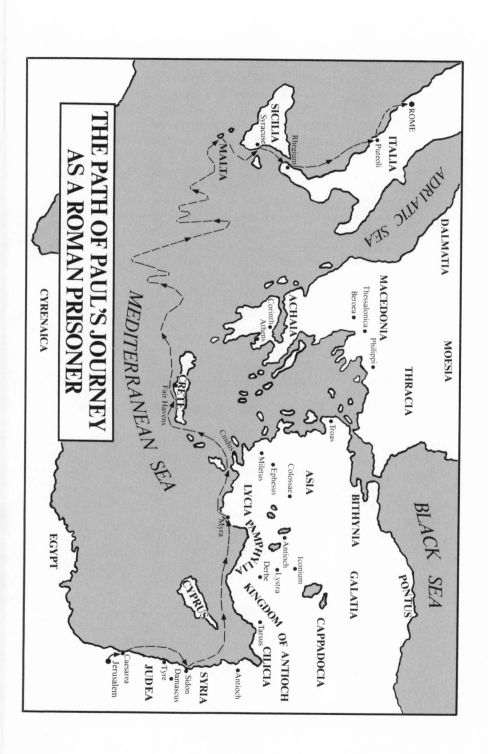

THE PATH OF PAUL'S JOURNEY
AS A ROMAN PRISONER

8

Paul, a Prisoner and a Witness in Rome

Before proceeding with the new developments which Luke reports in chapters twenty-seven and twenty-eight of Acts, it is desirable to devote a section to a review of Paul's attitude toward the Roman social order and another to an analysis of his uncompromising commitment to Jesus as Lord. The character of Paul's voyage to Rome will then be briefly treated and his interactions with the Jewish community of Rome studied in some detail. Insights from all of these sections will then be utilized in a concluding analysis of the ending of Acts, an analysis that will give careful attention to the manner in which Luke spotlights Paul, steadfastly loyal to Jesus, at the center of the stage.

1. PAUL'S ATTITUDE TOWARD THE ROMAN ORDER

To assess the portrayal that Luke has given in terms of Paul's stance toward the Roman social order, it is necessary to reflect upon Paul's attitude and conduct in a variety of circumstances within Acts. On the one hand, Luke shows Paul operating comfortably and even congenially within the framework of the Roman social order. Yet, on the other hand, he also portrays him withholding his ultimate allegiance from it.

As indicated within the preceding chapters of this study, Luke presents Paul undertaking extensive travels within Syria, Asia Minor, and Greece: all areas in which Roman rule was in effect. Signs of this control are abundantly present in Acts and Luke portrays Paul as being well aware of the realities of the Roman provincial system.

An interesting feature of the Acts narrative is that it makes so little reference to elements of Roman infrastructure such as roads and aqueducts and to various elements of Roman popular culture such as gymnasia, baths, and games.[1] Nevertheless, largely because the narrative portrays Paul interacting so naturally with various Roman military and political officers, Luke's readers rather easily form the impression that Paul is equally at home with the other aspects of Roman rule: Rome's economic and social, as well as its political innovations.

As a general rule Luke portrays Paul interacting cooperatively with the Roman officials he encounters. For example, Luke shows Paul addressing Roman military officers as well as Roman administrators quite respectfully. He holds sustained conversations with Lysias, Felix, Festus and Agrippa; and, in marked contrast with the Jesus of Luke's Gospel, the Paul of Acts is always ready to explain himself when asked to do so by a Roman official.

Within limits, Paul is also willing to cooperate with these officials' plans and procedures. Negatively, Luke does not characterize him as ever resisting arrest or attempting to escape from custody. Positively, Paul energetically cooperates with Lysias' plan to have him appear before the Sanhedrin and with Festus' efforts to have him appear before Herod Agrippa II at Caesarea.

As a means of highlighting Paul's generally cooperative attitude toward the Roman authorities and the order they maintained, it can be stated for the sake of emphasis that there is nothing in Luke's descriptions to suggest that Paul was in any way associated with the Zealot movement. Luke does not portray him expressing the opinion that it would be desirable for the Romans to withdraw from Judea much less showing any support for violent efforts to overthrow them. Also, in contrast to the Jesus described in the Gospel, the Paul of Acts makes no pronouncement on the subject of Roman taxes; nor does he instruct his disciples to avoid taking "the kings of the Gentiles" as their models.

Indeed, with the possible exception of one comment in which he speaks of being delivered into the hands of "the Romans" (28:17) in a way that seems to suggest that they were a group with whom he was not personally identified, Luke never shows Paul expressing even a mild criticism of the Romans or their order.[2]

On the other hand, while Paul is assuredly not anti-Roman in his outlook and generally behaves in a cooperative manner toward the Roman officers and officials he encounters, Luke also narrates a significant number of instances in which Paul acts assertively and boldly toward these same guardians of Roman rule. In addition, his indignant insistence that the magistrates of Philippi should come personally to release him and Silas, Paul's bold, challenging words to Festus should also be recalled: "I am standing before Caesar's tribunal, where I ought to be tried; to the Jews I have done no wrong, as you know very well" (25:10).

Then, too, in Acts 24:24–25 there is the image of Paul standing before Antonius Felix in his chains and presuming to argue with him about "justice and self-control and future judgment." Nor does Luke indicate that Paul was cowed by the greatness of the assembly in Caesarea and the fact that such notables as Herod Agrippa II and Bernice, and prominent Romans from the city were all assembled to help Porcius Festus judge him. As previously indicated, Luke shows Paul speaking boldly, testifying to his own conversion by the Lord Jesus and even seeking Agrippa's conversion. In the course of his speech Paul does refer to the embarrassing reality of his Roman chains; but, as the speech itself demonstrates, he does not allow them to intimidate him.

In addition to adverting to his bold, assertive conduct toward various

Roman authorities, any complete assessment of Paul's stance toward the Roman social order must also take into account the fact that Luke so fre-quently portrays him as a disturber of the Roman peace.

The number of cities and provinces in which Paul's activities resulted in public controversy and even rioting is extensive. Because of the controversy which developed from their preaching within the Jewish community at Pisidian Antioch, Paul and Barnabas ended up being driven out of that city and district (13:50). At Iconium the outcome of their preaching in the synagogue was that the whole city became divided and an effort was made to stone them (14:4–5). Then, after his initially successful preaching at Lystra, Paul's earlier opponents arrived on the scene and instigated a stoning that very nearly resulted in his death (14:19).

At Philippi the possessed girl's owners gathered a crowd for an attack upon Paul and Silas and the Roman magistrates themselves joined in (16:22). Then, at Thessalonica a group of unbelieving Jews who were jealous of Paul's preaching gathered some malcontents and succeeded in setting the city into an uproar, the crowd eventually attacking Jason's house in an effort to lay hands on Paul (17:5). The same group of Jewish opponents from Thessalonica also succeeded in inciting crowds against Paul at Beroea (17:13). At Corinth despite Paul's achievement in converting the head of the synagogue, those Jews who refused to believe eventually made a concerted effort to denounce Paul to the proconsul (18:12). Finally, when Paul was later once again preaching in Asia, resistance to his message resulted in an extensive uprising led by Demetrius. The entire populace of Ephesus became so agitated that the city clerk found it necessary to admonish them over the consequences they faced for such rioting (19:40).

To be sure, Luke's narrative makes it clear that Paul never deliberately stirred controversy or disturbed the public order in any of the provinces he visited. And the same is true regarding the near riot which ensued after he had returned to Jerusalem. Paul had no role in engendering the initial uprising; rather it was instigated by Jews from Asia who were mistaken in assuming that Paul had violated the temple precincts. Finally, although the gathered crowd rose up vehemently during the course of Paul's speech to them (at the mention of Jesus' instructions to him to go among the Gentiles), the speech itself was not for the purpose of rekindling the crowd's outrage but was rather for the purpose of justifying Paul's standing as an observant Jew.

It can thus be said that Luke's descriptions of the circumstances in which each of the foregoing incidents took place indicate that Paul did not have the intention of creating public disorder, of disturbing the Roman peace. Nevertheless, Luke's descriptions also make it clear that, although he did not intend it, public disorder ensued in virtually every place that Paul conducted his ministry.

Much of this disruption, although not all of it, was related to the fact that Paul's preaching frequently generated controversy in the Jewish communities he visited. As Luke's various accounts make clear, these internal disputes frequently spilled over into the public arena and resulted in city–wide turbulence and disorder. From the standpoint of a Roman concern for public order, it is this latter phenomenon, rather than internal controversy within a given Jewish community, that would be significant.

In addition to indicating that Paul's preaching in the Jewish communities of the Diaspora could and did lead to public disorders, Luke also reports two instances in which Paul's way of conducting his ministry in a totally Gentile setting similarly led to significant public upheavals. No members of Jewish communities were involved at Philippi or at Ephesus; yet, in both of these cities, Luke shows that Paul's ministry still served to engender major public controversies.

When Luke's various descriptions of Paul are scrutinized for their implications with respect to the Roman order, what emerges is the portrait of a disciple whose resolute proclaiming of Jesus significantly disturbs Roman rule within the provinces of Judea, Galatia, Asia, Macedonia, and Achaia, even though he himself is not anti-Roman.

The fact that Paul is, by Luke's account, so deeply motivated in his discipleship is also a factor that needs to be adverted on in the present context. For Paul's unsurpassed dedication is an important element in a hypothesis that can now appropriately be proposed. The hypothesis: Luke's Paul, though not anti-Roman and not seeking to contravene the Roman order around him, is nevertheless so zealous and so committed in his discipleship that he would be likely to refuse a Roman order obliging him to desist from his public ministry on behalf of Jesus.

Such a hypothesis obviously moves beyond the material contained in the reports that Luke has provided regarding Paul's activities. Within the narrative of Acts, Luke never places Paul in a situation where he is told by any Roman official that his proclamation of Jesus must cease due to the turmoil that it is engendering. Yet conjecture about such a scene does help to unveil some of the implications of the highly committed discipleship that Luke does attribute to Paul.

If the Paul of Acts were to receive such an order from a Roman official, what response could he be predicted to give to it? A negative reply, a refusal to obey such an order, is the only response that can be projected as consistent with all that Luke has narrated regarding Paul's commitment, his outlook, his approach. A negative response would also locate Paul within the "tradition" of Peter, John and the others at Jerusalem: "Whether it is right in the sight of God to listen to you rather than to God, you must judge; for we cannot but speak of what we have seen and heard" (4:19–20).[3]

2. PAUL'S PROCLAMATION OF JESUS AS LORD

Was the Paul presented in Acts dangerous to the social order that the Romans sought to maintain in their eastern provinces? The analysis presented in the previous section indicated the basis for an assessment that Luke's Paul did indeed constitute a *de facto* threat to the Roman order even though he never intentionally sought to disrupt Roman rule and was not anti-Roman in his outlook. It is now appropriate to add to this analysis considerations regarding Paul's reverence for Jesus as his "Lord" and his public use of the term "Lord" in carrying out the mission which Jesus had entrusted to him.

As the analysis of chapter four has already indicated, the impact that the risen Jesus made upon Paul at the time of his conversion was overwhelming. In both of the accounts of this experience that Luke portrays him giving, Paul indicates that at first he did not know who had so overwhelmed him. Yet he did know that it was someone of unprecedented power and he immediately used the term "Lord" in addressing this person, asking "Who are you, Lord?" (9:5; 22:8; 26:15). And, as Luke's subsequent reports make abundantly clear, from that time forward Paul never ceased to experience the power of this Lord, the power of the risen Jesus, in his life.

Luke portrays Paul's later life as the faithful carrying out of the ministry that was entrusted to him by Jesus. In the fulfillment of this ministry, Paul journeyed, frequently under the most difficult and threatening circumstances, throughout the provinces of Asia Minor and Greece. And in virtually every province that he visited, Paul gave faithful and forthright testimony on behalf of his Lord.

The terms and phrasing that Luke uses in detailing Paul's acknowledgment of "the Lord" and Paul's ministry on Jesus' behalf vary. The term "Lord" appears frequently in Paul's speeches. In addition Luke frequently describes Paul's activities in such terms as, "speaking boldly for the Lord" (14:3) and "teaching and preaching the word of the Lord" (15:35); he also indicates that Paul had the disciples at Ephesus "baptized in the name of the Lord Jesus" (19:5).[4]

In assessing these references to Jesus as "Lord" for what they imply with respect to Luke's positioning of Paul within the overall Roman framework, two further observations are in order. The first observation pertains to the *public* character of Paul's speech. There is nothing secretive or cautious about Paul's references to and proclamations about Jesus the Lord. Rather, Luke presents him speaking of Jesus quite boldly and at virtually any opportunity. As previously indicated, Acts provides ample indication that words spoken within the walls of synagogues could still have significant consequences for the public order. Even more so does the potential for public reaction exist when the speeches and proclamations take place in town squares and on city streets, settings in which the Paul of Acts frequently witnessed on behalf of Jesus.

Secondly, the fact that the Jesus to whom Paul refers in all of these speeches is obviously a *living* Lord is also a consideration to be underscored. In each of the instances mentioned above, it is clear that the Jesus of whom Paul speaks is not some noble and revered figure from the past. Rather this Jesus is a presently existing person who sometimes appears to Paul and gives him direction and encouragement. This living Jesus also exercises power in other ways. Many are the instances in which Luke portrays Paul's Jesus intervening, through Paul, to heal the sick and overcome evil spirits.

When appropriate attention is accorded these latter dimensions of his deep allegiance to the Lord Jesus, what becomes clear is that Luke's Paul will necessarily have a far different basis for assessing the Roman order than a person without such an allegiance. It is not difficult to conclude, for example, that the basis on which Paul evaluates the Roman order will differ significantly from the basis on which someone who is loyal to a pagan deity or someone without any religious loyalties will make such an assessment.

But what of the potential for differing assessments by someone like the governor Porcius Festus, a figure within Acts whose first and ultimate loyalty is to no other "lord" than the Roman emperor himself? That is an aspect of the question which remains to be examined.

In the present context it is appropriate to recall that "lord" is the very title that Luke reports Festus using when the governor speaks about the emperor and about submitting charges to him (25:26).[5] Particularly in light of the fact that *kyrios*, the Greek word underlying "lord," is the same exact word that Luke always portrays Paul using when he speaks about Jesus as "the Lord," Festus' reference is highly significant.

By convention the RSV and most English translations indicate that Festus' lord is not on the same level as Paul's Lord by capitalizing the English word when *kyrios* refers to Jesus or to God. This convention of translation serves to communicate that there is a distinct difference between the two "kinds" of lords. For clearly in Festus' statement, "But I have nothing definite to write to my *lord* about him" (25:26) *kyrios* designates a far different personage than it does when it appears in Paul's statements about, and references to, "the *Lord* Jesus Christ."

Within the framework of Acts, it is helpful to inquire concerning Festus' attitude toward the two "lords," Jesus and Caesar. Clearly it is to the emperor in Rome that Festus gives his fundamental allegiance. This emperor has given him his appointment as governor and the emperor possessed the authority to send him to virtually any part of the Roman world. Consequently, Festus adheres before all else to the emperor's decrees, procedures, and wishes.

In contrast with this foundational allegiance to the emperor, Festus manifests no allegiance whatsoever to Jesus. Even more basically, he does not even recognize Jesus or accord him any kind of standing. The "word of the Lord," the word of Jesus, has no claim upon Festus' loyalties. As a teaching regarding life and conduct, it is of no consequence to him. It is not in any way to be compared with a "word" or a "decree" of the emperor.

In contrast with Festus, it is obvious from what has been indicated above that Paul views Jesus as the "Lord" who is ultimately sovereign over his life. It is Jesus who accomplishes Paul's conversion and it is on Jesus' behalf that Paul undertakes extensive and arduous missions. It is Jesus' "word" that gives him fundamental meaning and direction, and for the sake of Jesus Paul is willing to accept great suffering and even the loss of his life.

What is the character of Paul's loyalty to the other "lord," the emperor, given his "foundational" loyalty to Jesus? In Acts Paul does possess what can be termed a "conditional" loyalty to the emperor. He does after all appeal for the personal judgment of Caesar and he does, in other ways as well, manifest a regard for the procedures which Caesar uses to rule. Nevertheless, Acts leaves no doubt that, in the event of a clash between these two loyalties, Paul's allegiance to Jesus would unquestionably take precedence over his allegiance to Caesar.

While no explicit clash between Paul's "foundational" loyalty to Jesus and his "conditional" loyalty to the emperor is ever described in Acts, the account of events at Thessalonica which Luke has included in chapter seventeen takes on added significance in the present context. It should now be recalled that Paul's Thessalonian opponents made the allegation that he acted disloyally to Caesar because of his deeper loyalty to Jesus, "another king." As previously noted, the denunciation was made in the following terms:

These men who have turned the whole world upside down have come here also, and Jason has received them; and they are all acting against the decrees of Caesar, saying that there is another king, Jesus [17:6b-7].

As previously indicated in section three of chapter six, Luke portrays the politarchs at Thessalonica as being "disturbed" by these charges and as requiring security from Jason and the others. Such a response does not necessarily establish that these officials accepted the premise that Paul's loyalty to Jesus was resulting in subversive conduct; Luke may simply be indicating that the authorities were proceeding cautiously in the face of a near riot.

However, inasmuch as the charges did have a plausible ring to them or, as in a previous figure of speech, did have the "color of truth" about them, that Luke may understand the politarchs' response as indicating that they considered the situation one of conflicting loyalties must still be retained as a possibility. Whatever the exact nuances that Luke intends to impart relative to the authorities' reaction to the charges, it is at least certain that he has shown Paul's enemies raising the issue of conflicting loyalties. Thus, it is established within the Acts narrative that at least some of Paul's contemporaries were alert to the *possibility* that deeply held allegiances to other lords could bring a person into conflict with the rule of Caesar.

When the results of the analysis made in the present section are added to those derived in the previous section, it can be stated by way of summary that Acts does not portray Paul as anti-Roman, but does portray him as a de facto disturber of the Roman peace. Secondly, at the same time that Luke's reports show Paul manifesting a conditional loyalty to the Roman emperor and his order, they also present him teaching widely concerning the "Lord" Jesus and manifesting a foundational loyalty to him.

Finally, while Acts never relates an instance in which Paul's foundational loyalty to Jesus actually clashes with his conditional loyalty to the emperor, such a clash is by no means unthinkable within the framework of Luke's work. Indeed, it can be hypothesized that, in the event of an order to desist from public preaching concerning Jesus or in some similar event involving a clash of allegiances, the Paul of Acts would without hesitation manifest his foundational loyalty to the cause of Jesus, his *Lord*.

3. NOTES CONCERNING THE MEDITERRANEAN VOYAGE

In describing the various "ministries" that he undertook during the course of what developed into an extremely perilous sea journey to Rome, Luke does not portray Paul referring to Jesus by name. Nevertheless, at several points Luke describes Paul as intensely loyal to God and as experiencing anew God's powerful presence in his life. Within the context of his relationship to God Luke also portrays Paul responding respectfully and cooperatively to the Roman centurion in charge of him and receiving at the centurion's hands remarkably kind treatment.

In terms of Luke's narrative sequence, the hospitable treatment afforded Paul by Julius the centurion, is actually illustrated first. When the ship on which the Roman group[6] was traveling reached Sidon, Luke relates that the centurion gave Paul leave to go ashore and be cared for by his friends, explicitly stating: ". . . Julius treated Paul kindly" (27:3a). Luke also indicates that this initial favorable rapport between Julius and Paul remained in effect throughout the journey. In 27:10–11 when Paul counseled against trying to sail for Phoenix, another harbor on Crete, Julius rejected Paul's advice for that of the ship's captain and owner; however, the sense of Luke's report is that Paul's counsel, the counsel of a prisoner, was given serious consideration.

Subsequently, Paul's prophecy of travail having been partially fulfilled, Luke indicates that the centurion complied fully with Paul's later urging that the sailors be prevented from abandoning ship (27:31–32). An even more noteworthy sign of Julius's high personal regard for his distinguished prisoner comes still later when Luke relates that the centurion prevented the soldiers from proceeding with their plan to kill the prisoners expressly because he wished to save Paul (27:42–43).[7]

Finally, it should also be noted that Luke's reports of the circumstances of the party's stay at Malta and at Puteoli portray Paul being given a considerable latitude. In the former setting Paul exercised a remarkable healing ministry. (These healings, among them the healing of Publius' father, have already been treated in chapter four.) In the latter, he received seven days' hospitality from "the brethren." Luke seemingly implies that the centurion's approval and cooperation were conditions for both of these favorable developments.

As indicated above, the present section of Luke's narrative also provides ample indications of God's continuing presence in Paul's life. Perhaps most significantly Paul receives a message at the height of the crisis from an angel who relates that God intends for Paul to give witness before Caesar[8] and that, as a consequence, the lives of all those with Paul would be saved (27:23–24). In reporting this vision to his shipmates Paul indicates his own confidence that God will bring them through to safety by enabling them to run aground on some island (27:25-26). And this is, in fact, the outcome which eventually occurs.

In addition to evidencing God's power present in Paul's life, these same passages also serve to indicate Paul's own ongoing gratitude and intense faithfulness to God. Despite the hardships and the dangers of the journey, Paul still manifests great faith that the God to whom he belongs[9] will stand by him and bring about what is according to divine plan "For I have faith in God that it will be exactly as I have been told" (27:25).[10] And he still continues to return thanks to God for what God is accomplishing in his life and in the lives of those around him (27:35).[11]

Almost as a parenthesis, it should also be noted that Luke's portrait of Paul in this section of the narrative integrates an important additional element: despite the fact that Paul is a Roman prisoner, he nevertheless engages in a form of ministry among the Gentiles.[12] Although Luke reports no converts from among the ship's crew or the soldiers[13] as a consequence of Paul's powerful witness among them and is similarly silent regarding a response of faith by any of the Maltese, it is still the case that he at least implicitly portrays Paul resuming a ministry "to the Gentiles" after a lapse of more than two years. And in light of these two reports, it can accordingly be said that Luke portrays Paul actively ministering among the Gentiles (as well as among the Jews) virtually from the time of his conversion until the end of Acts.

Luke thus describes Paul experiencing much travail on a journey across the Mediterranean, but eventually arriving in Rome with his fundamental allegiance to God and to Jesus and his conditional allegiance to the Roman order very much intact. The arduous trip has provided Paul with still further evidence of God's sovereignty over his own life, the lives of those around him, and the created world itself. The trip has also been an occasion for him to experience kindly treatment from a Roman centurion and to cooperate effectively with him in responding to the perils of the journey.

Will these same two elements of foundational allegiance to God and Jesus and conditional loyalty toward the Roman order be maintained as Paul now moves to the very heart of the empire? These questions provide the context for an assessment of Luke's final reports concerning Paul's ministry in Rome.

4. THE PRISONER PAUL'S INTERACTIONS WITH THE JEWISH COMMUNITY AT ROME

A somewhat surprising feature of Luke's description of Paul's stay in Rome is that, from the point of his arrival until the end of the narrative, Paul ceases to have direct contact with Roman officials. Remarkably, once Paul arrives in Rome, Luke makes no further mention of Julius the centurion and no other Roman official of comparable or higher level is presented assuming responsibility for Paul's case.

Nevertheless, despite the lack of any information regarding the official(s) now in charge of Paul's case, it is clear from Luke's reports that Paul's standing is still very much that of a Roman prisoner and presumably a prisoner facing capital charges.[14] Verses 28:16 and 28:23 indicate that the character of Paul's custody was such that he was allowed to reside in private lodgings. However, 28:16 also explicitly states that he was under the guard of a Roman soldier, and the wording used in 28:20 seems to indicate that Paul was handcuffed or in some other way chained to this soldier.[15] This latter passage makes it quite clear that Paul was at least bound with some kind of chain while in his lodging and that he received visitors in this condition.

Luke's account of this interval also proves somewhat surprising for the relatively brief mention that it makes of the Christian communities that were in existence in Italy and Rome prior to Paul's arrival there. As previously noted, in 28:14 Luke refers to "brethren," presumably members of the Christian community at Puteoli, who afforded Paul a hospitable welcome for a period of seven days. And Luke also indicates that, as the party drew near to Rome itself, "the brethren" from that city came out as far as two of the approach stations to meet them (28:15a).

In this latter scene Luke presents Paul being visibly moved by the presence of the disciples: "On seeing them Paul thanked God and took courage" (28:15b). However, from that point onward in his account Luke makes no further explicit mention of any contact between Paul and those Christians already living in Rome.[16]

If Luke's account of Paul's stay at Rome describes relatively little interaction between Paul and the other disciples and no interaction between Paul and any imperial representatives, what then is the focus of the narrative? In each of the two principal scenes that Luke describes, Paul's exclusive dialogue partners are the leaders and the members of the local Jewish community.

After indicating in 28:17a that Paul took the initiative in inviting a group of the local Jewish leaders to his lodging,[17] Luke then uses verses 28:17b-20 for an account of Paul's speech to them. In several respects this speech is a remarkable one. Unlike previous speeches by Paul before Jewish groups, this speech scarcely makes mention of Jesus.[18] Instead, Paul's address seems mainly designed to reassure the Jewish leaders regarding his own loyalty to Jewish tradition and to indicate to them that he has proceeded with good will. Implicitly, Paul's remarks also indicate that he harbors no great resentment or ill will toward any of the parties who have mistreated him in the past:

> Brethren, though I had done nothing against the people or the customs of our fathers, yet I was delivered prisoner from Jerusalem into the hands of the Romans. When they had examined me, they wished to set me at liberty, because there was no reason for the death penalty in my case. But when the Jews objected, I was compelled to appeal to Caesar—though I had no charge to bring against my nation. For this reason therefore I have asked to see you and speak with you, since it is because of the hope of Israel that I am bound with this chain [28:17b-20].

At the outset it should be noted that Paul's reference to his hearers as "brethren" and his mention of the customs of "our" fathers both function to affirm his relationship with Judaism.[19] Indeed, so expressly does Luke show Paul indicating his sense of belonging to the Jewish community that readers of Acts may well wonder whether Luke wishes to imply that Paul was concerned that his appeal to the emperor might have been used to discredit him within the Jewish community. One of the chief points which Luke shows him making within this speech seems to touch directly upon this matter: Paul states that he did not enter into this appeal because he sought in any way to harm the Jewish people; rather this step was one that he had been *compelled* to take.[20]

Nevertheless, Paul's emphasis upon his own standing as a Jew does not prevent him from referring later in the speech to "the Jews" as though they were a group in which he himself had no membership. In effect, however, this reference actually represents the continuation of the pattern of usage analyzed earlier in chapter five of this study. For, as that analysis established "the Jews" is actually a term used for designating those members, that portion, of the larger Jewish community who adamantly refuse to believe in Jesus. In this instance, it is clear from Luke's account that the high priest and his allies are meant. And clearly they are a group from which Paul is in fact now morally, as well as physically, distant.

It should be noted that there is also a certain "distancing" implied in Paul's report that he was handed over to "the Romans." Luke has indicated on many previous occasions that Paul is, by reason of his citizenship, himself a *Roman*. Yet as the analysis made in chapter seven of this study has established, Paul does not attach undue importance to his Roman status. Here then, is yet another instance in which Paul seems to place his Jewish and, a fortiori, his Christian identity before his identity as a Roman. Speaking to Jews who are at this stage of the proceedings open to his message, Luke's Paul seems to be bonded with them in such a way that "the Romans" are truly outside of the community in which Paul and his listeners participate.

If Paul's specific terminology thus indicates a certain distance between himself and the Romans, his speech as a whole does not lay great onus upon the Roman officials who have handled his case. From his comments in 28:20 about the chain that binds him, it is evident that Paul dislikes his status as a chained prisoner, yet he does not explicitly or directly associate his condition with the mishandling of his case by two Roman governors.

Indeed, the most explicit statement which Luke portrays him making about the Romans' conduct of his case is highly exonerating: "When they had examined me, they wished to set me at liberty, because there was no reason for the death penalty in my case" (28:18). Although it omits reference to the procedural and substantive malfeasance of both Felix and Festus, such a statement is not, strictly speaking, incorrect. For Luke's previous reports do imply that, left to their own devices, the two governors would likely have decided for Paul's release. Nevertheless, by making this his principal statement regarding the Romans' handling of his case, Luke's Paul does thereby emerge as being strikingly free from any bitter or harsh feelings regarding his treatment by Felix and Festus.

Similarly, viewed against Luke's previous descriptions of the chief priests' unceasing efforts to secure his demise, Paul's present summary of their role in his case is remarkable for its benignity. Paul indicates that he was "delivered prisoner" to the Roman authorities,[21] but he does not indicate who so "delivered" him. And, while he does blame "the Jews" for objecting to his release, the high priest and his allies are not mentioned by either name or position. In addition, there are no other criticisms of the priests' treacherous enterprises, nor any other forms of indictment against them to be found in Paul's overview. It can thus be said that, within this speech, Paul is remarkably free from residual bitter feelings toward the Jerusalem chief priests just as he is remarkably free from similar feelings toward the past and present Roman governors of Judea.[22]

As indicated previously in this section, Paul did not explicitly refer to Jesus in his initial address to the Jewish leaders. Nor did he refer at that time to the mission that Jesus had entrusted to him among the Gentiles. Typically, these two elements are almost always to be found in Luke's other descriptions of Paul's ministry within Jewish contexts.

Both of these elements are present, and prominent, in Paul's address to these leaders and to the other members of the local Jewish community who came to Paul's lodging for a second meeting.[23] Luke begins his account of the gathering with the following statement: "And he expounded the matter to them from morning till evening, testifying to the kingdom of God and trying to convince them about Jesus both from the law of Moses and from the prophets" (28:23).

For readers of Acts who readily recall the events which transpired in the wake of similar preaching by Paul at Pisidian Antioch (13:42–47), Corinth (18:6–8), and Ephesus (19:9),[24] what Luke now reports as the reactions of Paul's present Jewish audience hardly comes as a surprise. Upon hearing Paul's testimony some of those assembled became convinced. Others, however, refused to believe.

Luke then relates that, observing this reaction, Paul offered a final statement. Paul first cited a powerful prophetic text as a means of indicting those who would not accept his message; he then alluded to his own mission to the Gentiles, emphasizing *their* acceptance of God's salvation. The full text of these searing remarks is as follows:

The Holy Spirit was right in saying to your fathers through Isaiah the prophet: "Go to this people, and say, You shall indeed hear but never understand, and you shall indeed see but never perceive. For this people's heart has grown dull, and their ears are heavy of hearing, and their eyes have closed; lest they should perceive with their eyes, and hear with their ears, and understand with their heart, and turn for me to heal them." Let it be known to you then that this salvation of God has been sent to the Gentiles; they will listen [28:25b–28].

Quite obviously this stinging indictment marks a sharp contrast with the mild, non-vengeful summary that Luke presented Paul giving at the initial meeting. Indeed, in both content and tone, Paul's words here are far closer to those he spoke at Pisidian Antioch (13:46-47) and Corinth (18:6) than they are to his remarks at the previous Roman meeting. Particularly in light of their harshness, a central issue concerning this speech is whether Paul's criticism should be understood as applying to all of the Jews in his audience or only to those who refused to believe in his message.

Inasmuch as Luke has explicitly stated in 28:24, "And some were convinced by what he said, while others disbelieved,"[25] there would seem to be solid grounds for holding that Luke understands those present as having divided into two camps with respect to Paul's proclamation. Proceeding along this line, it would thus seem that Paul's indictment actually falls only upon those who steadfastly "refuse to believe" his proclamation. They and only they are the ones to have Isaiah's words directed against them. They alone are additionally indicted by Paul's notice that his message of salvation will be accepted by the Gentiles.[26]

Although it requires moving beyond the confines of the present passage, it is appropriate to observe at this point that Luke does, two verses later (28:30), portray Paul welcoming "all" (*pantas*) who approach his lodgings.[27] This reference seems to provide additional support for the conclusion that Paul has not, by reason of his reproach, ceased his ministry among the Jews, but has in fact only turned away from those who have now designated themselves as "unbelieving Jews."

With this report of Paul's second speech, Luke brings to a close the detailed part of his account concerning Paul's activities in Rome. He has shown Paul entering the city, apprising the Jewish community of his case and then, within the limits of his circumstances as a prisoner, resuming his preaching of Jesus. It is Luke's sense that, in a certain limited fashion, Paul's ministry is once again underway. He is preaching to the Jews, persuading some of them, indicting others for lack of belief, and he has announced his mission to the Gentiles. What now remains in Luke's account is only a brief summary, a summary that will, with many nuances, highlight Paul's resolute continuing allegiance to Jesus.

5. PAUL'S RESOLUTE, CONTINUING WITNESS

While the conclusion of Acts is only thirty-one Greek words in length, its relative brevity does not prevent Luke from leaving his readers with a striking closing image of Paul in steadfast witness to Jesus. Indeed, especially when the sentiments which Luke expresses through his last four words are properly understood, it can be seen that there is a kind of power and majesty present in the conclusion of Acts.

In the paragraphs which follow, Luke's closing description will be analyzed for what it indicates regarding the content of Paul's ministry, the circumstances in which he continued it, and the qualities of spirit with which he did so. The first parts of this analysis, those concerning the circumstances and the content of Paul's ministry can be effectively carried out by utilizing the RSV translation. However, because this translation does not render satisfactorily what Luke has written concerning the bold character of Paul's witness, an alternate translation of one of Luke's phrases will also be indicated. With this qualification—that alternate wording is going to be proposed for Luke's final phrase—the RSV translation for 28:30-31 can now be considered:

> And he lived there two whole years at his own expense, and welcomed all who came to him, preaching the kingdom of God and teaching about the Lord Jesus Christ quite openly and unhindered.

At the outset it is important to grasp that Luke's description implicitly asserts that certain key elements of Paul's situation continued to be in effect. With reference to the analysis made in the preceding section, Paul's circumstances can now be described according to the following schema:

(1) Paul continued[28] under the guard of a soldier, restricted to his quarters, and in some way chained.
(2) As a consequence of this confinement, Paul was prevented from the type of "free" ministry that he had conducted in other cities when he preached in synagogues and public places.[29]
(3) The area in which Paul was confined was not a cell in a prison but rather some type of private lodging that he himself presumably arranged for.[30]
(4) Paul was allowed to invite visitors to his quarters and to speak with them at some length. Nevertheless he remained chained and under guard during these meetings.

When these various factors are all adverted to, it is clear there are important elements of liberty in Paul's situation as Luke portrays it. Yet, at the same time there are obviously serious constraints that bind upon him. The contemporary term that is seemingly most apt as a characterization of the circumstances that Luke has described is the term, "house arrest."[31] Fundamentally, Paul's situation is that of a Roman citizen under house arrest; it is from this particular, limited situation that he continues to give "bold" testimony on behalf of Jesus.

It should be noted that Luke's closing passage also indicates that Paul's confinement continued for fully two years. This latter piece of information takes on additional significance when one of Luke's earlier references to such an interval of time is recalled. For Luke has previously reported in 24:27 that Paul's imprisonment under Antonius Felix lasted for two years. And when the two years of Paul's time as a prisoner in Rome are added to the two plus years of his earlier imprisonment, it becomes clear that Paul was in Roman custody for more than four years of his life.

Did Luke himself have knowledge of any events that befell Paul in Rome at the end of this two–year period? This question has long been an intriguing one for both scholars and lay readers of Acts and in chapter eleven of this study additional attention will be given to it. However, what needs to be emphasized at this point is that speculation about additional information that may have been available to Luke must not result in any lack of attention to the various elements that Luke has actually chosen to emphasize.[32]

To speak in the language of drama, what is of extreme importance in terms of the methodology of the present study are the various elements and features that are present on the stage as Acts comes to a close. Thus far, the analysis of the present section has largely concentrated upon the material circumstances in which Paul was situated. The ministries with which Paul was engaged and the qualities of spirit with which he engaged in them still remain to be discussed. And, inasmuch as both of these areas have great consequence for any assessment of the Lukan Paul's stance toward the Roman social order, it is well now to proceed with their analysis.

With respect to the contents of Paul's ministry during this period, Luke describes him as being engaged in two related activities: 1) Paul welcomed all who came to him; and 2) he continued preaching the kingdom of God and teaching about the Lord Jesus Christ.

For perspective on the welcome that Luke now portrays him extending, it should be recalled that, over the course of Acts, Paul's ministry has been directed to three principal groups. Depending upon the circumstances Paul can be found in Acts addressing: 1) those already Christian, 2) Jewish groups, and 3) Gentile groups. Luke seemingly intends to encompass members of all three of these groups in stating that Paul welcomed "all" (*pantas*) who came to him. In its plainest meaning, *all* has connotations of universality and seems to preclude any interpretation that Jews were not welcome at Paul's lodging.

The fact that the other features contained in Luke's closing all indicate continuity with what has preceded is an additional ground for holding that Luke here understands the continuation of Paul's ministry to receptive Jews as well as to members of the other two groups.

With respect to Luke's phrase indicating Paul's continued preaching of the kingdom of God and his teaching about the Lord Jesus Christ, two observations are in order. The first is that there is a certain fullness with respect to the ministry that is signified by such a description. In many respects Paul's entire previous course could be encompassed under the headings of preaching the kingdom of God and teaching about the Lord Jesus Christ.[33] By indicating that such was Paul's ministry in Rome Luke signifies that Paul was remaining faithful to the fullness of the mission that he had been entrusted with by Jesus.

Secondly, in light of the considerations adduced in section two of this chapter, the fact that Luke's closing image of Paul includes reference to his teaching on behalf of "the Lord Jesus Christ" and the fact that Paul's teaching takes place in Rome, the very home of Festus' "lord," is also highly significant.

Initially this juxtaposition of Paul teaching about "the Lord" in the central precincts of the emperor can prove somewhat startling. Yet, in reflecting upon this juxtaposition, a point to be stressed is that Luke does not portray Paul embarking upon some new activity here. Rather what Luke is showing is that Paul continued with his previous teaching without unduly deferring to his new location at the heart of the empire. Paul had taught concerning the Lord Jesus in the earlier stages of his ministry; he did so, Luke now reports, during this two-year period. Paul had previously witnessed on behalf of the Lord Jesus in the eastern Roman provinces; he also did so, Luke now reports, in the capital city itself.

As indicated previously, the RSV translation of Luke's Greek text provides a reliable guide to the nuances of Luke's meaning up until this point. However, the RSV's next phrase, "quite openly," fails to communicate the attitude and the outlook that Luke carefully attributes to Paul when he uses the words *meta pasēs parrēsias.*

Previously in section five of chapter three, considerable attention was given to Luke's use of the term *parrēsia* in describing the "bold" witness of the apostles and disciples in Jerusalem.[34] This word appeared first in 2:29 when Peter spoke *boldy* at Pentecost and secondly at 4:13 when Luke described the chief priests and their allies marvelling at Peter and John's *boldness.*

Significantly, *parrēsia,* accompanied by the same two Greek words that accompany it in the present passage, *meta* and *pasēs*, also appears in 4:29. In that case the RSV translators adopted the literal sense of the Greek phrase giving "with all boldness" as the translation for *meta parrēsias pasēs.* (Note that the adjective follows the noun here.) Yet strangely they departed from this precedent and opted for "quite openly" as the translation in 28:31.[35]

Not only do the same three Greek words appear both in 4:29 and 28:31 but the contexts *in which* they appear are also quite similar. In both instances the phrases indicate a response to a situation in which the political authorities are, to varying degrees, attempting to intimidate or hinder the disciples of Jesus from preaching publicly in his name. That there is a political context for *meta parrēsias pasēs* in chapter four of Acts is immediately evident. That there is a comparable context for *meta pasēs parrēsias* at the end of chapter twenty-eight becomes clear upon a moment's reflection.

In chapter four, Luke reports the following as a part of the Jerusalem community's prayer when Peter and John are released by the Sanhedrin:

> For truly in this city there were gathered together against thy holy servant Jesus, whom thou didst anoint, both Herod and Pontius Pilate, with the Gentiles and the peoples of Israel, to do whatever thy hand and thy plan had predestined to take place. And now, Lord, look upon their threats, and grant to thy servants . . . [4:27–29a].

The fact that Herod (Antipas) and Pontius Pilate are both named along with "the Gentiles and the peoples of Israel" as having acted against Jesus is in itself significant in terms of remote context. Now it is Jesus' disciples who find themselves in similar circumstances, subject to "threats" (*apeilas*)[36] by the ruling authorities and to real danger.

What is the specific object of the disciples' prayer in such a setting? It is not for an end to the dangerous circumstances or for retribution upon those who are responsible for the threats. As Luke's narrative continues, their prayer in this instance is for no other intention than . . . "to speak thy word *with all boldness*" (4:29b; emphasis added). And, as the following verses make clear, it is precisely this prayer which is answered. For the room in which they prayed was shaken "and they were all filled with the Holy Spirit and spoke the word of God *with boldness*" (4:31; emphasis added).

While Luke does not explicitly state that Paul was under "threats" in the way that the disciples in Jerusalem had felt themselves to be, has he not actually painted Paul's situation as a Roman prisoner in comparable and even stronger terms? Like Peter and John, Paul experienced arrest at the hands of the ruling authorities. Like Peter and John, he was brought before their tribunals and interrogated. And like Peter and John's situation at the time of the community's prayer, there are ominous elements, evidenced by his guard and his chain, present in Paul's situation.

While the parallels are not exact, Paul's circumstances, as Luke describes them, are clearly those in which the quality of boldness is greatly to be desired. And it is exactly this quality that Luke ascribes to Paul in full measure. Read in the context of the community prayer described in 4:24–30, Luke's description in the present passage can only be understood as a tribute to Paul. For the fact that Paul witnessed to the Lord Jesus in difficult and even ominous circumstances *with all boldness* is no small achievement and not one to be lightly esteemed.

One word, Luke's final word still remains to be treated. In Greek it is *akolutos*, a rare adverb that the RSV translates as "unhindered."

Given the other instances in which *akōlutōs* and its root, *kōluō,* are used by Luke and by other ancient authors, "unhindered" may well be the best literal translation for the term.[37] However, used as the final word of Acts, it seems highly probable that Luke intended it to underscore the boldness which he attributed to Paul in the preceding phrase. It would thus be important to understand the word "unhindered" as describing the resoluteness with which Paul continued his preaching and teaching and as indicating that his status as a prisoner and his chains did not have the effect of intimidating, deterring, or hindering him from this witness.

As a general rule such an understanding of *akōlutōs* is not to be found in the standard commentaries on Acts. For the most part these commentaries espouse the view that, with his final word, Luke is drawing attention to the benign attitude of the Roman authorities toward Paul. Luke means to say, these commentators argue, that the Roman authorities were actually allowing Paul to preach and teach and minister "unhindered."[38]

Such an interpretation does not, however, take into account what Luke has previously related regarding Paul's Roman chains and his resentment of them. It also fails to appreciate that, in the verses immediately preceding, Luke has implicitly indicated that Paul continued to be bound with the very chain that he resented.

To repeat this point, to interpret *akōlutōs* to mean that the Roman officials were not hindering Paul requires that Luke, in his final word, asked his readers to minimize the significance of Paul's status as a Roman prisoner. According to such an interpretation Luke closed his account by asking his readers to understand that, although Roman officials kept Paul under guard and in chains for two years and prevented him from preaching publicly during this period, they were favorably disposed toward him and were not hindering him. Such an interpretation requires an extremely high level of disjointedness and clumsiness in Luke's "imaging" of Paul and his surroundings.

In contrast, the interpretation of *akōlutōs* as meaning "unhindered" in the sense of *not being internally hindered* results in no such problems with respect to the consistency of Luke's "imaging" of Paul. According to this interpretation, Luke closes with Paul physically bound by a Roman chain, yet not dispirited or broken by his circumstances.[39]

The meaning of the paragraph above which stated that Luke uses *akōlutōs* to underscore and intensify what he has already expressed by means of the phrase *meta pasēs parrēsias* is now more readily apparent. For, in effect, Luke is imparting his closing image of Paul through two adverbial forms which convey essentially the same idea. His intimation that Paul did not allow himself to be hindered is, in effect, an intensification of the image that he has already conveyed to his readers in telling them that Paul continued to teach "with all boldness."

In most English translations, the RSV among them, the function and meaning of *akōlutōs* as an intensifier of *meta pasēs parrēsias* has not been adverted to. (And, as noted above, *meta pasēs parrēsias* has itself frequently been improperly translated.) In order to communicate this point unmistakably, a comma is inserted between these two adverbial elements in the translation which follows. Luke's closing sentence is thus effectively translated into English in the following way:

AND HE LIVED THERE TWO WHOLE YEARS AT HIS OWN EXPENSE, AND WELCOMED ALL WHO CAME TO HIM, PREACHING THE KINGDOM OF GOD AND TEACHING ABOUT THE LORD JESUS CHRIST *WITH ALL BOLDNESS, UNHINDERED.*

9

Jesus, the Disciples of Jesus,
and Roman Rule

With the analysis of Paul's continuing witness in Rome now completed, it is appropriate to review what Luke has presented and to draw comparisons regarding the social and political approaches of Luke's main characters. Accordingly, after a preliminary section on methodology, the principal section of this chapter will present a series of comparisons between the social and political stance of Jesus and the stances of his leading disciples. Reflections concerning the compatibility between Roman rule and the Christian "Way" will then conclude the chapter.

1. METHODOLOGICAL CONSIDERATIONS

In a chapter elaborating comparisons between Jesus' social and political stance and that of his disciples, it is important to note at the outset that Luke has clearly indicated that Paul's conversion occurred with blinding suddenness. Unlike the apostles (and other members of the Jerusalem community) Paul was not associated with Jesus during the time of his public ministry. Consequently he did not have the same exposure to Jesus' teachings or experience Jesus' interactions with various groups and authorities in the way that the original disciples did.

Nevertheless, while indicating that the circumstances of Paul's formation as a disciple were different, Luke quite obviously does portray Paul as a fully mature disciple and shows him interacting confidently with many groups and teaching boldly in Jesus' name. Indeed, the implicit meaning of the accounts of Paul's conversion that Luke includes within his narrative is that Paul, no less than the apostles and the Jerusalem disciples, knows Jesus as Lord. It is thus clearly methodologically feasible to take Paul's social and political stance seriously and to ask how closely it corresponds to that of Jesus just as it is feasible to ask the same question about the apostles' stance.[1]

Did the apostles and the other disciples at Jerusalem adopt a social and political approach that corresponded closely to that adopted by Jesus? Did Paul adopt a social and political stance which closely resembled that of his Lord? Undoubtedly readers who have taken care to assess the material presented above in chapters two through eight from the standpoint of the material summarized in chapter one will already be disposed to answer these two questions affirmatively. And rightly so.

Nevertheless, it is conceivable that Luke's descriptions in Acts might not indicate a fundamental correspondence between the disciples' approach and that of their Lord. And indeed, as the analysis which follows will establish, there are certain areas in which Luke's apostles and Luke's Paul do not evidence continuity with the Jesus of Luke's Gospel.

Inasmuch as the present study has been conducted largely in terms of the headings that were used in *Jesus, Politics, and Society,* the task at this point is primarily one of placing the conclusions reached regarding the apostles and Paul alongside of those previously reached for Jesus. In addition to utilizing the principal headings which have been used to describe the social stance of Luke's Jesus, comparisons will also be instituted in reference to Jesus' and the disciples' responses to various political authorities and also in reference to the respective outcomes which befell them.

For the purpose of expediting an analysis that might otherwise be too repetitious, the findings that are made under each of these headings will only be presented in summary fashion. It is left to the reader to review the material presented in chapter one and in the intervening chapters when a more nuanced appreciation of the contrasts between Jesus' approach in a specific area and the approach of the apostles and/or Paul is desired.

2. AREAS IN WHICH THE APOSTLES' STANCE CORRESPONDS WITH THAT OF JESUS

Considering the various areas in the same basic sequence that was used for chapter one, the present section begins with a consideration of the apostles' stance with respect to the sick. Here it can be simply stated that, in the persons of Peter and Philip, Luke portrays the apostles carrying forward with a concern for the sick and a healing ministry that is comparable to that described for Jesus in the Gospel.

Similarly, in regard to the affirmation of women, Samaritans, and Gentiles, and a reaching out to them, Luke also portrays the apostles and the Jerusalem community adopting an approach that is at least roughly continuous with the approach initiated by Jesus. Women are welcomed as believers as the Christian movement develops in Jerusalem and in Samaria. And by reason of the initiatives undertaken by Philip and then by Peter, Samaritans and Gentiles are also brought into relationship with the Jerusalem community.

In regard to the use of material possessions, Peter and the others at Jerusalem continue to witness to Jesus' basic teaching that material resources are not to be accumulated by individuals but are rather to be directed to the needs of others.

Luke also portrays them expressing reservations about silver and gold and indicating that such items are not among their resources. Significantly, the Jerusalem disciples also embark upon a highly communitarian approach to the material resources that were originally the personal possessions of each member. Such a practice does not violate the spirit of Jesus' approach and may actually be regarded as an embodiment of his approach in the specific circumstances of Jerusalem; however there is no teaching of Jesus within Luke's Gospel that specifically encourages such a community-of-goods arrangement.

In the area of service and humility it is noteworthy that within Acts, Luke never shows the apostles seeking to be "great" and actually reports instances in which they distanced themselves from honors and acclaim. Indeed, in one instance, Luke shows the apostles rejoicing in the fact that they had been found worthy to suffer "dishonor" for the name of Jesus.

In terms of an opposition to injustice, the apostles and disciples manifest continuity with Jesus in their willingness to speak out publicly regarding unjust conduct. However, at the same time, there is also a certain discontinuity between their stance and Jesus' in that they do not speak concerning the same forms of misconduct that he addressed. Instead, with respect to the subject area of the chief priests' malfeasance, the apostles' emphasis is upon the grave injustice perpetrated in the killing of God's servant, Jesus. (Further comments on the apostles' stance in this area will be given in the section which follows.)

With respect to the rejection of violence, it is significant that in Acts there is no mention of the disciples using or possessing swords or other weapons. Nor, apart from the reports concerning the violent end to which God brought Ananias and Sapphira, is there any indication of the apostles and disciples initiating or becoming involved in violent activities. With reference to their internal community life, Luke portrays a situation of great harmony and joy. Significantly, the word, "forgiveness" does not appear at all in Acts except in Stephen's grace-filled plea for the forgiveness of those executing him.

Luke's presentation of the apostles' stance toward the political authorities is primarily focused upon their interactions with the high priest and the Jerusalem Sanhedrin. As indicated above, these leaders were political as well as religious figures since, under Roman rule, they had responsibility for the public order of Jerusalem in addition to their more specifically religious responsibilities of officiating at the temple and interpreting the Jewish law.

In their two principal interactions with the Sanhedrin, Luke portrays Peter and John (and the other apostles) adopting a stance that corresponds closely to Jesus' own "evaluative" stance. Peter and John first pose the question of whether it is right for them to obey the Sanhedrin rather than God. Then, on a subsequent occasion, after they have preached publicly in spite of the Sanhedrin's order, they state: "We must obey God rather than human beings."

In addition, it should be recalled that Luke also relates Herod Agrippa I's deadly interventions against James and Peter. No dialogue is reported, but the larger context suggests the possibility that, in this instance as well, the apostles refused to give unqualified obedience and loyalty to the orders of a political ruler.

3. AREAS IN WHICH THE APOSTLES DO NOT REFLECT JESUS' APPROACH

The fact that the Greek words for "the poor" and for "tax collectors and sinners" do not appear at all in the text of Acts has already been remarked upon in chapter two. Luke thus does not portray the apostles expressing the concern for these groups that Jesus did.

Inasmuch as Luke describes the life of the Jerusalem community as being characterized by generosity and joy and states that there was not a needy person among them, it is easy to overlook the fact that he is silent about any specific ministry to the poor or to tax collectors and sinners. Yet this is actually the case. As a result, there is a distinct contrast with the situation of the Gospel where Jesus draws attention to the plight of the poor and the standing of tax collectors and sinners, counseling that surplus possessions should be distributed to the former and indicating that the latter should be brought into table fellowship.

Related to the subject of the apostles' attitude toward the poor is the subject of their attitude toward the rich. Luke does portray Peter and the others of the Jerusalem community expressing disapproval over Ananias and Sapphira's duplicitous conduct with respect to their possessions. However, beyond this, there is nothing else in Luke's descriptions of the apostles which corresponds to Jesus' criticisms of riches and the rich. Indeed, given the frequency with which such criticisms appear upon the lips of Jesus in the Gospel, it is significant that neither *ploutos* ("riches") nor *plousios* ("wealthy") are ever part of the apostles' vocabulary in Acts.

An additional point of discontinuity has already been adverted to in the preceding section's analysis of the apostles' approach to injustice and corruption. It was indicated at that time that the apostles did speak publicly against the unjust execution of Jesus and thus did demonstrate their concern to challenge the chief priests and those allied with them.

Nevertheless, Luke does not portray the apostles taking up the subject of the chief priests' corrupt practices at the temple, an issue that Jesus addressed extremely forthrightly within the Gospel. It should also be noted that Luke never depicts any of the Jerusalem disciples criticizing the corrupt practices of the scribes and the Pharisees or speaking publicly, as Jesus did, concerning the case of a corrupt judge who refused to render proper justice to a widow.

4. THE APOSTLES' STANCE AND ROMAN RULE

With the completion of the above comparisons between the social and political stances of Jesus and the apostles, the way is now clear for a summary assessment concerning the stance of Luke's apostles and the realities of Roman rule. In their social values and practices and in their approach toward the political authorities, the apostles' stance is similar enough to Jesus' and dissimilar enough from the stance of those who administered Roman rule (and those who were the compliant subjects of it) to be assessed as constituting at least a potential danger to Roman rule. Luke's apostles do not minister to tax collectors and sinners as Jesus did, and they do not admonish the rich and criticize the corrupt practices of other groups in the same way that he did, yet clearly their social and political stance closely resembles his. And thus, to the degree that his stance represented a potential danger to the Roman order, so too does theirs.

5. AREAS IN WHICH PAUL'S STANCE CORRESPONDS WITH THAT OF JESUS

Paul's ministry to those who were sick or in some way handicapped has been detailed above in sections one and two of chapter four. Summarizing, it suffices to say that both Jesus' concern for the sick as well as something of his miraculous healing power are both manifestly present in Paul's own ministry.

With respect to the affirmation of women, Samaritans, and Gentiles and a reaching out to them, it has already been seen that Acts superabounds with reports of Paul's activities on behalf of the Gentiles. Significantly, in addition to a number of incidental reports indicating that Paul addressed his preaching to women as well as to men, Luke also portrays Paul interacting in a highly affirmative way with Lydia at Phillippi and also with Priscilla at Corinth. In comparison with Jesus Paul gives considerably less attention to the Samaritans. While Jesus made pronouncements regarding a good Samaritan and a gratitude-filled Samaritan, Luke's only report about Paul and this group comes in 15:3 where he indicates that Paul and Barnabas passed through Samaria reporting the conversion of the Gentiles and giving joy to the disciples there.

In regard to the use of material possessions, Luke portrays Paul living simply, supporting himself by the work of his own hands, and in different ways evidencing a concern to share his resources with other community members and disciples. Here, too, there is definite general continuity with Jesus' own approach. In this context it should be recalled that Luke also describes more than one instance of economic turmoil being engendered as a result of Paul's proclamation of the gospel.

Although the terms "service" and "humility" do not appear on the lips of Paul in Acts as frequently as they appeared on the lips of Jesus in the Gospel, Paul's memorable words to the Ephesian elders at Miletus are in themselves sufficient to establish general correspondence. There Paul reminded his hearers how from his very first day among them he had been "...serving the Lord with all humility..." These sentiments are also reflected in other comments and conduct that Luke attributes to Paul.

With respect to the degree of his continuity with Jesus in the area of opposition to corruption and injustice, a great deal hinges upon the interpretation that is placed upon Paul's interactions with the high priest at the time of his appearance before the Jerusalem Sanhedrin. In other speeches, notably at Pisidian Antioch, Paul did not hesitate to speak publicly concerning the unjust killing of Jesus and, for this reason, he is in general continuity with a Jesus who did not hesitate to decry unjust conduct publicly.

However, is the Paul of Acts also in continuity with Jesus on the issue of the high priest/chief priests' corruption and on the related issue of their illegitimacy in office? Based upon the interpretation given above to Paul's "white-washed wall" epithet and to his rejoinder that he did not realize that he was in the presence of a true high priest, continuity is seemingly to be affirmed on these specific points as well.

Under the heading of the rejection of violence, it is clear from several reports that Paul is still capable of angry outbursts even after his conversion. Also, Luke never portrays Paul emphasizing the role of forgiveness in Christian discipleship and does not portray him ever achieving reconciliation with Barnabas after their "sharp contention."

Nevertheless, Luke's Paul does not retaliate or seek vengeance against his opponents—even those who attempt to kill him. Instead, he consistently moves forward in his ministry without harboring harsh feelings or grudges. Then too the noteworthy events which transpired at Philippi should be recalled: Paul, with God's help, befriended and eventually made a disciple of the jailer appointed to guard him.

In regard to the approaches that Luke portrays Jesus and Paul respectively adopting toward the political authorities, a certain basic similarity is once again to be seen. Jesus' approach has previously been described as "evaluative." Although several of the specific features are different, Paul's approach can also be viewed as having an evaluative cast to it.

It should be recalled that, within Acts, Paul's fundamental allegiance to Jesus his Lord always takes precedence over any other allegiance including any loyalties to Festus' "lord," the emperor. This allegiance is manifested in Paul's dealings with the political authorities at every stage. He maintains it despite the proceedings against him and his associates at Philippi, Thessalonica, Ephesus, Jerusalem, and Caesarea.

When they are carefully assessed, the three instances in which Paul invokes his rights as a Roman citizen do not shadow the brightness of this deeply held allegiance to Jesus. Nor does the fact that Paul cooperates so forthrightly with the Roman officials overseeing his case. For Paul's cooperation clearly has its limits, and, in the same surroundings in which he cooperates with his judges, Paul also confronts these officials with higher standards of right and wrong.

6. AREAS IN WHICH PAUL DOES NOT REFLECT JESUS' APPROACH

Luke makes no mention of Paul addressing "tax collectors and sinners" in his ministry. And, while he does portray one instance in which Paul expresses his commitment to aid "the weak," the wording of the passage seems to suggest that it is the weak within the Christian community at Ephesus who are meant.

Luke also makes no mention of Paul adopting any of the key features of Jesus' stance with respect to the rich. (Again, the Greek words for "riches" and "the rich" do not appear in Acts.) Paul's preaching does not contain anything comparable to Jesus' criticism of the rich and his counsel to them that they must distribute their surplus possessions.

Also, while Luke does describe Paul's stringent criticism of the high priest and those allied with him on the Sanhedrin, he does not depict Paul publicly citing the moral failings of any other social group or class. Thus, there is no instance in Paul's ministry in which he criticizes the scribes and the Pharisees for their hypocrisy and deceit. Nor is there any instance in which he publicly refers to (even for purposes of illustration) the conduct of unjust judges.

In these areas, then, Luke does not portray Paul adopting the approach that he has previously attributed to Jesus. In addition, one other area of significant divergence—Paul's strikingly different conduct at his trials—should also be noted.[2]

In contrast with a Jesus who responds rather tersely and noncommittally to Pilate's single question and not at all to any of those asked by Herod Antipas, Paul obviously looks upon his trials before Felix, Festus, and Herod Agrippa II as opportunities to testify to the calling he has received from the risen Jesus, to justify his own conduct, and even, if possible, to convert those hearing his case. In contrast to Jesus who evidences little interest in the procedures that are being followed in his trials, Paul keeps careful track of the proceedings. Also in contrast with Jesus, Paul acts aggressively to counter the chief priests' legal and extra-legal efforts against him and assertively challenges Festus himself regarding his conduct of the case.

7. PAUL'S STANCE AND ROMAN RULE

Although the social practices and the approach to the political authorities that Luke attributes to Paul do not exactly match those which he attributes to Jesus, there is still a high level of correspondence between the general social and political stance that Luke describes for each figure. (This correspondence becomes even more evident when a conceptual contrast is made with the stances that can be attributed to those who administered Roman rule or those who were compliantly subject to it.) Accordingly, to the approximate degree that Jesus' own stance represented a *potential* danger to the Roman order, so can it be concluded that Paul's stance constituted a similar *potential* danger.

There is also one additional factor, a point referred to in chapter seven but not referred to in the sections above, that should be adverted to at this point. As a consequence of his reports detailing Paul's activities in a wide range of cities and provinces, Luke portrays him as a de facto disturber of Roman rule in a much more pronounced way than he does Jesus or the apostles. Paul, by reason of the extensive travels and activities that Luke attributes to him (and not because of a qualitative difference in his social and political stance), thus emerges in the later chapters of Acts as much more of an *actual* danger to Roman rule than was true with respect to Jesus or the apostles in the earlier stages of Luke's writings.

8. THE COMPATIBILITY OF THE CHRISTIAN MOVEMENT OF LUKE-ACTS WITH THE ROMAN SOCIAL ORDER

As analyzed at length in *Jesus, Politics, and Society* and as adverted to at several junctures in the present study, the Jesus of Luke's Gospel espoused social values and practices that were greatly at variance with those sanctioned by the ruling Romans and also adopted an "evaluative," nondeferential stance toward various Roman officials. In combination, these two aspects had the consequence of positioning him as someone potentially dangerous to Roman rule. While his stance was not that of the Zealots, it still involved enough divergence from Roman sanctioned values and patterns that, if a sufficient number embraced it, the Roman provincial order would itself have been jeopardized.

In like manner the present analysis has also established that, within Acts, both the apostles and Paul adopted social values and practices and an attitude toward the political authorities that were generally similar to Jesus'. Consequently their social and political approaches also differed significantly from the approaches of those who administered Roman rule and those who were compliantly subject to it.

To the degree that these disciples of Jesus can be regarded as constituting a "movement" within the eastern provinces, this movement must itself also be regarded as carrying within it the potential for serious challenges to the Roman order. For if such a movement were given sufficient time to recruit new members and to transmit its values and its practices, the Roman empire (or any similarly based social order) could not avoid serious disruption.

Essentially, then, the question of the conceptual compatibility between the Christian movement described in Luke-Acts and the Roman social order is a question to be analyzed from the standpoint of competing social practices and competing approaches to political authority. There is, however, one additional way in which the question of compatibility can be studied: an examination can be made of the treatment which the officials of the established order accorded to the leaders of the new movement. Luke's writings also provide the basis for an assessment from this latter vantage point.

The particular circumstances of each figure's case have been discussed above in considerable detail and it must be recalled that, particularly in the case of Jesus, the motives and processes which resulted in his death are, in Luke's account, complex. However, even when all of the mitigating factors are properly respected, it is still a remarkable feature of Luke-Acts that Jesus and James are put to death, that Peter is very nearly executed, and that Paul is imprisoned and chained for over four years—all by the decisions of various Roman officials.

When this latter point—that various Roman officials dealt so severely with Jesus and his leading disciples—is added to earlier considerations about the controversies that surrounded Paul and the other disciples,[3] it becomes even more obvious that the Christian "Way" which Luke is describing is not a way characterized by calm and placidity. In a word, while Luke's Christians very evidently adhere to Jesus' teachings concerning "the things that make for peace," they hardly manage a peaceful entry into the world controlled by Rome.

And the implications of these points for the widely held view that Luke wrote for reasons of "political apologetic"? Such a question raises a larger question about the range of concerns that may have motivated Luke to provide the reports that he did. These and related questions are now appropriately responded to in the final two chapters of this study.

10

Not Political Apologetic or Ecclesial Apologetic

With the close of the preceding chapter, the basic task of interpreting the text of Acts, actually the text of Luke-Acts, has largely been completed. There is, however, a related task still remaining and it will be the function of this chapter and the one following to accomplish it. The task in question is that of analyzing the concerns and purposes that influenced Luke in the writing of his two volumes.

As indicated above and in *Jesus, Politics, and Society,* Luke has provided a rich and stimulating account of the social and political stance of Jesus and his leading disciples. But what motivated him to do so? What influenced him, in Acts, to give so much attention to the social and political involvements of Paul and the apostles? In the present chapter it will be argued, negatively, that Luke was not motivated by a concern for either "political apologetic" or "ecclesial apologetic." Chapter eleven, a largely constructive chapter, will then analyze two of the major concerns that very probably did have an influence upon Luke's presentation.

1. PRELIMINARY CONSIDERATIONS REGARDING POLITICAL APOLOGETIC

Particularly in a classical frame of reference "defense" or "justification" are the primary meanings of the word "apology" and it is in this sense that "apologetic" is used by New Testament commentators in the term, "political apologetic." In effect, those New Testament scholars who assert that Luke wrote for reasons of political apologetic (and at the present time, this is by far the majority position) thus argue that one of Luke's purposes in writing was to defend or justify the Christian movement before the political authorities. In other words Luke was allegedly concerned to insure that Roman officials reading Luke-Acts would come away from this work favorably disposed toward the Christianity of Luke and his fellow Christians.[1]

Frequently those who espouse this view are influenced by the conclusions that they have reached regarding the situation of the Christian movement within the Roman empire at the time when Luke composed his works.[2] However, from the standpoint of this study, a much more significant feature of their position is the arguments that they put forward with respect to Luke's presentation in Acts. For advocates of this view expressly claim that *the text of Acts* reveals in several ways that political apologetic was one of Luke's preoccupations.

2. ASSERTIONS CONCERNING POLITICAL APOLOGETIC IN ACTS

In the subsections which follow, three of the principal assertions that advocates of the political-apologetic position have made with respect to Luke's work in Acts will be presented. In order to avoid an undue repetition of previous discussions regarding specific passages, these interpretations will be presented, for the most part, without reference to the exegesis which is said to substantiate them. Nevertheless, no significant supporting argument on behalf of a given interpretation will be omitted from the analysis which follows. And it is to be hoped that such comprehensiveness at the level of concepts[3] will more than compensate for the fact that relatively little attention is being given to detailed exegesis at this juncture.

A. Luke Presents the Christians of Acts as Law-Abiding and Harmless

The claim that Luke portrays the Christians of Acts as law-abiding and harmless is one of the general assertions frequently made by proponents of political apologetic and should be regarded as being of fundamental importance for the theory as a whole.

Luke does not show the Christians of Acts actively (or even passively) ever opposing Roman rule: some authors may formulate the claim in this way as well. The supporting argument that Luke never shows any of the disciples following the approach of the Zealots may then also be made. And more specifically, it may also be emphasized that Luke never shows the apostles or Paul ever questioning Roman taxation or criticizing any other Roman policy or practice.

But what of the disruptions that Acts does show Paul and the disciples becoming involved in? An argument that some proponents of political apologetic make on this point is that, within Acts, any public controversies which do occur are shown to be instigated by Jewish troublemakers.

Similarly, another argument sometimes expressed is that whenever any public disorder does come to the attention of Roman authorities, Acts makes it clear that these officials exonerated the disciples of illegal activity. Thus, for example, Paul was excnerated by Gallio in Corinth, and Festus and Herod Agrippa II later agreed that Paul had done nothing meriting Roman imprisonment.

B. Luke Portrays Paul Esteeming His Roman Citizenship and Responding Cooperatively to Roman Officials

In addition to arguing that the Roman authorities never find Paul guilty of illegal activity, proponents of political apologetic are also apt to argue that Luke's description of Paul's own stance was designed to make a favorable impression upon the Roman officials who were among his readers. Here the principal assertion is that Paul's attitude toward his Roman citizenship and toward the various Roman authorities he encountered would have established that Paul himself (and, by implication, others in the Christian movement) was well disposed towards things Roman.

With respect to Paul's citizenship, the argument that is most frequently made is that Paul takes a considerable pride in his standing as a citizen and does not hesitate to invoke his Roman rights. Secondly, it may be argued that Paul adverted to the fact that he was a citizen as a result of his birth, something that made him even more legitimate in Roman eyes.

Concerning Paul's attitude toward the Roman authorities, a frequently made argument is that Paul recognizes the authority of these officials and shows them respect and deference. Secondly, it is also emphasized that Paul responds energetically and enthusiastically when any of these officials asks him to explain his views and his conduct. Finally, advocates of political apologetic are also disposed to argue that Luke shows Paul retaining his confidence in the Roman authorities right until the very end of Acts. Indeed, Paul's appeal to Caesar is taken as an indication of his abiding confidence in the emperor's personal fairness and justice.

C. Luke Portrays the Roman System Itself Favorably within Acts

Over and beyond their specific claims that Luke shows Paul taking a positive stance toward his Roman citizenship and toward Roman officials, proponents of political apologetic also frequently argue that Acts portrays the Roman system itself in favorable terms. Here the thrust of the argument is that Roman officials reading Acts would have been pleased with Luke's favorable reports concerning various aspects of the system that they themselves administered.

Typically, advocates of political apologetic contend that Roman legal, military, and economic institutions are impressively portrayed within Acts. Regarding legal institutions, a common assertion is that whenever Paul is brought within Roman jurisdiction, orderly procedures are followed. Indeed, it is alleged that Luke emphasizes the orderliness and fairness of "Roman justice" by dotting his account with scenes exemplifying "Jewish chaos." Here reference is typically made to the scene before Gallio's tribunal and the scene in which Claudius Lysias brings Paul before the Jerusalem Sanhedrin.

Concerning military institutions a frequent argument is that Luke describes Lysias and the centurion Julius both functioning wisely and effectively in complex and dangerous situations. After commenting on the passages describing the conduct of these two officers, it is not uncommon for proponents of political apologetic to argue that Acts recognizes the positive role played by the Roman army and appreciates the security and order which the Roman forces brought to the provinces.

With respect to economic institutions it is also asserted that the Acts narrative presumes the presence of roads, harbors, etc. that were constructed and developed by the Romans. Accordingly, Roman officials who read Acts would conclude that the new Christian movement was fully acclimated to both the realities and the benefits of Roman rule. Christianity was thus not something that happened "in a corner."[4] Rather it was a religious movement that had developed publicly and openly in the empire, happy to avail itself of the benefits and opportunities provided by the empire.

3. CRITICISM OF THE POLITICAL-APOLOGETIC POSITION

From the standpoint of the preceding chapters of this study, there are two major criticisms to be made of the political-apologetic position. The first criticism, to be elaborated in the three subsections which follow, is that the principal claims advanced by proponents of political apologetic fail to be established in a careful reading of the text of Acts. The second criticism, to be presented in the last subsection of this section, is that the political-apologetic position overlooks or underemphasizes important elements that are *manifestly* present in the text of Acts.

A. Acts Does Not Present Christians as Law-abiding and Harmless

An important characteristic of the political-apologetic theory, and one that undoubtedly helps to explain why the theory has gained such wide acceptance, is that it references, and proposes to explain, so many passages in Acts. While some of the specific interpretations which proponents of this theory make do have merit, what invariably proves to be the case is that there is not enough evidence to sustain even one of the theory's principal claims.

Such is the case, for example, with respect to the first major claim made by advocates of the theory. It can and should be granted that Acts does not portray the disciples questioning Roman taxation or engaging in any other form of anti-Roman activity. However, what then needs to be emphasized is that such a limited conclusion does not serve to establish the more general and more important claim that Luke actually presents the Christians as law-abiding and harmless.[5]

From the standpoint of imperial officials, the fundamental determination to be made regarding any new movement was whether or not it helped Rome's territories to be *pacata atque quieta,* "settled and orderly." This point was noted in the opening chapter of this study and it is a point that is appropriately emphasized in the present context. For while Roman officials reading Acts would have perceived that Christianity was not anti-Roman in character, it can hardly be said that these officials would have regarded the Christian movement as conforming to and contributing to the "peace and order"[6] that were critical to the continuance of Roman rule.

When Acts is read quickly from beginning to end, one of the strongest impressions left with the reader concerns the large number of public controversies that the principal figures in the Christian movement became involved in. At an early stage of the proceedings, the apostles themselves came into conflict with the chief priest-dominated Sanhedrin because of their public activities within Jerusalem. Later James and Peter were arrested and James executed by Herod Agrippa, presumably for the same type of public activity.

And then there is the figure of Paul, Paul who so dominates the second half of Acts. In province after province and city after city, essentially the same story repeats itself. Paul arrives on the scene and begins to conduct a ministry on behalf of Jesus. Then, however, controversy of one form or another erupts; and, if the dispute has not been public at the outset, it eventually becomes so. The political authorities enter the picture and take some form of action concerning Paul. Paul then voluntarily or involuntarily leaves the area only to resume his ministry in another setting.

Clearly what could not have escaped the attention of a Roman official reading Acts in even a cursory fashion is "the chain of disruption" that Luke portrays as an effect of the proclamation of the Christian message by the apostles and Paul.

Nor is it feasible to argue that Luke has nuanced his reports to show that, when such controversies arose, it was due to the agitation of Jewish troublemakers.[7] For the narrative of Acts makes it clear that the various troubles did not begin until Paul himself arrived on the scene. In addition, Acts also shows clearly that Paul's activities resulted in major controversies even in strictly Gentile settings. Such points as these would not have failed to register upon Roman officials who took the time to give careful consideration to Luke's text.

Finally, in light of what is actually shown by Luke's reports of Paul's trials, it is also not feasible to argue that Luke shows high Roman officials formally exonerating Paul from any illegal activity or wrongdoing in connection with these public disorders.[8] As indicated previously Paul is not actually exonerated by Gallio, but is rather the beneficiary of the proconsul's bias. Nor is he ever convincingly or effectively exonerated by the two Roman governors who try his case.

In summary, what Acts indicates on the subject of Christianity's alleged harmlessness is that, while not anti-Roman, the apostles and Paul were highly dedicated disciples of Jesus who were not easily dissuaded from preaching in his name even though controversy and turbulence might result. As a consequence they were far from congenial figures in terms of the principal objectives of Roman rule. While Paul was not a "law-breaker" in the usual sense of that term, he was constantly embroiled in public controversy and, within Acts, the charge that he is an agitator and troublemaker persistently dogs his steps.

B. Paul's Attitude toward His Roman Citizenship and His Cooperation with Roman Officials Are Highly Qualified in Acts

The appropriate responses to be given to the claims of the political-apologetic position regarding Paul's citizenship and regarding his attitude toward Roman officials are similar. For in each instance a principal argument can be granted—Paul's Roman citizenship is prominent within Acts and Paul also does adopt a generally cooperative stance toward the Roman officials who become involved in his case. Nevertheless, it must also be recognized that, in each of these areas, there is much more to Luke's portrayal than proponents of political apologetic commonly recognize.

To begin with the subject of citizenship, the basic response which needs to be articulated is that, when all of the relevant passages are carefully considered, it can hardly be maintained that Luke portrays Paul as a typical citizen with traditional loyalties to the emperor and the imperial order.[9]

Rather, Luke actually portrays Paul taking an approach to his Roman standing that could only have impressed a Roman reader of Acts as highly unorthodox and even as troublesome. For one thing, there is the pattern of Paul being reluctant to mention his citizenship in public settings and only doing so in private to Roman officials who were failing to treat him properly. And secondly, how could a Roman official reading Acts not have been startled when instead of indicating to Lysias that he was a Roman citizen, Paul volunteers with considerable pride that he is a citizen of Tarsus![10]

Paul's continuous references to Jesus as his "Lord" is also a feature of the Acts narrative that serves to delimit his regard for his Roman status. What Acts thereby establishes is that Paul, in contrast with Lysias and Festus, does not take the emperor as his ultimate sovereign.[11] Clearly Paul's continuous advertences to Jesus as his "Lord" could only have proved disconcerting to Roman officials who were accustomed to think that a loyal citizen's first allegiance belonged to the emperor and his decrees.

In their comments upon Paul's interactions with Roman officials in Acts, proponents of political apologetic have emphasized Paul's cooperative stance toward Roman officials, and rightly so. Yet here too what must be recognized is that when Roman officials in Luke's own day read everything else that Luke relates concerning him, they would undoubtedly not have been overly sanguine about their own prospects for dealing with the likes of Paul.

For, manifestly, the Paul of Acts is independent and assertive. Indeed, far too independent and assertive for normal Roman tastes.[12]

What Roman governor reading Acts would not have been jarred by Luke's report that, at one stage of his interactions with Felix, governor of Judea, Paul lectured him concerning "justice and self-control and future judgment" (24:25)? In the same vein how could one of Paul's subsequent declarations not have proved even more disturbing to Roman officials? "I am standing before Caesar's tribunal, where I ought to be tried; to the Jews I have done no wrong, as you know very well" (25:10). Such was the rebuke that Paul tendered to Festus and it must be presumed that Roman officials of Luke's day could only have viewed the prisoner who voiced such sentiments as a troublesome figure indeed.

Finally there is the specific issue of Paul's attitude in making his appeal to the emperor. What Luke actually indicates regarding Paul's expectations in making such an appeal is appropriately considered at this juncture even though this material also pertains to the subsection which follows on Luke's portrayal of the Roman system.

Regardless of whether it is argued that Roman officials reading Acts would have perceived Paul as ultimately cooperative with the highest Roman authority or argued that Paul's appeal showed these officials that he retained his confidence in the Roman system, the fundamental assumption made by proponents of political apologetic is that Luke shows Paul appealing to the emperor confident that he will receive justice.[13] Indeed so pervasive is this assumption within New Testament scholarship that it at first glance seems almost fictive to suggest that Paul does not seem to expect justice from the Caesar to whom he appeals.[14]

Where does Paul, either in making his appeal or in speaking about his situation while a prisoner under appeal, ever indicate that he expects to receive justice from the emperor? Framing the question in this way effectively shifts the burden of proof to those who would assume that Luke presents Paul's appeal to Caesar as a step toward justice.

As Luke portrays the situation, Paul is convinced that he will not receive justice if he allows Festus to retain jurisdiction over his case. He thus reacts instinctively and angrily to avoid the transfer of his case to Jerusalem. Yet in availing himself of the only alternative available to him, Paul utters no elaborating comment to the effect that he knows he will be vindicated by the emperor. He makes no allusion to the emperor's wisdom, the emperor's discretion, the emperor's justice. Indeed, the only words Luke portrays Paul speaking at this juncture are the minimal words necessary to prevent Festus' treacherous proposal from taking effect.

The counter-argument now being advanced, the counter-argument that Luke actually shows Paul making his appeal to Caesar without a definite expectation that he will receive justice in Rome, receives additional support when the character and contents of Paul's speech to the leaders of the Jewish community in Rome are recalled.

As Luke describes this speech, Paul does not allude to the emperor's fairness or his justice as factors that motivated him to make his appeal. Nor does he state anything to the effect that he judged his chances for acquittal to be far better with the emperor himself. Instead, the basic explanation that Paul gives for his decision is negative, that it was forced upon him by the circumstances. It was a decision that he was *compelled* to take.[15]

In addition, it should also be noted that there is nothing at all within Paul's speech which implies that he anticipated a favorable outcome when the emperor would finally adjudicate his case.

Indeed given the claims that have traditionally been made by the supporters of political apologetic, Paul's failure to attribute higher standards of justice to the emperor and his failure to predict vindication as a consequence of the emperor's intervention must be considered as a highly significant silence on Luke's part. A certain care should always be exercised in assessing the import of an author's silence in a particular area; but in this instance, Luke's silence unmistakably functions to deny tenability to yet another facet of the political-apologetic position.

C. Luke Does Not Portray the Roman System with Particular Favor

From the analysis made above regarding the particular circumstances which compelled Paul to appeal to the emperor and from the preceding analysis made regarding his treatment at the hands of Tiberius Felix, it seems evident that supporters of political apologetic have departed from the actual data in asserting that Luke has portrayed the Roman system of justice favorably within Acts.[16]

Luke does indicate that the protections which Roman law afforded to citizens enabled Paul to avert mistreatment on three occasions. And it can be pointed out that `Acts portrays the Roman citizen, Paul, receiving much better treatment than that previsouly accorded to the Roman subject, Jesus.

Nevertheless, in the end Paul experienced more than four years of imprisonment without having an effective verdict rendered in his case and Luke makes it strikingly clear that this outcome was due to the corruption of his judges. It was Festus' desire to do a favor to Paul's enemies, just as previously it had been Felix's desire to receive a bribe and to grant a concession (favor) to Paul's opponents, that resulted in this indefinite period of confinement.

Finally, it is spurious to argue that Luke intended various passages illustrating "Jewish disorder" to enhance (by way of contrast) the justice of the Roman system that he described in other scenes.[17] The fact that once in Corinth and once in Jerusalem groups of Paul's Jewish opponents failed to act in concert when they had an opportunity to press their case against him does nothing to palliate the fact of two Roman governors' misconduct of Paul's case. And indeed, looking at the Acts narrative as a whole, what is remarkable is not so much "Jewish disorder" but rather the relentless and highly successful effort that Paul's chief-priestly adversaries mounted against him.

While mistaken in their assessment regarding Luke's portrayal of Roman judicial practices, it should not be thought that proponents of political apologetic completely misinterpret the contents of Acts in arguing that the Roman system is favorably portrayed. For within his narrative Luke does provide, through his favorable reports concerning the conduct of two Roman officers toward Paul, a generally positive view of the Roman army.

Nevertheless, to affirm that Luke depicts two Roman military officers acting in a disciplined and highly responsive fashion is not as significant an affirmation as it might seem to be at first glance. For it must immediately be asked whether Luke's favorable presentation in this area would have had the effect of counter-balancing, in the minds of his readers, the negative impression that his presentation in the judicial area would have left with them.

In other words, would Roman officials reading Acts have been so impressed by the positive portrayal afforded their military personnel that they would have allowed this to overshadow the largely unfavorable portrayal of their provincial governors?

When the issue is framed in these terms it seems evident that a negative response has to be given. For inasmuch as Luke's descriptions of Roman military officers are interspersed among his descriptions of Roman provincial officials, it is difficult to see how a Roman official reading Acts could have been favorably impressed by the one without being simultaneously distressed by the other.

Nor, realistically, is it possible for advocates of political apologetic to argue that there is other data within Acts to support their contention that Luke has portrayed the Roman system favorably. To modern readers who are themselves highly mindful of Roman achievements in such things as road building, harbor construction, and engineering, it can be somewhat surprising to discover that there is virtually no explicit recognition accorded to these accomplishments within Acts. Nevertheless, as indicated above in chapter eight, Acts mentions no Roman roads, no Roman aqueducts, no Roman navigational techniques, and nothing of the other aspects of Roman economic life.

Clearly none of these things is deprecated within Acts, and Luke's second volume can hardly be said to be hostile to Greco-Roman civilization. However, what is required for the sake of the political-apologetic case is simply not present: an obvious enthusiasm for the benefits afforded by and through the Roman system.

D. Data That Is Particularly Damaging to the Political-Apologetic Position

One method for assessing the validity of the political-apologetic theory is to identify and schematize the principal interpretations that it makes and then to assess these interpretations in the light of a close reading of the reports that Luke has included in Acts. This method has been employed in the preceding sections and it has now been shown that the principal claims made by proponents of the political-apologetic theory are not sufficiently enough grounded in the Acts narrative to justify the acceptance of the theory.

A second method of responding to the political-apologetic position is to begin by immediately identifying the principal elements in Acts that are acrimonious to the view of Luke's purposes that the political-apologetic theory presumes. While there are some conclusions from the preceding sections that will be repeated under this second approach, there are also new points to consider and the line of development is itself different enough to justify the relatively brief analysis that will be made in the following paragraphs.

The first feature of the Acts narrative that is especially damaging to the political-apologetic position is the statements on the subject of political allegiance that Luke attributes to Peter and the apostles early in the narrative. Roman officials reading Acts would have encountered these two statements in Luke's very first descriptions of the apostles' contacts with political authority:

Whether it is right in the sight of God to listen to you rather than to God, you must judge; for we cannot but speak of what we have seen and heard [4:19-20].

We must obey God rather than human beings [5:29].

The fact that proponents of the political-apologetic position envision high Roman officials as the recipients of Luke's words should not be overlooked in assessing the significance of these two statements. For presumably such officials would have had responsibility for enforcing, and even formulating, the empire's policies and laws. As a consequence, such a clearly and emphatically expressed position by the leaders of the Christian movement could only have engendered among officials a certain wariness regarding the stance that members of this movement would be inclined to adopt toward the Roman authorities and their order.[18]

Furthermore, it is not the case that Acts presents these statements as abstract principles that lacked any reference to real-life situations. Quite the contrary. For according to the narrative, Peter and John, the other apostles including James, and no less expressly Paul himself all embodied these principles in their lives and ministries. This then is the second feature of Acts that is particularly damaging to the political-apologetic position: Luke's narrative consistently shows the apostles and Paul obeying and witnessing to God's word without regard for the concerns, and even the harsh reactions, of the political authorities.

It is thus the case that Peter and John exemplified these principles when they refused to obey the Sanhedrin's orders to cease preaching in Jesus' name and were willing to accept whipping and imprisonment as a consequence. Similarly, James and Peter were also presumably living out these principles when they came into conflict with Herod Agrippa I, suffering imprisonment and, in James' case, death. And, over and over again, Paul behaved in a manner consistent with these principles when he steadfastly continued to proclaim Jesus despite being denounced before a variety of political officials.

The third feature of Luke's account that significantly contravenes the political-apologetic position is closely related to the second and also reinforces the meaning of the apostles' early statements. It is nothing else than the great amount of turbulence and public controversy that Acts portrays following in the wake of the proclamation of the Christian message.

As detailed above, Acts provides abundant testimony regarding the disruptive effect of Paul's preaching. However, it should be noted that disruption was also a consequence of the apostles' preaching in Jerusalem. And, indeed, while it may be supposed that Roman officials reading Acts would be confused about many of the disputes in which Paul and the apostles became embroiled, it should not be thought that such confusion would have had the consequence of leaving them favorably disposed toward the Christian movement.[19]

Rather, even without being able to determine who was right or who was wrong in the various disruptive situations described in Acts, these officials would still very probably have taken the impression that the leadership of the Christian movement had a penchant for becoming embroiled in controversy. And, read in the light of the principles that the apostles had already enunciated, these latter reports could only have given rise to still further suspicions on the part of these officials.

In addition to these three features, Luke has also included a reference in the first chapter of Acts that would have undoubtedly contributed to uneasiness on the part of Roman officials. At 1:13 when he lists the eleven apostles, Luke specifically identifies Simon as *ho zelōtēs* ("the Zealot").

On the supposition that his Roman readers were well familiar with the violent efforts of the Zealots to overthrow Roman rule in Judea,[20] it is hard to imagine a single reference that Luke could have made that would have had more potential for discrediting Christianity in Roman eyes. This point has already been remarked upon in *Jesus, Politics, and Society* in relation to Luke's identification of Simon as a Zealot at 6:15 of the Gospel.[21] However, inasmuch as Luke himself has repeated this controversial term in Acts—thus making it highly improbable that any Roman official could have finished reading Luke's two volumes without adverting to this connection—it is an observation that deserves to be stressed again in the present context.

There are thus at least four elements in the narrative of Acts which argue strongly against the view that Luke wrote for reasons of political apologetic. Taken together the apostles' dramatic statements that their first allegiance belongs to God, the manifestly disruptive consequences of the disciples' preaching of Jesus, and the consistent refusal of the apostles and Paul to be constrained by various political authorities characterize the type of movement that could only have aroused Roman officials' suspicions and made them uneasy.

And similarly, if Luke had in fact been trying to encourage Roman officials to tolerate Christianity, he would have been foolish to link the leadership of the Christian group with the Zealot movement, a movement known to be explicitly anti-Roman in its outlook and violent in its character.[22]

Luke thus did not write for reasons of political apologetic. When passages in Acts that are said to support such a theory are analyzed carefully, they scarcely provide a modicum of support for it. And Luke also includes within his narrative easily noticed reports and references that can only be regarded as thoroughly counterproductive to the accomplishment of such an objective.

4. THE THEORY OF ECCLESIAL APOLOGETIC

Although it does not have the same degree of support that the political-apologetic position has heretofore commanded, the related theory of "ecclesial apologetic" also deserves consideration as a conceptually plausible interpretation of Luke's purposes in writing. Inasmuch as its advocates appeal to many of the passages cited by proponents of political apologetic, it is appropriate and efficient to discuss this theory's claims an appendix to the preceding discussion.

As its name indicates, the ecclesial-apologetic theory agrees with the political-apologetic theory in affirming that Luke wrote with a view to accomplishing an "apology." This theory also agrees that the apology involved in two entities: Luke's fellow Christians and the Roman empire itself. However the new theory diverges with respect to the *direction* of the apology. For what proponents of ecclesial apologetic actually argue is that Luke was concerned to explain the empire in favorable terms *to his fellow Christians* and to encourage *them* to adopt a positive stance toward the Roman authorities.[23]

How did Luke accomplish this apology in Acts? Advocates of ecclesial apologetic see signs of Luke accomplishing this purpose in two of the areas are appealed to by proponents of political apologetic: Luke's portrayal of Roman justice[24] and his portrayal of Roman military personnel.[25] In addition, proponents of this interpretation may also appeal to passages in Acts in which Luke shows prominent Roman officials responding favorably to the Christian message.[26]

Taken together these arguments delineate a conceptually plausible position. However, just as previous analysis indicated that the conceptually plausible political-apologetic position foundered upon the hard data of Acts, so now does the same outcome occur when the ecclesial-apologetic position is carefully scrutinized with reference to what Luke has actually written.

First, as established above, the argument that the narrative of Acts portrays Roman justice in highly favorable terms cannot be substantiated. At several junctures Luke does portray Roman officials as being committed to certain procedures pertaining to justice; but, as the later scenes in Acts unfold, justice is not the outcome that Paul receives.[27] Indeed, he suffers mistreatment at the hands of two Roman governors and, as Acts ends, he has been in Roman chains for over four years and still has not been vindicated.

Secondly, while Luke does indicate that Paul was treated favorably by two military officers, Lysias and Julius, proponents of ecclesial apologetic distort and overemphasize this favorable portrayal in arguing that Luke wished his fellow Christians to conclude that the gospel was thereby "saved" by Rome.[28]

Actually it is Luke's sense that Lysias was primarily intent on quelling a disorder when he arrested Paul; thereafter his treatment of Paul is what might be expected of an officer who finds that he has taken a Roman citizen prisoner. And even though Luke does show Julius manifesting an unusual degree of concern for Paul, it is still too much to claim that Luke wished his readers to understand that Julius was acting in order to enable Paul to fulfill his commission to bear witness to Jesus in Rome.[29]

Similarly, with respect to the attitudes that Roman officials display toward Christian preaching, it is certainly true that there are passages in Acts in which Roman officials favorably respond to the Christian message. The centurion Cornelius is the first of these in chapter ten; he is followed by the proconsul Sergius Paulus in chapter thirteen. And, in addition, in chapter twenty-four Luke also portrays Tiberius Felix giving an initially favorable response.[30]

However, when these passages are read in the context of numerous other passages in Acts, it can hardly be said that Luke is suggesting to his readers that the Roman authorities in general are favorably disposed toward the Christian message. Cornelius and Sergius Paulus do embrace the gospel; but, on the other hand, Herod Agrippa I persecutes and executes its messengers. And while Felix is initially receptive to Paul's message, he is, in the end, even more receptive to a bribe. The point is: the response is mixed. Some Roman officials accept the Christian message, others do not; still others actively persecute those who preach it.[31]

It is thus the case that when account is taken of all the elements and nuances that are present in Luke's narrative, the ecclesial-apologetic position, like the political-apologetic position, falls to the ground for lack of sufficient supporting data.

Luke does portray Paul receiving favorable treatment from two Roman officers and he does portray a centurion and a proconsul coming to Christian faith. Nevertheless, given his other reports regarding the misconduct of other Roman officials and the lack of a just resolution of Paul's case, it seems evident that Luke did not write in order to persuade his fellow Christians to look favorably upon the Roman authorities. Political apologetic was not Luke's purpose; but, on the other hand, neither was ecclesial apologetic.

11

Allegiance to Jesus and Witness before Kings and Governors

If Luke wrote neither for reasons of political apologetic nor for reasons of ecclesial apologetic, then what were the concerns that did influence him to write? Building upon the analysis that has been made in the preceding chapters and keeping in mind that the focus of the present study is upon Christian conduct in the context of Roman rule, the task of the present chapter is to propose a theory regarding the factors that actually did motivate Luke.

In the first section of this chapter a three-part theory of Luke's concerns will be presented and elaborated. Then, in section two, the proposed theory will be discussed from the standpoint of various methodological considerations that are important to *any* theory of Luke's purposes. Finally, in a concluding section the theory that has been developed will be related to the conclusion of Acts and to two of the objections which have traditionally been raised against Luke's ending.

1. ALLEGIANCE AND WITNESS: A THEORY OF LUKE'S PURPOSES

Whatever sources of information that Luke had available to him, it was, in the end, his own responsibility to determine what to present and how to present it. And it is for this reason that considerations regarding Luke's own purposes have considerable importance. What was Luke actually trying to accomplish through his writings? What impressions did he hope to have others take from them? The theory now to be proposed seeks to respond to these and to other related questions.

At the outset it is important to recognize that the present theory is somewhat complex in its formulation and encompasses three separate, although closely related, assertions. The theory's first assertion is that Luke wrote to express and share his own personal commitment to Jesus. Its second is that he wrote to provide his fellow Christians with guidance for their exercise of Christian discipleship within the context of Roman rule. Thirdly and more specifically, the theory also asserts that Luke wrote to provide the Christians of his day with perspective and guidance regarding the trial witness of Christians before various political officials.

If separate terms were to be utilized to provide for each of these assertions, then the theory now being proposed might have the short-form designation of the "allegiance-conduct-witness" theory. However, inasmuch as the term "witness" can be understood to encompass the testimony that disciples give in the conduct of their daily lives as well as the special form of testimony given at hearings and trials, it is possible to abbreviate further and to describe the theory simply as the "allegiance-witness" theory of Luke's purposes in writing. This latter designation will be adopted as the theory is now presented in amplified form.

Under the heading of "allegiance," the proposed theory asserts that Luke actually wrote with two distinct, albeit closely related, concerns in mind. On the one hand the Gospel and Acts fairly breathe Luke's deep commitment to Jesus and it must be supposed that his own personal allegiance to the risen Lord was a powerful factor motivating him to write.[1] And on the other hand, Luke presumably also had an abiding concern to strengthen his readers in *their* allegiance to Jesus. This, too, is a dimension that seems constantly present in the narrative even if it is not something that Luke ever explicitly states.[2]

Regarding the "witness" part of the theory, it is also highly probable that Luke wished to provide his readers with information that they would find useful in their own lives as disciples of Jesus within the framework of Roman rule. From even a casual reading of the Gospel, it seems evident that Luke was concerned to present Jesus' teaching and his conduct in considerable detail. And the same is also true with respect to Acts where the narrative is replete with reports of how the disciples taught and conducted themselves in Jesus' name.

To what precise degree Luke himself believed that the conduct he attributed to Jesus should be normative for the Christians of his own time and later generations is a matter for further discussion.[3] But it is seemingly beyond doubt that Luke felt that his reports about Jesus' stance and his descriptions of the approach followed by Jesus' leading disciples would be highly instructive to and highly valued by the members of his audience.

Luke seemingly had specific concerns within each of the seven headings that were used above to schematize the stance of Jesus in the Gospel and the disciples in Acts. It can also be presumed that he wished his readers to be particularly well informed regarding two themes which delineated, in a fundamental way, the social stance adopted by Jesus and his disciples. The first theme: Jesus and his disciples operated in terms of priorities and concerns that were sanctioned by God. The second theme: because of their priorities and concerns Jesus and his followers sometimes came into conflict with the Roman order even though they themselves were not anti-Roman revolutionaries as the Zealots were.

And reflection about Luke's purposes in these two thematic areas leads easily into reflections regarding the final major area of the allegiance-witness theory and the subject of Christians' witness in their trials before Roman officials. Here the theory asserts that Luke was generally concerned to alert his readers to the fact that witness before political officials constituted an extremely important part of their heritage.[4] In addition, Luke presumably also had a number of specific insights that he wished to communicate to his readers.

Before attempting to present these latter highly specific insights, it is well to indicate that increasing caution is called for as a theory becomes steadily more detailed in its interpretations. For, clearly, there is less of a basis for attributing a particular concern to Luke when only one or two texts can be cited. Nevertheless, the nature of Luke's reports is such that it is still fully plausible to argue that the following points were among his particular concerns:

(1) Luke wished his readers to appreciate that Jesus himself had experienced trials before Rome officials and he wished them to know that Jesus had explicitly predicted that his disciples would have comparable experiences at the hands of the Roman authorities.

(2) Secondly, Luke's readers should also know that Jesus had given specific instructions regarding the approach that the disciples should follow upon such occasions (these specific instructions will be considered in section two, below).[5]

(3) Further, the members of Luke's audience should also be well aware of the fact that a significant number of Jesus' leading disciples had themselves been brought to trial before Roman officials of varying ranks.

(4) Fourthly, Luke wished his readers to know that considerably different outcomes were possible when such hearings and trials took place. Severe punishment and even death were possibilities, but it was also possible that the charges might be rejected or misinterpreted. Or there might be delays due to corruption and intrigue.[6]

(5) However, whatever they had experienced at their trials and whatever the outcomes that materialized, Jesus and his leading disciples had all remained steadfast in their witness. This faithfulness was the quality that Luke wished to have his readers recognize and appreciate above all else.

From the foregoing considerations, it is now apparent that the "allegiance-witness" theory which is being proposed is far from limited in its scope. On a general level, the theory speaks in terms of allegiance to Jesus and the basic social and political stance of Jesus and his disciples. On a more specific level, it speaks of Christian witness before Roman officials at various hearings and trials.

The allegiance-witness theory thus proposes that Luke had both of these types of concerns in his mind, the more specific as well as the more general, when he set out to write. The task which now remains is to assess the validity of this theory in the light of several important methodological criteria.

2. SUPPORTIVE METHODOLOGICAL ARGUMENTS

The task of determining appropriate methodological criteria for evaluating various theories regarding Luke's purposes is not an easy one, and the evaluative questions which will now be elaborated are not the only ones conceivable. Nevertheless, used with circumspection, the three methodologically-oriented questions which follow can serve as a highly effective instrument for evaluating the merits of any given theory.[7]

Is the proposed theory consistent with and congruent with what Luke has actually presented in Luke and Acts? Does the proposed theory fit plausibly with the life-setting of the audience that Luke was presumably addressing? Given what is probable concerning Luke's sources, can it be shown that Luke utilized any of them in a way that is confirmatory of the proposed theory? These three methodological questions will now be utilized to evaluate the allegiance-witness theory of Luke's purposes in writing.

A. Congruence with the Contents of Luke and Acts

Of the three criteria, the first regarding congruence with the contents of Luke and Acts is clearly of decisive importance. Indeed, should a particular theory fail to meet this standard, its success with respect to any other criterion is of little consequence.[8]

It is also clear that a systematic presentation with reference to this question would involve a careful study of virtually the whole of Luke's two volumes. Yet, in effect, such a study has been conducted in the preceding chapters with reference to Acts and in *Jesus, Politics, and Society* with reference to Luke's Gospel. And, accordingly, it is now left to the reader to consider the degree to which these previous analyses substantiate the claim that Luke held specific concerns in the areas of "allegiance," "conduct," and "witness," when he proceeded to write his works.

There is, however, one additional feature of Luke's presentation that deserves to be noticed in the present context, a feature which pertains to the extensive treatment that Luke accords to Paul's interactions with various political authorities in the last half of Acts. Once it becomes apparent just how expansive Luke's presentation is in this particular area, the allegiance witness theory is rendered all the more plausible. Indeed, without the benefit of this theory, Luke's careful detailing of so many political controversies could almost seem disproportionate.

Although Luke does describe the apostles being arraigned before the Sanhedrin on two separate occasions and also indicates that James and Peter were severely dealt with by Herod Agrippa I, an initial awareness that Luke is devoting a significant proportion of his narrative to the subject of trials is not likely to come to readers of Acts until after they have encountered Luke's descriptions of Paul's activities in Macedonia, Achaia, and Asia. And indeed a full appreciation regarding just how much of his narrative Luke devotes to this subject cannot really be had until Luke's descriptions of Paul's experiences in Jerusalem and Caesarea have also been assimilated.

In chapter sixteen Luke gives considerable attention to Paul's dealings with the magistrates at Philippi. At the beginning of chapter seventeen the events involving Paul, Jason, and the politarchs of Thessalonica are described and serve as the culmination of Paul's ministry there. In chapter eighteen, Luke then reports the hearing (actually the "non-hearing") held before Gallio as the end-event of Paul's ministry in Corinth. This episode is then followed in chapter nineteen by the lengthy report of the controversy which ensued at Ephesus and the assessment that the clerk of the city ultimately made of Paul's conduct.

At that point, for almost two chapters, there is a lapse in Paul's contacts with the political authorities. Then, however, at the end of chapter twenty-one, Paul is arrested by Claudius Lysias and begins a long period as a Roman prisoner. During this interval, which actually lasts until the end of the book, Paul is involved in a hearing before the Sanhedrin, in a trial before Tiberius Felix, in a personal encounter with Felix, in a trial before Porcius Festus and in a review hearing before Festus and Herod Agrippa II.

All in all then, Luke describes Paul giving explicit or implicit witness to Jesus before various political officials and in various political circumstances no less than nine times.[9] That Luke portrays this form of witness as such a significant dimension of Paul's ministry during this period must be regarded as remarkable on its own terms. It becomes even more noteworthy when it is recognized that, as this dimension of Paul's ministry comes to greater prominence, another hitherto extremely important aspect of Paul's ministry gradually recedes. For the converts that Paul makes in Ephesus at 19:18–20 are actually the last that he makes within Acts. Luke does not ever portray him again winning such a full-hearted response.[10]

Indeed to speak in terms of "images," it is no exaggeration to say that as Luke gradually unfolds his narrative, the image of Paul as a great missionary is replaced with the image of Paul as a Roman prisoner and the image of Paul as a witness before Roman officials.[11]

As indicated above, without the benefit of the allegiance-witness theory, Luke's portrayal of Paul's numerous hearings and trials might be considered somewhat "disproportionate." However, when this theory is assumed, there is no mystery as to why Luke has included such material so abundantly within his account. Luke included these numerous reports because he himself was extremely interested in detailing just how Jesus and his disciples conducted themselves before a variety of Roman officials.

B. Congruence with the Presumed Circumstances of Luke's Audience

Since Luke wrote from a specific place and over a particular span of time and since he almost certainly had his audience in mind as he wrote, it is incumbent upon anyone who proposes a theory of Luke's purposes to show that the proposed theory congrues well with Luke's own circumstances and those of his audience.

There is, however, a significant obstacle to the accomplishment of this step: the fact that so little is certain with respect to Luke's time and place of composition! Did Luke write sometime in the early 60s or as late as the late 90s; or did he write, as many scholars would maintain, close to the year 70? Did Luke write from Syrian Antioch, or Ephesus, or Caesarea, or perhaps even from Rome itself? On these questions of specific time and place, there is little by way of consensus within New Testament scholarship.[12]

Nevertheless, there are two features of Luke's situation regarding which certainty is possible and both of these features congrue well with the premises and assertions of the allegiance-witness theory. First, it is virtually certain that Luke himself and at least the central members of his intended audience were Christians. Secondly, it is also virtually unassailable that both Luke and his readers were living out their Christian lives in social and political circumstances that were essentially unchanged from those in effect for Jesus and his leading disciples.

Inasmuch as the dimension of Luke's own personal faith commitment to Jesus has already been emphasized in the opening section of this chapter, no further elaboration is called for in the present discussion. Similarly, at this juncture only two points need to be briefly made regarding the assertion that Christians comprised at least the core of Luke's readership.

The very character of Luke and Acts as volumes which consistently advert to faith in Jesus and consistently portray the realities of lives based upon faith attests to the fact that Luke envisioned his fellow disciples and perhaps those who were drawing close to faith as the recipients of his writings. In addition, a significant insight regarding Luke's audience can also be derived from the arguments utilized in the preceding chapter to refute the political-apologetic theory. For if Luke did *not* write to curry favor with pagan officials, then seemingly it must have been to Christian groups that his accounts were directed.

There is, however, considerably more which needs to be said on the subject of the common social and political context that Luke and his readers shared with Jesus and the first disciples. Fundamentally this context was that of the enduring Roman empire. And it is no minor insight to recognize that *whenever* Luke wrote, the Roman empire still endured. *Wherever* he and those he addressed lived, they surely lived within the context of Roman rule.[13]

The perduring Roman empire. The continuing framework of Roman rule. What would these realities have meant in practice for Luke, a Christian writer with allegiance-witness purposes? Seemingly the first point to observe is that Luke could presume that his readers, would easily understand the social and political setting of the events that he was relating to them. For regardless of the dates which are assigned to Luke's work, it is obvious that his readers would have still understood the Roman provincial system, that they would have been familiar with the traditional Roman objectives of peace and order, and that they would have been well aware of the ways in which governors and other Roman officials carried out their mandates.

And secondly, the fact that his readers' circumstances were in such close continuity with the circumstances of Jesus in Judea and the circumstances of Paul in Achaia and Judea could only have confirmed Luke in the conviction that his readers would find reports about Jesus' approach and Paul's stance highly relevant to their own deliberations about the demands of Christian conduct. In other words, what Luke wrote concerning Jesus' teachings about "the things of Caesar" and what he wrote concerning Jesus' outcome under Caesar's governor—such reports would have immediate interest for disciples who were trying to work out their own approach within the continuing empire.[14]

And similarly with respect to what he wrote concerning the apostles' approach and Paul's testimony. Luke must surely have known that his reports would have immediate appeal for disciples striving to manifest their own commitments to Jesus in situations which closely resembled those experienced by Peter, John, and Paul.

Did Luke write for the purpose of sharing his own faith in Jesus and to encourage his readers to a still deeper allegiance to their common Lord? Did he write to provide his readers with information that would be highly useful to them as they sought to live and witness to Jesus within the context and the framework of the Roman empire? Did he wish to make them aware, in considerable detail, of the type of witness that Jesus and his leading disciples had given before "kings and governors"?

The foregoing analysis of the circumstances of Luke's readers does not establish that these were actually Luke's conscious purposes. But, manifestly, such a setting in life for him and his readers could easily have persuaded Luke regarding the relevance of providing such information. Or, alternately expressed, Luke's appreciation for such factors in the life situation of his audience could well have given him the assurance that a work providing such material would be highly valued and enduringly appreciated.

C. Confirmation from Luke's Handling of His Markan Source

What sources did Luke have available to him when he composed his works? Can it be shown that Luke's way of utilizing any of these sources supports the theory of his purposes now being proposed? While it is legitimate to try to demonstrate that Luke has utilized his sources in a manner that is consistent with the allegiance-witness theory, it must be recognized at the outset that only tentative conclusions are possible.

Part of the difficulty has to do with the fact that there is considerably less than universal agreement as to the number and character of the sources that Luke possessed for each of his volumes. With respect to Acts it is often asserted that Luke used a number of oral and written sources in developing his account.[15] Nevertheless, Luke's final draft is written in such a way that it has proved impossible for scholars to identify any of these sources with certitude let alone to determine any modifications that Luke may have made in utilizing one or more of them.

With respect to the Gospel the present writer, along with many other commentators, is persuaded that Luke had Mark's Gospel, a collection of sayings ("Q"), and other reports about Jesus ("L") as sources for his work.[16] However, even if such a starting point is assumed, there are still major obstacles to be overcome before insights regarding Luke's purposes can be derived.

First, of the sources just identified, only one of them, Mark's Gospel, exists in such a form that Luke's manner of appropriating it can be readily established. And secondly, even after it has been determined that Luke has added to, subtracted from, or otherwise modified one of Mark's reports, the reason for which he did so may not be obvious. For Luke may conceivably have made a modification for a purpose that actually has little to do with the purposes entertained in a given theory.

Bearing these cautions in mind, it is still valid and even imperative to have any theory of Luke's purposes assessed with reference to Luke's use of Mark's Gospel. Indeed, should it be shown that Luke's utilization of Mark is not consistent with a particular theory, then the viability of that theory would be impaired. No such negative outcome results when the present theory is so evaluated, however. For in three critical instances, Luke's utilization of Mark's account provides significant confirmation for the tenets of the present theory pertaining to the subject of Christian witness before Roman officials.

Proceeding chronologically, the first instance of a significant modification occurs at Luke 21:12–19 where Luke seemingly presents in his own fashion material that occurs at Mark 13:9–13, material regarding Jesus' instructions to the disciples concerning their future testimony before various officials. The precise process which Luke followed in presenting his own account of Jesus' instructions is far from certain; but what is clear is that he was not satisfied simply to incorporate Mark's report into his own narrative without alteration.[17]

What is also clear, upon a close verse-by-verse comparison of the two accounts (here the reader's attention is directed to the discussion carried out in the accompanying notes), is that Luke's report portrays Jesus giving a significantly fuller guidance to the disciples regarding the approach that they should follow and the developments they should anticipate in their encounters with such rulers.[18] In addition, it is also evident that Luke wished his readers to understand that Jesus' instruction pertained to the time before the period of cataclysmic upheavals.[19] This latter point, an important one is easily observed within Luke's text:

> But *before all this* they will lay their hands on you and persecute you, delivering you up to the synagogues and prisons, and you will be brought before kings and governors for my name's sake. This will be a time for you to bear testimony. Settle it therefore in your minds, not to meditate

beforehand how to answer; for I will give you a mouth and wisdom, which none of your adversaries will be able to withstand or contradict. You will be delivered up even by parents and brothers and kinsmen and friends, and some of you they will put to death; you will be hated by all for my name's sake. But not a hair of your head will perish. By your endurance you will gain your lives [Luke 21:12-19; emphasis added].

If the report just cited can justifiably be regarded as surpassing Mark's report with respect to the data that it communicates relative to allegiance-witness concerns, two of Luke's passages regarding the particulars of Jesus' own appearances before a governor and a tetrarch also significantly surpass Mark. The first of these passages pertains to the charges against Jesus. The second pertains to Jesus' interrogation by Herod Antipas.

Clearly, any report regarding the proceedings against Jesus at his Roman trial would be of interest to a writer with allegiance-witness concerns. Yet in reading Mark's trial account, the only statement that Luke would have found regarding the allegations against Jesus would have been the brief reference in Mark 15:3 that the chief priests accused him "of many things."

While the exact approach which Luke followed at this juncture cannot be known with certainty, it is again obvious that he was not content merely to repeat what Mark had stated.[20] Instead he took steps to provide his readers not only with one but actually with two reports regarding the charges that the chief priests and their allies lodged against Jesus:

We found this man perverting our nation, and forbidding us to give tribute to Caesar, and saying that he himself is Christ a king [Luke 23:2].

He stirs up the people, teaching throughout all Judea, from Galilee even to this place [Luke 23:5].

The fact that Luke's articulation and elaboration of these charges can so easily be explained in terms of the allegiance-witness theory must be regarded as still another point in favor of this theory. Indeed, it is difficult to envision any other construction that explains Luke's modifications in this matter nearly as plausibly.

The same assertion cannot be made regarding Luke's decision to include in his narrative a report regarding an appearance of Jesus before Herod Antipas. For in this instance, the character of the material included is such that Luke may have conceivably been interested in it for several different reasons. The passage, for which there is no parallel or reference within Mark's Gospel, reads as follows:

And when he learned that he belonged to Herod's jurisdiction, he sent him over to Herod, who was himself in Jerusalem at that time. When Herod saw Jesus, he was very glad, for he had long desired to see him, because he had heard about him, and he was hoping to see some sign done by him. So he questioned him at some length; but he made no answer. The chief priests and the scribes stood by, vehemently accusing him. And Herod with his soldiers treated him with contempt and mocked him; then, arraying him in gorgeous apparel, he sent him back to Pilate [Luke 23:7–11].

What motivated Luke to provide his readers with this additional report? From the perspective of the allegiance-witness theory, it can be generally asserted that he did so because he wished to give his readers further data regarding the meaning of faithful witness before Roman officials. More specifically, it may also be argued that Luke simply wanted his readers to appreciate that Jesus had had to appear before more than one Roman official and that in his appearance before Herod Antipas he did not answer the questions the tetrarch put to him.

In a previous study the present writer has advanced the argument that Luke may have decided to include this passage in his narrative because it allowed him a further opportunity for emphasizing the relentless way in which the chief priests pressed their case against Jesus.[21] And indeed it should not be supposed that other plausible explanations regarding Luke's purposes in this matter are hereby foreclosed. For as mentioned above, Luke's actual purposes may be well beyond those envisioned by a given theory.

Nevertheless it is far from inconsequential that Luke's inclusion of this passage can be so plausibly explained from the allegiance-witness perspective. It is, as has been demonstrated, the third major passage for which a plausible interpretation can be given. In the first case Luke significantly modified Mark's report to include further relevant data. In the second case, he elaborated and greatly particularized something that Mark only adverted to in general terms. And in the present case he provided his readers with important allegiance-witness data that was completely unavailable to them within the boundaries of Mark's Gospel.

3. THE PROPOSED THEORY AND THE ENDING OF ACTS

In addition to its strengths with respect to the three methodological criteria discussed in the previous section, the allegiance-witness theory also manifests strength in terms of its ability to interpret the ending of Acts.[22] And in light of the fact that Luke's conclusion has sometimes been criticized for an alleged lack of climax and an alleged lack of completeness,[23] it is more than appropriate to bring the present study to its own conclusion by demonstrating that, when viewed from the perspective of the allegiance-witness theory, the ending of Acts has more than adequate amounts of both of these qualities.

Characteristically those who allege that the conclusion of Acts lacks climax argue that Luke fails to show Paul exceeding in Rome the achievements he has earlier made in various provincial cities.[24] Such an outcome, these critics assert, frustrates the expectation which Luke's previous reports have engendered regarding the highly significant endeavors which awaited Paul's arrival in the capital of the empire.

But is it true that Luke fails to show Paul engaging in any particularly significant endeavor at the ending of Acts? Seemingly such an assertion is not well established within the text itself—at least when Luke's account is regarded from an allegiance-witness perspective. For, from this perspective, there is a significant climactic element present in Luke's account of Paul's arrival and ministry in Rome as a consequence of the fact that Paul stands ready to give faithful and uncompromised testimony before the empire's highest official.

To see this point more clearly, it is important to observe that the encounters which Paul has previously had with various provincial officials effectively prepare the way for such a "summit" encounter with Caesar. And, in addition, there is the fact that, earlier in his account, Luke has portrayed Paul receiving divine visions guiding him to judgment and testimony before the emperor. In the first of these visions the risen Jesus indicated to Paul that he would have the responsibility of testifying in Rome. In the second vision the angel told him that it was specifically to Caesar that his testimony would be given:[25]

Take courage, for as you have testified about me at Jerusalem, so must you bear witness also at Rome [23:11].

Do not be afraid, Paul; you must stand before Caesar; and lo, God has granted you all those who sail with you [27:24].

And yet within Acts Paul does not actually give testimony before the emperor. Why does Luke not end with Paul physically present before Caesar's tribunal? Why does he not report the emperor's verdict on Paul's case? It is at this point that a reply to the criticism that the conclusion of Acts is anticlimactic necessarily evolves into a response to the charge that Luke's ending lacks completeness.[26] For in order to confirm the argument that the end of Acts possesses a suitable degree of climax, it is necessary to establish that Luke's ending also manifests an appropriate degree of completeness.

Once again the perspective afforded by the allegiance-witness theory is crucial. What emerges when Acts and its conclusion are viewed from this perspective is: (1) that Luke's ending shows Paul's faithful testimony before Caesar to be complete *in principle,* and (2) that Luke's ending indicates that Paul's "ordinary" ministry on behalf of Jesus continues for the immediate future. In other words, viewed from the perspective of the allegiance-witness theory, there are two subtly related aspects present in Luke's ending, a dimension indicating that Paul's uncompromised testimony before Caesar is assured and a dimension indicating that Paul's faithful ministry of preaching and teaching continues for the time being.

Without a doubt the aspect of Luke's work which signals that Paul's faithful testimony before Caesar is complete in principle is the more difficult of the two aspects to grasp. For with respect to this aspect there are insights which must be gained regarding the fact that Paul will indeed appear before Caesar and regarding the fact that, when he does testify, he will prove to be utterly faithful.

What elements within the narrative indicate that Paul will eventually stand before the emperor? The first, obvious point to be grasped is that as Acts closes Paul is in close geographical proximity to the emperor's tribunal. He is personally in Rome and remains under the guard of a Roman soldier. And presumably the particular features of his case are being weighed by the imperial officials into whose jurisdiction Julius has delivered him.

In addition, Luke also indicates that there are divine as well as institutional influences acting upon Paul. For Paul has not come to Rome through mere happenstance and he is not, as it were, bobbing in the water as Acts ends. Instead, on one level he is being propelled to the emperor as a result of the appeal process that is underway. He himself initiated this process, but Festus, the governor of Judea has implemented it, preparing the necessary reports and sending Paul to Rome in Julius' custody.[27]

And on a higher level Paul is inexorably being propelled to the emperor's tribunal because the risen Jesus desires him to give testimony there. Indeed, God has safeguarded him throughout a perilous journey in order that he might give this very witness.

What elements within the narrative indicate that Paul will testify with complete faithfulness when he eventually does appear before Caesar? Here, too, what Luke has previously reported regarding Paul's earlier trials and what he reports concerning the character of Paul's situation in Rome both indicate that Paul's testimony will be faithful and uncompromising.

Paul before Claudius Lysias and the Jerusalem Sanhedrin. Paul before Tiberius Felix. Paul before Porcius Festus and then before Festus, Herod Agrippa II and an assembly of notables. In not one of these instances did Paul ever fail to testify faithfully to Jesus his Lord. In not one of these instances did he ever allow the power of those before whom he stood to prevent him from explaining his own allegiance to Jesus and defending the course that his life had taken since the time of his conversion.

It is only when Luke's previous reports regarding Paul's encounters with various Roman officials are carefully reflected upon that the pattern and the significance of the faithful testimony which Paul has given prior to his arrival in Rome become evident. And to these previous reports Luke then adds a description which highlights Paul's fidelity to his Lord during the time of his ministry in Rome. Once again he portrays Paul as fully faithful, teaching about Jesus with all boldness and refusing to let himself be intimidated or bowed down by the constraints placed upon him.

In such a fashion, through his descriptions of Paul's previous trials and his description of Paul's continuing ministry in Rome, Luke indicates in unmistakable terms a pattern of uninterrupted faithfulness. And it is this pattern which is operational as Acts ends. Does Paul's faithfulness extend in principle to his coming appearance before Caesar? From all that has preceded, it would seem unalterably Luke's sense that Paul's faithful testimony is indeed assured.

By way of a preliminary concluding note it may also be suggested that there are sound reasons for affirming that Luke himself, a writer with allegiance-witness concerns, would surely have regarded the ending that he fashioned as fully satisfactory. For on the one hand Luke had shown that Paul's fidelity to Jesus had never wavered; he had indicated to his readers that in all of his encounters with Roman officials, Paul had never compromised, nor been compromised in, his allegiance to Jesus.[28]

And on the other hand, the aspect of Acts' final scene under which Paul continued in faithful "ordinary" ministry while he awaited trial would also have commended itself to Luke. For, in effect, such a description enabled Luke to give his readers final encouragement to continue in their own "ordinary" ministry on behalf of Jesus without undue anxiety regarding the more specialized calling of giving testimony to Jesus before Roman officials.[29]

If such concerns led Luke to commend his work to his readers with just such a conclusion,[30] what response might his original readers well have had when they reached the end of his second volume? As an interpretation with which to conclude the present study, it is perhaps not inappropriate to suggest again that Luke's readers could only have received all that he wrote, including his ending, with unqualified appreciation.

Just as they were deeply moved by Luke's Gospel accounts concerning "all that Jesus began to do and to teach," so must they have been encouraged to continue in faithful witness to their risen Lord by all that Luke related in his second volume concerning the apostles and Paul.

And may it not be supposed that Luke's closing descriptions concerning Paul would have particularly engaged them? Whatever their time and place, whatever their particular circumstances, how could they not have been inspired to manifest within their own lives the same faithfulness and the same resoluteness which Paul himself had manifested in his own surpassing witness to the risen Jesus, the Lord who had called them all?

Abbreviations

Multi-Author Collections, Dictionaries, Periodicals

AATRT   *Les Actes des Apôtres: Traditions, rēdactions, thēologie.* Edited by J. Kremer. Gembloux: Duculot, 1979.

BAGD   W. Bauer, *A Greek-English Lexicon of the New Testament and Other Early Christian Literature.* Translated and adapted by W. Arndt and W. Gingrich; revised and augmented by W. Gingrich and F. Danker. Chicago: University of Chicago Press, 1979.

BC   *The Beginnings of Christianity.* Volumes I–V. Edited by F. Foakes Jackson and K. Lake. London: Macmillan, 1920–1933.

BL   *Bibel und Leben*

BTB   *Biblical Theology Bulletin*

CBQ   *Catholic Biblical Quarterly*

DNT   X. Léon-Dufour, *Dictionary of the New Testament.* Translated by T. Prendergast. New York: Harper and Row, 1980.

DR   *Downside Review*

ET   *The Expository Times*

ETR   *Études Théologiques et Religieuses*

IDB   *The Interpreter's Dictionary of the Bible.* 4 Volumes and Supplement. Edited by G. Buttrick. New York: Abingdon, 1962.

INT   *Interpretation*

JBL   *Journal of Biblical Literature*

LANP   *Luke-Acts: New Perspectives from the Society of Biblical Literature Seminar.* Edited by C. Talbert. New York: Crossroad, 1984.

LSJ	H. Liddell and R. Scott, *A Greek-English Lexicon.* Revised and augmented by H. Jones. Oxford: Clarendon Press, 1968.
NT	*Novum Testamentum*
PILA	*Political Issues in Luke-Acts.* Edited by R. Cassidy and P. Scharper. Maryknoll, New York: Orbis, 1983.
PLA	*Perspectives on Luke-Acts.* Edited by C. Talbert. Danville, Virginia: Association of Baptist Professors of Religion, 1978.
PP	*Past and Present*
RE	*Review and Expositor*
RSR	*Revue des Sciences Religieuses*
RTR	*Reformed Theological Review*
SLA	*Studies in Luke-Acts.* Edited by L. Keck and L. Martyn. Nashville: Abingdon, 1966.
TDNT	*Theological Dictionary of the New Testament.* 9 Volumes. Edited by G. Kittel and G. Friedrich. Translated and edited by G. Bromily. Grand Rapids: Eerdmans, 1964–1974.
TS	*Theological Studies*
ZG	M. Zerwick and M. Grosvenor, *A Grammatical Analysis of the Greek New Testament.* Rome: Biblical Institute Press, 1981.

Commentaries and Studies

Barrett	C. K. Barrett, *Luke the Historian in Recent Study.* Philadelphia: Fortress, 1970.
Bruce	F. F. Bruce, *The Book of Acts.* Grand Rapids: Eerdmans, 1981 (reprint).
Cadbury/*Book*	H. Cadbury, *The Book of Acts in History.* London: Black, 1955.
Cadbury/*Making*	H. Cadbury, *The Making of Luke-Acts.* London: SPCK, 1968.
Cassidy/*Jesus*	R. Cassidy, *Jesus, Politics, and Society: a Study of Luke's Gospel.* Maryknoll, New York: Orbis, 1978.
Cassidy/*Motive*	R. Cassidy, "Luke's Audience, the Chief Priests, and the Motive for Jesus' Death," in PILA, pp. 146–67.

Conzelmann/ *Apostel*	H. Conzelmann, *Die Apostelgeschichte*. Tübingen: Mohr, 1963.
Conzelmann/ *Theology*	H. Conzelmann, *The Theology of St. Luke*. Translated by G. Buswell. New York: Harper and Row, 1960.
Degenhardt	H. J. Degenhardt, *Lukas, Evangelist der Armen*. Stuttgart: Katholisches Bibelwerk, 1965.
Dupont/*Actes*	J. Dupont, *Les Actes des Apôtres*. Paris: Cerf, 1964.
Dupont/ *Nouv. Études*	J. Dupont, *Nouvelles Études sur les Actes des Apôtres*. Paris: Cerf, 1984.
Dupont/ *Salvation*	J. Dupont, *The Salvation of the Gentiles*. Translated by J. Keating. New York: Paulist, 1979.
Fitzmyer/*Acts*	J. Fitzmyer, *Acts of the Apostles* (introduction; commentary on chapters six through twenty-eight) in *Jerome Biblical Commentary*. Edited by R. Brown, J. Fitzmyer, and R. Murphy. Englewood Cliffs, New Jersey: Prentice-Hall, 1968.
Fitzmyer/*Gospel*	J. Fitzmyer, *The Gospel According to Luke*. 2 Volumes. Garden City, New York: Doubleday, 1981.
Gasque	W. Gasque, *A History of the Criticism of the Acts of the Apostles*. Grand Rapids: Eerdmans, 1975.
Haenchen	E. Haenchen, *The Acts of the Apostles*. Translation revised by R. Wilson. Philadelphia: Westminster, 1971.
Hengel	M. Hengel, *Acts and the History of Earliest Christianity*. Translated by J. Bowden. Philadelphia: Fortress, 1980.
Hull	J. Hull, *The Holy Spirit in the Acts of the Apostles*. London: Lutterworth, 1967.
Jervell	J. Jervell, *Luke and the People of God*. Minneapolis: Augsburg, 1972.
Johnson	L. Johnson, *The Literary Function of Possessions in Luke-Acts*. Missoula, Montana: Scholars Press, 1977.
Juel	D. Juel, *Luke-Acts: the Promise of History*. Atlanta: John Knox, 1983.
Lake and Cadbury	K. Lake and H. Cadbury, *The Acts of the Apostles* (volume IV of *The Beginnings of Christianity*).

Maddox R. Maddox, *The Purpose of Luke-Acts*. Edinburgh: Clark, 1982.

Marshall H. Marshall, *The Acts of the Apostles*. Grand Rapids: Eerdmans, 1980.

Martin R. Martin, *Acts*. London: Scripture Union, 1978.

Munck J. Munck, *The Acts of the Apostles*. Garden City, New York: Doubleday, 1967.

Neill W. Neill, *The Acts of the Apostles*. Grand Rapids: Eerdmans, 1981.

Neyrey J. Neyrey, *The Passion According to Luke: a Redaction Study of Luke's Soteriology*. New York: Paulist, 1985.

O'Neill J. O'Neill, *The Theology of Acts in Its Historical Setting*. London: SPCK, 1961.

O'Toole/*Climax* R. O'Toole, *The Christological Climax of Paul's Defense*. Rome: Biblical Institute Press, 1978.

O'Toole/*Unity* R. O'Toole, *The Unity of Luke's Theology*. Wilmington, Delaware: Glazier, 1984.

Rackham R. Rackham, *The Acts of the Apostles*. London: Methuen, 1901.

Ricciotti G. Ricciotti, *The Acts of the Apostles*. Translated by L. Byrne. Milwaukee: Bruce, 1957.

Schille G. Schille, *Die Apostelgeschichte des Lukas*. Berlin: Evangelische Verlagsanstalt, 1983.

Schmithals W. Schmithals, *Die Apostelgeschichte des Lukas*. Zurich: Theologisches Verlag, 1982.

Schneider G. Schneider, *Die Apostelgeschichte*. 2 Volumes. Freiburg im Breisgau: Herder, 1980.

Sherwin-White A. N. Sherwin-White, *Roman Society and Roman Law in the New Testament*. Oxford: Clarendon Press, 1963.

Talbert C. Talbert, *Acts*. Atlanta: John Knox, 1984.

Tiede D. Tiede, *Prophecy and History in Luke-Acts*. Philadelphia: Fortress, 1980.

Walaskay/   P. Walaskay, " 'Kai Houtōs Eis Tēn Rōmēn Ēlthamen': The
Dissertation   Political Perspective of St. Luke." Duke University Dissertation, 1973.

Walaskay/*Rome*   P. Walaskay, *"And So We Came to Rome": The Political Perspective of St. Luke.* Cambridge: Cambridge University Press, 1983.

C. Williams   C. Williams, *The Acts of the Apostles.* New York: Harper and Brothers, 1957.

Williams   D. Williams, *Acts.* New York: Harper and Row, 1985.

Wilson   S. Wilson, *Luke and the Pastoral Epistles.* London: SPCK, 1979.

Notes

Chapter Two: The Social Stance of the Apostles and the Jerusalem Community

1. In contrast with studies of Acts which might treat everything pertaining to Luke's descriptions of Peter and the other apostles, his portrayal of Stephen, Philip, and the seven, and his reports concerning James the brother of the Lord, the present work focuses upon the social and political stance that Luke attributes to all of these figures as well as to the other members of the Jerusalem community. It is clear from even a cursory reading of Acts that Luke provides a great deal of information regarding the characteristics of leadership in the early community and, when appropriate, these descriptions will be adverted to in what follows. However, in terms of its primary concern, the present study is more interested in the stances that Luke shows Peter and Stephen adopting toward the Sanhedrin than in his reports concerning the relationship between the apostles and the seven.

2. See Schneider, I, pp. 304-310, for a helpful excursus, "Die Wundererzählungen." In this excursus (as well as in the others he provides in his commentary), Schneider includes a useful chronological bibliography of other studies on the topic being treated before proceeding with his own analysis.

3. Clearly the absence of *ptōchos* from Acts is of major consequence for any attempt to assess Luke's presentation in Acts and to characterize Luke's personal concerns and/or those of the community for whom he wrote. Nevertheless, the absence of this term is a phenomenon that appears to have been overlooked in the vast majority of commentaries (including those by Lake and Cadbury, Bruce, Conzelmann, Haenchen and Marshall; also that by Schmithals who states, p. 10, that a concern for the poor is one of Luke's redactional tendencies) and in a number of important specialized studies including those by Degenhardt and Johnson.

To his credit, Schneider notices the non-occurrence of *ptōchos* and seeks to explain it in his excursus, "Besitz und Besitzverzicht" (Schneider, I, pp. 290-295). However, it must be said that his own attempted explanation—that Luke may have been influenced by the statement of Deuteronomy 15:4 that there would be no poor in the messianic community—leaves much to be desired and signals that caution is necessary in speaking about the presumed influences that Luke's community(ies) exercised upon his writing.

4. This is the meaning given by LSJ. Especially since this is the only appearance of *endeēs* in the New Testament, it is not clear on what basis BAGD gives "poor, impoverished" as the primary meaning.

5. See Haenchen, p. 160 and n. 8.

6. For reflections concerning other aspects and dimensions of the summaries, see Dupont/*Salvation*, pp 85-102. See also K. Lake, "The Communism of Acts II and IV-VI and the Appointment of the Seven," BC-V, pp. 140-151.

7. It has frequently been observed that Luke is not reluctant to include more than

one description of the same event within his narrative. For example, there are two descriptions of Cornelius' conversion (10:1-48 and 11:4-18) and three of Paul's (9:1-19; 22:6-21; 26:4-18).

8. In addition to indicating that Barnabas played a key role in introducing Paul to the apostles in Jerusalem, Luke also reports in chapter eleven that Barnabas was instrumental in bringing Paul to Antioch. Luke's own description of Barnabas contains high praise: " . . . for he was a good man, full of the Holy Spirit and of faith" (11:24).

9. In his article "Ananias, Sapphira, and the Right of Property," *DR,* Vol 89 (1971) pp. 225-232, J. Derrett indicates that, legal considerations notwithstanding, the conduct of Ananias and Sapphira in this passage struck at the very integrity of the church.

10. So Marshall, p. 84 and p. 109, n. 1.

11. Within Acts the RSV five times translates *diakonia* as "ministry"(1:17; 1:25; 6:4; 20:24; 21:19), once as "relief"(11:29), and once as "mission" (12:25). Acts 6:1 is the single instance, within Acts and the New Testament, in which *diakonia* is translated as "distribution."

Because of the various meanings possible for *diakonia,* there is no little difficulty in understanding what Luke intends to convey when he states that the Greek-speaking members of the community criticized the Hebrew-speaking members because their widows were being neglected in the daily *diakonia.* Interpretation is particularly complicated by the fact that *diakoneō* as an infinitive appears with *trapetzais* in the next verse and then is again used as a noun in verse four.

In the RSV the translation of these three forms of *diakoneō* is as follows: the daily *distribution* (v.1), to *serve* tables (v.2), and the *ministry* of the word (v.4). The translators have thus understood the passage to indicate that there was a daily distribution taking place and to indicate that Peter did not want to reduce the apostles' emphasis upon the ministry of the word for the sake of giving more attention to serving (food) at tables.

It should be noted that, in suggesting the image of a daily distribution of food, the RSV has moved beyond what is actually indicated in the text. An additional factor arguing against the translation of *diakonia* as "distribution" is that, when Luke wants to describe the actual allocation of material resources in 2:45 and 4:35, he does not use any form of *diakoneō.* Rather in the first instance he uses *diameridzō* and in the second *diedidōmi.*

While it is difficult to propose a fully satisfactory alternative, the possibility that Luke actually had in mind some other type of daily ministry, not necessarily involving food or even a ministry directed exclusively to widows, should not be ruled out. Along this line it can be proposed that Luke actually wanted to describe a daily visitation which sometimes involved monitoring and responding to the economic situation of the members. Such an interpretation becomes more plausible if *trapetzais* in v. 2 is interpreted as a reference to the tables connected with banking as in Luke 19:23.

12. As mentioned in n. 1, above, the present study is not so much concerned with precisely identifying the leadership patterns of the Jerusalem community as it is with analyzing the social and political stance generally attributed to prominent individuals and the community as a whole. Nevertheless, as a possible clarification of Luke's meaning, Marshall's suggestion, p. 204, that in Luke's view the "seven" eventually became known as "the elders" should be noted here. See Haenchen, p. 375, for a further discussion of the difficulties involved; Haenchen notes that the present reference functions to prepare for the prominent role that the elders play in chapter fifteen.

13. Haenchen, pp. 377-379, suggests that oral traditions reaching Luke fused two of

Paul's journeys and that Luke further compounded the matter by supplying the explanation that the collection was taken because of a famine. In contrast, Marshall, pp. 204-205, argues that there is no real conflict between what is contained in the present passage and what is narrated in the second chapter of Galatians. Fundamental to the difference between Haenchen and Marshall on this point are their basic differences regarding the nature and character of Luke's "portrait" of Paul. See Haenchen, pp. 112-116, and Marshall, pp. 42-44.

There is, of course, a long-standing prior dispute concerning the appearance of Paul (as well as that of Peter and others) in Acts. In BC-II, p. 384, n. 2, A. McGiffert cites and translates Jülicher's controversial 1894 observation that, within Acts, "Paul is not Judaized and Peter Paulinized, but both are Lucanized, that is Catholicized." In his *A History of the Criticism of the Acts of the Apostles* W. Gasque traces the principal lines of the discussion of these and other issues as it has been conducted from the 16th century to the present era.

14. K. Lake, BC-V, p. 141, takes for granted that a breakdown occurred in the "communistic" practices and theorizes about the factors which contributed to this development. Neill, p. 146, conjectures that one of the reasons why the Jerusalem church was poor and in need of a collection was "because of the pooling of resources in the early days."

15. Without elaborating this point, Juel, pp. 87-89, correctly notices that the disciples in Acts "seem less interested in outcasts than we might have anticipated" and also correctly emphasizes that, instead of focusing upon non-observant Jews, discussions regarding table fellowship in Acts focus upon Gentiles. Perhaps because they are omissions, the absence of references to these groups has not been recognized in many of the standard commentaries and special studies on Acts.

16. Q. Quesnell, "The Women at Luke's Supper," in PILA, p. 61.

17. Haenchen, pp. 338-339, directs attention to the fact that Luke's description of Tabitha as *mathētria* represents the only New Testament example of the term for "disciple" in the feminine. C. Parvey, "The Theology and Leadership of Women in the New Testament," in *Religion and Sexism,* ed. R. Ruether (New York: Simon and Schuster, 1974), pp. 144-145, concludes that Luke wished to portray Tabitha as a figure of central importance in the congregation at Joppa.

18. Although the Acts narrative makes mention of Jesus' activity in Galilee at two other points (10:37 and 13:31), this is the only instance in which there is an indication of a Christian community there.

19. While noting that, if the Ethiopian is not understood to be a Gentile, there is a break in Luke's description of a progressive movement toward the Gentiles, Haenchen, p. 314, concludes that Luke leaves the eunuch's status undetermined. Marshall, p. 160, holds that the eunuch was a Gentile but notes that Luke is here recounting the conversion of an individual returning to a distant country.

20. In his article, "Ethiopian Eunuch," in IDB, II, p. 177, F. Gealy indicates that the word *aithiops* sometimes meant "burnt faced" or "swarthy faced" and thus designated dark-skinned persons. "Burnt-face" is also given as a primary meaning of *aithiops* in LSJ. I am indebted to Rev. Ronald Spann for originally drawing my attention to this question during a seminar on Acts in the spring of 1983.

21. It should be noted that *pais* is used to designate David in v. 25 and also to designate Jesus in v. 27 and v. 30. This usage contrasts with the use of *doulos* for the disciples' designation of themselves. The RSV uses "servant" in translating both of these terms.

22. It will be seen below that both Stephen and Paul are charged with offenses against the temple. No reproaches against Peter or the other disciples concerning their attitude toward the temple or its related practices are recorded in Acts. Indeed, that they are frequently in attendance at the temple is a characteristic of Luke's portrayal of Peter and the other members of the community. See 2:46; 3:1; 5:19-21; 5:42; 21:23-26.

23. For a discussion of the various difficulties which complicate the interpretation of Luke's account and the present writer's effort to resolve them see Cassidy/*Motive,* pp. 150-152, and the references cited. The discussion in Johnson, pp. 111-119, is also highly relevant.

24. As indicated in Cassidy/*Jesus,* pp. 3-4, and Cassidy/*Motive,* pp. 146-147, there can frequently be multiple dimensions of meaning contained within a particular Lukan verse or passage. The present verses from Peter's speech provide one more illustration of this phenomenon.

As noted in the text, Peter's allusion to Jesus' death as the fulfillment of a plan of God does have the effect of mitigating the severity of the charges that he has made against his listeners. This is a dimension of meaning that is of particular interest in the present context.

However, at the same time, Luke is also providing his readers with the interpretation that Jesus' death was an element in the plan of God (for the argument that such a presentation of Jesus' death is actually a characteristic of the Lukan writings, see Tiede, pp. 97-103), and it is possible that such a consideration may even be of paramount interest to Luke here. However, what must be remembered in interpreting this as well as other passages is that the presence of one dimension of meaning does not preclude the presence of other important dimensions.

25. In 4:5 Luke identifies these three groups and specifically names Annas the high priest and three others of the high priestly family. His reference to the "council room" (*synedrion*) in 4:15 suggests that the apostles were before a formal meeting of the Sanhedrin although this is not stated. Later, in describing the second arrest of the apostles, he states explicitly that the high priest convened a meeting of the Sanhedrin (5:21).

26. A lack of appreciation for the fact that Stephen's speech is not an indictment of all Jews but rather an attack upon the high priest and his associates would seem to be an important factor contributing to several failures to assess correctly the character of the speech. For example, Haenchen speaks of a "grim portrayal" of the Jewish people (p. 289) and refers to the speech as an "anti-Jewish diatribe" (p. 290). Similarly Marshall, p. 132, states that one of the speech's purposes is "an attack on the Jews for their failure to obey the revelation given to them in the Old Testament and their rejection of the Messiah and the new way of worship which he brought."

In the present writer's interpretation, the audience for the speech and its conclusion are the keys which unlock its structure and thrust. As Luke presents it, Stephen's speech is primarily an attack upon the high priest and the other Sanhedrin members, an attack in which he decries the fact that they, *and not the Jews as a people,* have surpassed the worst elements in the preceding generations and have murdered God's Righteous One.

27. The underlying Greek is: *tou dikaiou hou nun humeis prodotai kai phoneis egenesthe.* Preferable to the RSV in allowing the character of *prodotai* and *phoneis* as epithets to be more readily recognized is Johannes Munck's Anchor Bible translation. Munck gives: " . . . and you now living have become his *betrayers* and *murderers* . . . " (emphasis added).

28. It must be emphasized that, once it is properly understood, Luke's report of

Stephen's speech delivers a severe jolt to readers of Acts. Stephen's incendiary ending is carefully prepared for in the earlier sections of the speech, but it is only after the ending has been assimilated that it is possible to re-read the opening passages and perceive the way in which Luke shows Stephen laying the ground for the inflammatory denunciation with which he will end.

Clearly, it is an understatement to say that Luke portrays Stephen throwing caution to the winds. Stephen is alone, facing serious charges before a hostile or at least potentially hostile Sanhedrin council. Perhaps under the influence of a vision (see Luke's preliminary comment in 6:15), Stephen proceeds to do nothing less than charge the council members with the murder of Jesus! He does not offer a direct defense against the charges facing him (and within the speech proper, he does not even testify to the resurrection of Jesus). Instead he launches a devastating and ultimately martyrdom-provoking attack upon his judges. Such is the striking portrayal of Stephen given by Luke in this passage.

29. In chapter five, in connection with the analysis of Luke's presentation regarding Paul's opponents, the identity of Stephen's opponents will also be discussed.

30. It has frequently been noted that Stephen's call for forgiveness echoes Jesus' plea from the cross in Luke 23:34. For a detailed analysis of other points of similarity in Luke's portrayal of the deaths of Jesus and Stephen, see C. Talbert, "Martyrdom in Luke-Acts and the Lukan Social Ethic," in PILA, pp. 99-110. See also O'Toole/*Unity*, p. 138.

31. Within Acts this is the only instance in which *eirēnē* ("peace") is explicitly associated with Jesus. For an analysis of the various meanings of *eirēnē* in the Lukan writings, see W. Swartley, "Politics and Peace (*Eirēnē*) in Luke's Gospel," in PILA, pp. 18-37.

Chapter Three: The Political Stance of the Jerusalem Community

1. Lake and Cadbury, pp. 41-42, argue that Luke is mistaken in stating that Annas was high priest at this time. Rather, Annas was deposed by Valerius Gratus in A.D. 14 and Joseph Caiaphas held the office until A.D. 36 when Jonathan (not John) was appointed by Vitellius, the legate of Syria.

In contrast, Bruce notes, p. 98, that the term "high priest" could appropriately be used of former as well as present holders of the office. He then argues that it is not inappropriate for Luke to describe Annas as the high priest and suggests that Luke may have understood Annas to have had the real power in the situation even though he was emeritus.

2. Marshall, p. 148, leans toward the interpretation that Luke infers the occurrence of a spontaneous act of mob violence. However, he also conjectures that the Sanhedrin may have had special permission to carry out executions owing to the absence of a Roman governor at that time. Haenchen, p. 295 n. 2 and p. 296, believes that Luke tries to infer that the Sanhedrin was proceeding in a legal fashion but that the trial of Stephen was actually "a piece of lynch law." He notes subsequently (p. 684 n. 5, in reference to verse 26:10) that Luke does credit the Sanhedrin with the power of execution.

3. Sherwin-White, pp. 35-43, draws upon his extensive knowledge of Roman legal regulations and Roman provincial administration to shed light on several key New Testament descriptions of the Sanhedrin's activity under Roman rule. Nevertheless, the issues raised above in the text (as well as other related points) still remain unresolved. Seemingly the present situation would be greatly helped by a study attempting a direct

comparison between the Jerusalem Sanhedrin's activities and those of local officials and councils at Thessalonica and Corinth, other leading provincial cities in which local institutions functioned with some degree of autonomy while ultimately being "supervised" by a Roman governor. Obviously the situations are not exactly comparable (for example, the situation of Thessalonica and Corinth as the capitals of *senatorial*, as opposed to *imperial*, provinces must immediately be recognized). However, a sustained analysis might well place the situations that Luke portrays in Acts, particularly those at Jerusalem and Caesarea, in clearer perspective. See section one of chapter six, below, for a preliminary effort to identify some of the features of Roman provincial rule in the cities which figure prominently in Acts.

4. That the phrasing of the apostles' reply is such as to admit of a wide range of applications is also seen by Maddox (p. 45): ". . . the formulation of Peter's principle in 4:19 and 5:29 points beyond the immediate situation and indicates how Christians are to regard any authorities at all."

5. Except for the use of inclusive language for *anthropois,* this translation closely accords with the translation, "It is necessary to obey God rather than men," given by Lake and Cadbury, p. 59.

6. ZG, p. 367, points out that *peitharchein* is derived from *peithomai,* "obey," and *archos,* "chief person in authority." The Greek thus draws particular attention to the issue of who actually possesses authority in the situation. That person is the one to be obeyed.

7. Luke portrays these words as having an infuriating effect upon many on the Sanhedrin (5:33), and even the subsequent intervention that he portrays Gamaliel making (5:34-39) contributes to the reader's impression that the apostles' words and conduct seemed to be challenging the entire social order to which the Sanhedrin members were committed. In persuading his fellow council members *not* to kill the apostles, Gamaliel nevertheless likens them to Theudas and Judas the Galilean, figures fully committed to revolutionary activity.

8. When Socrates was offered release if he would give up the pursuit of truth, Plato states that he answered: "I shall obey God rather than *you*" (*The Apology,* 29D; emphasis added). Although Socrates' reply could, by extension, be applicable in other contexts, the apostles' second reply to the Sanhedrin is, in its formulation, a general statement of principle and thus it is broader in scope than either Socrates' reply or Peter and John's previous reply in 4:19-20.

9. H. Schlier, *"Parrēsia, parrēsiazomai,"* in TDNT, and S. Marrow, *Speaking the Word Fearlessly* (New York: Paulist, 1982), pp. 65-67. I am indebted to Rev. William Kellerman for first drawing my attention to *parrēsia's* political consequences.

10. The only other place in Acts in which *parrēsia* is accompanied by the adjective, *pasēs,* is at 28:31, in the final phrase of Luke's work. In the treatment to be accorded to that final verse in chapter eight of this study, all the occurrences of *parrēsia* in its noun and verb forms will be listed and additional comments will also be made regarding "threats" *(apeilēs)* as the context for the disciples' prayer for boldness in the present verse, 4:29.

11. J. Hull, p. 145, notes the connection between this boldness and the Holy Spirit's presence.

12. As noted above, Luke does provide a listing of the high priest and the other high-priestly members of the Sanhedrin in 4:5-6. However, with regard to the introduction of the Roman governors and client kings, there is nothing in Acts which compares to 3:1-2 of the Gospel. Acts is also silent about Pilate's recall to Rome. His involvement in the

death of Jesus is referred to by Peter in 3:13, by the assembled Jerusalem community (in prayer at 4:27), and by Paul in 13:28; however no additional information about him is given in these instances.

From Josephus and other ancient sources, a considerable amount of information is available regarding the career of Herod Agrippa I. Basing themselves on these sources, F. Jackson and K. Lake, "The Background of Jewish History" in BC-I, pp. 14-28 (see also H. Cadbury's short article, "The Family Tree of the Herods," and an accompanying chart in BC-V, pp. 487-489), summarize that Agrippa I was one of the three grandsons of Herod the Great and the Hasmonean princess, Marianne. When his father, Aristobulus, was executed in 7 B.C. (by Herod the Great, his father!), his mother, Bernice, had Agrippa raised in Rome where he was the companion of Drusus, the son of Tiberius.

A series of reverses in Rome resulted in Agrippa's return to Judea, but his lack of character and further reverses resulted in his return to Rome, the displeasure of Tiberius, and consignment to prison! However, Caligula, upon succeeding his great uncle as emperor, set Agrippa free and gave him the tetrarchy of his uncle, Philip, and the title of *king*. Subsequently, Agrippa also secured Galilee and the other territories of his uncle, Antipas, by alleging to Caligula that Antipas had plotted against Tiberius and had intrigued with the Parthians. (During this period the governors who were serving as Pilate's successors in Judea were Marcellus and then Marullus.)

Agrippa managed to survive in the controversy Caligula created by proposing to have a statue to his honor erected in the Jerusalem temple and after Caligula's murder he threw his support on the side of Claudius. As a consequence Judea and Samaria were subsequently granted to him with the result that he reigned over virtually the same kingdom that his grandfather, Herod the Great, had governed.

At an earlier stage of his career, Agrippa I married his cousin, Cypros, who was also of Hasmonean stock. Among their five children were Herod Agrippa II (who will play a leading role in Luke's account of Paul's second trial before Festus), Bernice (who accompanied her brother at this trial) and Drusilla (whose second marriage was to Felix, the Roman governor who first presided over Paul's case).

13. Along with many others, Ricciotti, p. 184, observes that Luke's main concern at this point in Acts is to present Peter's life-threatening situation and his miraculous deliverance from it. Nevertheless the significance that James's execution possesses for Luke should not be underestimated. For, as a consequence of his (sometimes) elliptical manner of expression, Luke frequently encompasses worlds of meaning within a phrase of a clause that is, grammatically speaking, only "introductory."

14. Examples of those who favor such a view are Rackham, p. 176, who distinguishes between the penalty of stoning for "legal offenses" and the penalty of beheading for political disloyalty, and Ricciotti, pp. 184-185, who believes that Luke's report that decapitation was the form of execution indicates that James was guilty of a "political" as opposed to a "religious" offense. See also Williams, p. 199. In contrast, for a presentation of the view that James was executed on the Sanhedrin's orders and by stabbing with the sword (as opposed to beheading), see J. Blinzler, "Rechtsgeschichtliches zur Hinrichtung des Zebedaiden Jakobus," in *NT*, Vol 5 (1962) pp. 191-206.

15. See section three of chapter five below for a further analysis of how Luke uses this term to designate those "unbelieving" Jews who reject the message of the risen Jesus and oppose Paul for proclaiming it.

16. Later in the narrative (25:1-3) Luke portrays the chief priests and their allies acting in a similar fashion in an effort to further their plot against Paul. The governor,

Festus, had only been in the province three days before Luke shows this group approaching him and treacherously urging him to send Paul to Jerusalem.

17. It is manifestly the sense of the passage that Herod intends Peter's death even though he is proceeding against him differently than he did against James. See Martin, p. 39, for the view that the phrase *anagagein auton* ("to bring him out") itself implies an intended execution.

18. It is not an exaggeration to state that Luke portrays Herod treating Peter as an extremely high-risk prisoner. The Greek describes Peter being handed over to four squads of four soldiers and Haenchen, p. 382, holds that this refers to the Roman practice of having the (four) soldiers on watch relieved after three hours. Luke's description in 12:6 of the way in which the soldiers positioned themselves should also be noted: "Peter was sleeping between two soldiers, bound with two chains, and sentries before the door were guarding the prison."

In this context Peter and the other apostles' miraculous escape from "the common prison" (so the RSV; the Greek is *terēsei dēmosia* and ZG, p.365, indicates that the latter term has the meaning: "belonging to the state, public") in 5:18-23 should also be recalled. In that instance too, Luke indicates that sentries were positioned at the doors of the prison.

Chapter Four: The Social Stance of Paul

1. As a Roman citizen Paul presumably possessed three Latin names with "Saul" as a Jewish name also given him at birth (perhaps in honor of David's predecessor, Saul). Paul's full name may thus have been _____/_____ Paulus Saul (so Haenchen, p. 399, n. 1) with "Paul" more likely to be used in a Roman context and "Saul" within normal Jewish life.

Within Acts Luke makes a definite change at 13:9 when he shifts from the use of "Saul" to the consistent use of "Paul." Up until this point, "Saul" is always the name that Luke uses; afterwards, "Paul" is used exclusively except for those later passages which look back to events that occurred at the time of Saul's conversion. However, exactly why Luke makes such a shift at this point is not certain and has long been a matter of discussion. In addition to Haenchen's treatment of this question, see also that by Schneider, II, p. 21 and p. 122 n. 37.

2. In addition to the treatment afforded by Hull, the excursus on the Holy Spirit by Neill, pp. 52-60, also sheds light on this and related activity by the Holy Spirit within Acts.

3. In 19:13-17 Luke reports that itinerant Jewish exorcists undertook to use the name of Jesus for their own purposes, saying, "I adjure you by the Jesus whom Paul preaches." However, in the case of the seven sons of Sceva, a high priest, the attempt backfired disastrously.

4. Luke's portrayal of Paul's raising of Eutychus provides a parallel for his previous account of Peter raising Tabitha (9:36-43). Indeed, as Dupont and many others have pointed out, there are numerous parallels in Luke's descriptions of Peter and Paul. Cf. Dupont/*Nouv. Études*, pp. 173-184.

5. Translating *tōn asthenountōn* as "the weak" instead of as "the sick" does not result in any great shift of meaning and the listings in LSJ and BAGD indicate that the Greek may refer to physical or mental illness or weakness in general. Still, inasmuch as the RSV translates every other occurrence of *astheneō* and its forms as "sickness," it may have been preferable to do so in this instance as well. Cf. Lake and Cadbury, p. 263.

6. In *Les Actes*, p. 180, Dupont comments that this passage reflects the teaching of Jesus at 6:38 and 14:14 of Luke's Gospel. He adds that the idea expressed corresponds to the French proverb, "One who gives to the poor, lends to God" ("Qui donne au pauvre prête à Dieu").

7. *Chreia* is the same term that Luke uses in his summaries describing the life of the Jerusalem community indicating that distribution was made to all as "any had need" (2:45 and 4:35). There are nine other instances in which this word appears in Luke-Acts. With the exception of 6:3 where the translation is "duty," the RSV always uses some form of the word "need" in making the translation.

8. The word Luke uses here is *paidiskēn*. According to LSJ, the primary meaning is "young girl, maiden" with "young female slave, bondsmaid" and "prostitute" as secondary meanings. The RSV adopts "slave girl" as the translation in this passage but at 12:13 of Acts and 22:56 of the Gospel (the only other places where *paidiskēn* appears in the Lukan writings) "maid" is the rendering adopted.

9. For a sample of a magical text from a later period and reflections concerning the character of the magical books that Luke refers to here, see A. Deissmann, *Light from the Ancient East* (Grand Rapids: Baker, 1927), pp. 254-264.

10. At 16:10-17, at 20:5-21:18, and at 27:1-28:16, the author of Acts shifts from the usual third-person format to an account given in the first-person plural. These "we-passages" are easily noticed within the larger narrative and have attracted extended comment from scholars. Haenchen, pp. 86-87, 503, adopts the position that the "we-passages" represent eyewitness accounts (written or oral) that came into Luke's possession at a later time. Luke then chose to indicate to his readers the eyewitness character of these particular accounts by using "we-language" when he incorporated them into his narrative. In contrast, without taking a position as to whether Luke himself was a participant in the events described, Marshall, pp. 38-39, holds that these sections are based on material composed by a participant in the actual events and that Luke did not change the "we-style" in which these reports were initially presented. Bruce's position is along these latter lines but he explicitly holds (p. 328 n. 22) that Luke (the author of Acts) was himself present at the events described in the "we-sections."

11. Along with others, N. Flanagan, "The Position of Women in the Writings of St. Luke," *Marianum,* Vol 40 (1978), pp. 295-296, notes that the "we-sections" of chapters 16, 17, and 18 are particularly rich in their reference to the place of women in Paul's ministry.

12. Reflecting upon Luke's description of the roles played by Lydia and Priscilla as well as others, N. Flanagan, ibid., p. 297, concludes that Luke has given a memorable presentation regarding "the participation of women in the citizenship of the Church, in its sufferings, its ministry, and its growth."

13. The title, "The Great Missionary to the Gentiles," is an appropriate one for Paul in Acts (in contrast with "The Apostle to the Gentiles") for the reasons given in the text and in recognition of Luke's general practice of reserving the title of "apostle" to the Twelve. It should be noted, however, that both at 14:4 and 14:14 Luke refers to Barnabas and Paul as apostles. (Also in 22:21, when he portrays Paul recounting how the Lord sent him to the Gentiles, the word which is used, *exapostelō,* signals apostolic activity. Similarly in 26:17 when Paul is recounting the instructions the Lord gave him at his conversion, the term *apostellō* is used.) In the light of these and other factors it is clear that, while Paul is not technically an apostle according to Luke's scheme, he is a figure of extreme importance for Luke and Luke in various ways clearly associates him with the apostolic ministry.

For recent reflections on the nuances and implications of Luke's presentation regarding "apostles," see Schneider's excursus, "Die zwölf Apostel als 'Zeugen,' " Vol I, pp. 231-232 and the excursus, "Der Apostelat nach Lukas" in Schille, pp. 310-314.

14. As the narrative of Acts unfolds, Paul is shown to carry out his mission to the Gentiles in various stages. While there are considerable nuances that must be respected in all of Luke's reports concerning his efforts and while it must be remembered that Luke shows Paul simultaneously pursuing a ministry to the Jews, it can still be useful to think of his ministry among the Gentiles according to the following schema: 1) initial ministry to the Gentiles in the eastern provinces in chapters thirteen and fourteen; 2) confirmation of this ministry by the apostles and elders at Jerusalem in chapter fifteen; 3) continuation of and expansion of this ministry in the eastern provinces in chapters sixteen to twenty; 4) interruption of ministry due to imprisonment at Jerusalem and Caesarea in chapters twenty-two to twenty-six; 5) limited resumption of this ministry in Malta and in Rome in chapter twenty-eight.

15. Paul and Barnabas are "sent out by the Holy Spirit" from Antioch in 13:4. In 16:6 they are "forbidden by the Holy Spirit" from preaching in the province of Asia. (Despite being prevented from a ministry in Asia at this point, Paul does subsequently visit Ephesus and engages in an extremely rich ministry there and indeed throughout all of Asia. See 18:19-21; 19:1-41, especially 19:10 and 19:26; 20:1; 20:17-38.) In 16:7-8 the "Spirit of Jesus" does not allow them to go into Bithynia and so they proceed to Troas. In 16:9-10 Paul receives a vision in which a "Macedonian man" appears to him and he then concludes that God was calling him to preach the gospel in that territory.

16. Acts 18:9-10 relates that the Lord appeared to Paul at Corinth and stated, "Do not be afraid, but speak and do not be silent; for I am with you, and no man shall attack you to harm you; for I have many people in this city." As a consequence, Paul decided to stay in Corinth for a year and six months.

17. At 19:21 Luke indicates that Paul "resolved in the Spirit" to return once again to Jerusalem (in 11:30 he and Barnabas carried famine relief to Jerusalem; in 15:2-4 he, Barnabas, and others from Antioch traveled there for the "Jerusalem council"; also in 18:22 Luke seems to indicate that Paul stopped in Jerusalem before going down to Antioch—so Marshall, pp. 301-302 and Haenchen, p. 544) and he portrays him undertaking and continuing this journey despite clear indications that suffering awaited him at its end.

In his address to the Ephesian elders at Miletus, Paul states (20:22-23): "And now, behold, I am going to Jerusalem, bound in the Spirit, not knowing what shall befall me there; except that the Holy Spirit testifies to me in every city that imprisonment and afflictions await me." Subsequently when he arrives in Tyre, the disciples there advise him "through the Spirit" that he should not go on to Jerusalem (21:4). Finally, at Caesarea, Luke reports another instance of prophetic activity by Agabus. Binding his own hands and feet with Paul's girdle, he states: "Thus says the Holy Spirit, 'So shall the Jews at Jerusalem bind the man who owns this girdle and deliver him into the hands of the Gentiles' " (21:11).

18. At the same time that Paul "resolved in the Spirit" to return to Jerusalem, he also envisioned a journey to Rome: "After I have been there, I must [*dei*] also see Rome" (19:21). The note of necessity regarding Rome that is here indicated by *dei* is also similarly indicated at 23:11 when the risen Lord later appears to him, stating, "Take courage, for as you have testified about me at Jerusalem, so you must [*dei*] bear witness also at Rome." It is also similarly indicated in Paul's later report to his shipmates concerning an angel's message (27:24): " . . . Do not be afraid, Paul; you must [*dei*] stand before Caesar . . . "

A point of related interest is that within Acts there are also two instances in which *dei* (indicating necessity) is used in reference to Paul's sufferings. In 9:16 the risen Jesus speaks to Ananias in reference to Paul stating: " . . . for I will show him how much he must [*dei*] suffer for the sake of my name." And in 14:22 Luke portrays Paul exhorting the disciples at Iconium, Lystra, and Antioch concerning their common sufferings "saying that through many tribulations we must [*dei*] enter the kingdom of God."

19. Paul utilized or at least visited synagogues in the following places: Cyprus (13:5), Pisidian Antioch (13:14), Iconium (14:1), Thessalonica (17:1-2), Beroea (17:10), Athens (17:17), Corinth (18:4), and Ephesus (18:19 and 19:8).

20. "Worshipers of God" (*sebomenoi tou theou*) and "God-fearers" (*phoboumenoi tou theou*) are terms that appear in Acts with reference to Gentiles who took part in study and worship at synagogues without necessarily adopting the Jewish law in such matters as circumcision, diet, and temple sacrifice. They are to be distinguished from "proselytes" (*prosēlutoi*), born Gentiles who became fully converted to Judaism, adopting the whole of Jewish law including, for men, circumcision (Acts 6:5 indicates that Nicolaus of Antioch was such a proselyte). See Williams, p. 107, and Haenchen, p. 346, for further discussion of the appearance of these groups in Acts.

21. Luke indicates that Paul received favorable responses from Jews in the following places: Pisidian Antioch (13:43), Iconium (14:1), Thessalonica (17:4), Beroea (17:11), Corinth (18:4), Ephesus (18:20 and 19:9). He received a favorable response from "worshipers of God" at Iconium (14:1—so Haenchen, p. 419), Philippi (16:14), Thessalonica (17:4), Beroea (17:12—so Williams, p. 291), Athens (17:17), and Corinth (18:4).

22. Unbelieving Jews eventually forced Paul to leave the synagogue and/or the city at: Pisidian Antioch (13:50), Iconium (14:6), Thessalonica (17:10), Beroea (17:14), and Ephesus (19:9). The reactions and behavior of these and other "unbelieving" Jews will be analyzed more fully in chapter five.

23. Citing the harsh conclusions of Paul's speeches at Pisidian Antioch (13:46), at Corinth (18:6), and also at Rome (28:25-28), F. Hahn, *Mission in the New Testament* (London: SCM, 1965) p. 134, argues that Paul was not free to go to the Gentiles until the Jews of the Diaspora had rejected his preaching. However (in addition to the factors cited in the text and in the following note), the fact that Luke never portrays Paul allowing opposition tendered him by unbelieving Jews in one location to deter him from evangelizing Jews in other parts of the Diaspora must be seen as a powerful argument against such an interpretation. For within Acts, there is no definitive rejection of the Jews.

Indeed, right after he speaks strongly to the unbelieving Jews of Pisidian Antioch and announces his intention to go to the Gentiles, Luke portrays Paul traveling to Iconium and preaching in the synagogue there with the result that a "great company" of Jews and God-fearers believed (14:1). A similar pattern manifests itself after Paul's harsh words to the unbelieving Jews of Corinth: Luke then portrays him journeying to Ephesus and commencing to preach in the synagogue as usual.

In light of these factors, the overall sense of Luke's portrayal seems to be that Paul's words to the unbelieving Jews at Pisidian Antioch and Corinth mean that he will no longer preach *to them* and that they will regret their unbelief when they subsequently hear of Paul's efforts among the Gentiles and the other Jews to whom Paul will preach. In chapter eight, a similar interpretation will also be advanced concerning Paul's rebuke to the unbelieving Jews of Rome. He will no longer preach *to them,* i.e., to *that* group of unbelieving Jews. Rather he will preach to the Gentiles and to "all" (including other favorably disposed Jews) who will listen.

24. At Cyprus, the very first station on his initial missionary journey, Paul did not experience any rejection from unbelieving Jews before he began preaching to Sergius Paulus, the Roman proconsul for the island. In 13:5 Luke reports that Paul and Barnabas "proclaimed the word of God in the synagogues of the Jews" but he does not report that they received any response (positive, negative, or both) as a result of their efforts. It is thus the case that by reason of his belief (13:12) Sergius Paulus, a Gentile and a high Roman official, became Paul's first convert.

Luke's descriptions of Paul's ministry at Lystra and Derbe indicate that in those instances too, he did not make his preaching to the Gentiles contingent upon prior rejection by unbelieving Jews. At Lystra Luke does not mention any visit to a synagogue. Rather the sense of his account (14:8-14) is that Paul had begun to preach publicly to a predominantly or even exclusively Gentile crowd (evidenced by their reverence for Zeus and Hermes and the presence of a priest of Zeus). As a consequence of Paul's miraculous healing of a (presumably Gentile) man who had been crippled from birth and his subsequent teaching, some of those assembled were converted (evidenced by the gathering of *disciples* around Paul in 14:20 after he had nearly been stoned to death through the machinations of unbelieving Jews from Pisidian Antioch and Iconium).

In his brief description of Paul's subsequent visit to Derbe (14:20-21), Luke again makes no mention of any preaching in synagogues or to Jews. Rather he succinctly states that Paul "preached the gospel to that city." This latter phrase, *to that city,* seemingly indicates that Paul was engaged in the same type of public preaching, presumably to a Gentile populace, that he had undertaken at Lystra.

25. In describing Paul's ministry at Athens, Luke states (17:17): "So he argued in the synagogue with the Jews and the devout persons, and in the market place every day with those who chanced to be there." Clearly Paul is not described here as having experienced rejection from unbelieving Jews before directing his preaching to the Gentiles. Rather the overall sense of Luke's portrait of Paul at Athens is that Paul was particularly influenced by the panoply of idols that he saw (17:16). And, as a consequence, when he received the opportunity to speak before a large number of Gentiles at the Areopagus, he instructed them at length (17:22-31) concerning the true God who does not live in earthly shrines.

26. The phrase "serving the Lord" translates *douleuōn tō kuriō* and represents the only instance in which Paul specifically speaks of himself as the Lord's servant. However, note also 16:17 where the demon within the young girl cries out that Paul and Barnabas are "servants" (*douloi*) of the most high God.

27. The reports at 9:1-2 and 22:5 both indicate that Paul had been officially authorized by the high priest and the Sanhedrin to conduct persecutions against the disciples.

28. This part of Paul's charge may be based on Leviticus 19:15. So Haenchen, p. 638.

29. The only reference to a "whitewashed wall" in the biblical literature occurs in the Book of Ezekiel. ("Whited sepulchres" is an image that occurs in Matthew's Gospel at 23:27, but this is not a directly relevant reference.) Ezek. 13:10-l2 reads as follows: "Because, yea, because they have misled my people, saying, 'Peace,' when there is no peace; and because, when the people build a wall, these prophets daub it with whitewash; say to those who daub it with whitewash that it shall fall! There will be a deluge of rain, great hailstones will fall, and a stormy wind will break out; and when the wall falls, will it not be said to you, 'Where is the daubing with which you daubed it?' "

Marshall, p. 363, cites the Zadokite Document (8:14) as an indication that this metaphor was still alive in the New Testament period and suggests that Paul was adapting it for his own purposes. Bruce, p. 451, holds that the application here is that someone who behaved as Ananias did was bound to come to grief.

30. Munck, p. 223, Schille, p. 426, Neill, p. 228, and Marshall, p. 364, are among those commentators who affirm in some way that Paul's reply should be understood as an ironical rejoinder, rather than as an apology.

31. In the version of the "ironic" interpretation now being proposed, emphasis is given to the possibility that Luke understands Paul's reply as raising the issue of Ananias' legitimacy in the high-priestly office. If this interpretation is correct (and presuming the correctness of the interpretation proposed for Paul's previous "white-washed wall" retort), then there are definite parallels to be seen between Paul's challenge to the high-priestly group and that made by Jesus.

For, as indicated in chapter one of this study and in Cassidy/*Motive*, pp. 146-163, the Jesus of Luke's Gospel challenges the high-priestly group on the grounds of their corrupt practices but even more fundamentally with respect to their legitimacy in office. In brief Luke may understand Paul to be paralleling the Jesus who protested against the priests' "den of thieves" practices and likened them to "wicked tenants" soon to be expelled from the vineyard. In comparison, Paul alludes to corrupt practices when he castigates the high priest as a "whitewashed wall" and he alludes to illegitimacy in office when he replies that he has difficulty in seeing Ananias as a (true) high priest. Admittedly the idea of a Jesus-Paul parallel rests upon less than obvious interpretations for 23:3 and 23:5. On the other hand such a view does provide a coherent interpretation for a scene that others besides Conzelmann/*Apostel*, p. 137, have found "illogical and unimaginable."

32. At this point Luke does not report any response from the high priest (see below for comments upon the response that Ananias and his allies subsequently make). The "witness" which he now portrays Paul embarking upon seems to continue logically with the line of thought that Paul had begun to express before being slapped on the mouth: Paul's good conscience is founded in the resurrection of Jesus.

33. Some interpreters have commented that Luke presents a less than flattering portrayal of Paul in showing him strategically making reference to his standing as a Pharisee. Munck, p. 223, notes in reply that it does not detract from Paul's stature to show him attempting to win Pharisees over to what is actually centrally related to their theology.

34. The RSV here translates *diaspasthē* as "torn in pieces." In Mark 5:4, the only other appearance of *diaspaō* in the New Testament, the translation is "wrenched apart," referring to the Gerasene demoniac's activity in wrenching apart his chains. Citing Hosea 13:8 in the Septuagint, Williams, p. 385, states that Paul was in danger of being torn to pieces "as by a beast at its prey."

Whatever the exact nuances of the Greek, two points are not to be overlooked here: 1) Luke is indicating here that Paul's opponents are intent on, and are on the verge of, doing him bodily harm; 2) given that the high priest has already ordered Paul physically struck and Paul has responded to him in the sharpest possible terms and given that scribes of the Pharisees have spoken in Paul's defense, it is clearly the sense of the passage that the high priest and those aligned with him are the ones who want to tear Paul in pieces.

Although the subject of Paul's various opponents and his dealings with them will be examined more carefully in a subsequent chapter, it is well to note here that this is the first direct contact that Luke has portrayed Paul having with any of the high-priestly group since the time that he had actually been deputized to conduct a persecution against the Christians. Viewed against this background the sense of what Luke presents here is that Paul is now in danger of being "torn to pieces" by those with whom he was formerly allied in (see following note) "ravaging" the church.

35. The RSV translates *elumaineto* (*hapax legomenon*) as "ravage." LSJ indicates several meanings for this term including "outrage, maltreat" (someone or a group), "inflict indignities or outrages," and "cause ruin." According to Williams, p. 137, this term can express the image of a wild beast tearing its meat.

36. The Greek underlying the italicized clause is *hos tautēn tēn hodon ediōxa archi thanatou*. Williams, p. 370, argues that verses 22:20 and 26:10 provide sufficient warrant for accepting these words as indicating that Paul actually persecuted individuals to the point of death. Even if the phrase "to the death" is only expressing Paul's intention, the overall sense of the passage as indicating forceful violent behavior on Paul's part remains undisturbed.

37. The actions that Paul catalogues in this passage indicate the extent and the violence of his persecution. However, the words *perissōs te emmainomenos autois ediokon* (translated in the text as "in raging fury against them, I persecuted them . . .") add extremely important information regarding the anger and the hatred which Paul says drove him. ZG, p. 444, proposes translations such as "boiling over with rage against [them]" or "my fury against them knowing no bounds" which emphasize Paul's anger even more than the RSV rendering.

38. In light of the way in which Luke portrays Paul's earlier and later "contentions" with other Christians somehow being worked through (in particular, see 15:1-31 regarding the initial dispute over circumcision, 16:3-4 where Paul circumcises Timothy and then faithfully communicates the decision taken at Jerusalem to the communities he and Timothy visit, and 21:18-26 for the steps that Paul took at James' behest), his indication of an unreconciled situation between Paul and Barnabas is all the more startling. Even the fact that Silas, Barnabas' replacement, is well credentialled does not suffice to ameliorate the effects of this estrangement. (In 15:22,27 Silas, along with Judas Barsabbas, is sent to Antioch by the Jerusalem leaders to indicate the decision taken. And in 15:32 Luke reports: "And Judas and Silas, who were themselves prophets, exhorted the brethren with many words and strengthened them." The RSV also gives the following at the margin [15:34]: "But it seemed good to Silas to remain there.")

39. Luke does indicate that Paul proclaimed "forgiveness of sins" (*aphesis hamartiōn*) to have been achieved by Jesus (at Pisidian Antioch at 13:38 and before Agrippa and Festus at 26:18). However, forgiveness as an aspect of discipleship and community life is, somewhat surprisingly, not emphasized or even adverted to by Luke's Paul.

40. Although Paul does not leave his jail surroundings until the magistrates come personally to release him, the final words which Luke portrays his jailer speaking to him are "go in peace" (*poreuesthe en eirēnē*) (16:36).

Chapter Five: The Non-Roman Opponents of Paul

1. Maddox, p.37, argues that Luke shows this to be Paul's position when he portrays him making numerous Gentile converts without ever reporting that these converts were obligated to keep the law.

2. In subsequently reporting that Paul circumcised Timothy in deference to the sensitivities of "the Jews that were in those places" (16:3), Luke portrays Paul as fully concerned to anticipate and avoid controversy regarding the validity of the law for Jewish Christians.

3. This is thus the second instance in which Luke portrays Paul faithfully adhering to the directives given by James and those associated with him in the leadership of the Jerusalem community. As indicated previously, 16:4 portrayed Paul carrying out the decisions reached by "the apostles and elders who were at Jerusalem."

4. Noting the difficulties it presents, Haenchen, p. 574, refers to 19:33 as *crux interpretum.* His own suggestion is that Luke understands the crowd to have made no distinction between Jews and Christians. As a consequence the Jews present felt themselves threatened and put Alexander forward as a spokesperson. Then, although some in the crowd informed him about the basis for the turbulence, he was not allowed to speak.

5. In 20:1 Luke reports that, after the uproar had ceased, Paul sent for the disciples and encouraged them as a prelude to his departure for Macedonia. However, inasmuch as Luke has previously indicated that Paul already had plans to go to Macedonia and Achaia and had sent Timothy and Erastus on ahead of him (19:21-22), Paul's departure from Ephesus at this point seems due more to his own disposition than to the pressure generated by Demetrius.

6. By listing them first, Luke seemingly implies that the Gentiles are no longer simply being manipulated at this point; rather they are now leading participants in the efforts against Paul. The "rulers" (*archousin*) mentioned may be rulers from the Gentile as well as the Jewish group (Haenchen, p. 421 n. l) or Jewish leaders alone. (Williams, p. 234, thinks that Luke does not mean that the city magistrates participated.)

7. Marshall, p. 239, holds that the Jews from Antioch and Iconium first persuaded the Lystrian townspeople against Paul and then carried out the assault themselves. As indicated previously in section five of chapter four, Luke seems to suggest that the townspeople themselves are all Gentiles.

8. In 14:2 Luke writes: "But the unbelieving [*apēithesantes*] Jews stirred up . . ." He also uses *ēpeithoun* ("disbelieved") in 19:9, reporting: ". . . but when some were stubborn and *disbelieved*. . . ."

9. See Cassidy/*Jesus,* pp. 70-71 and notes, for indications of how Luke is sensitive to distinctions between and among various Jewish groups and individuals.

10. As indicated below in the text, Jews who reject his message seek to kill Paul in Damascus, Iconium, and Lystra. In addition "Hellenists" (as indicated in n. 13 below, presumably Jews from the Diaspora now residing in Jerusalem) seek to kill him in Jerusalem and, at a later stage, so do "Asian Jews" and others with them.

11. As described below, Paul is forced out of Pisidian Antioch, Thessalonica, and Beroea, and forced to alter his planned departure from Greece.

12. Both at Corinth and at Ephesus, Paul was forced to move his base of operations out of the synagogue as a consequence of hostility from those Jews who rejected his preaching. At Corinth he was also later denounced to the proconsul who took no action against him.

13. In "Once More, Who Were the Hellenists?" *ET,* Vol 70 (1959), p. 101, C. Moule argues for a distinction between Jews who did not speak Greek and Jews who did (Hellenists) and for a corresponding distinction between Jewish Christians who did not speak Greek and Jewish Christians who did (also Hellenists).

Moule believes that these distinctions facilitate the interpretation of both 6:1 and 9:29. In the former instance Luke is distinguishing between two groups within the Christian community. In the latter he shows Paul controverting with, and running afoul of, a particular group of Jews who knew Greek and were presumably conversant with Greek culture.

In "Not Jewish Christianity and Gentile Christianity but Types of Jewish/Gentile Christianity," *CBQ*, Vol 45 (1983), p. 75, R. Brown outlines a somewhat comparable set of distinctions even though his criteria for determining membership within a particular type are different from Moule's. Brown then gives particular attention to the impact of the conversions that Luke portrays being achieved by "Hebrew Christians" and "Hellenist Jewish Christians."

Specifically, on the "Hellenists" of 9:29, W. Schmithals, *Paul and James* (London: SCM, 1965), p. 27, is persuasive on the point that Luke understands them to be Jews from the Diaspora. It should also be noted that in 22:18, Paul recounts to the Jerusalem crowd that the risen Jesus told him to depart Jerusalem quickly because a not clearly specified "they" would not accept Paul's message and would presumably do harm to him. From the context it cannot be demonstrated that Luke understands this "they" to refer to the "Hellenists" named in 9:29, but the possibility of such congruence should be noted.

14. The Greek rendered by "the leading men of the city" is *tous prōtous tēs poleōs*. Williams, p. 229, suggests that the magistrates of the city may be among those designated by this term.

15. Inasmuch as Luke subsequently portrays them recognizing Trophimus (a native of Ephesus), there are good grounds for holding that Luke understands these Jews to have been some of Paul's opponents from that city.

16. That there is a considerable degree of similarity between the charges made here against Paul and those made against Stephen in 6:11,13-14 should be noted.

17. When Paul later reviews events for Agrippa II, he indicates the following concerning the motive for the attempt on his life (26:19-21): "Wherefore, O King Agrippa, I was not disobedient to the heavenly vision, but declared first to those at Damascus, then at Jerusalem and throughout all the country of Judea, and also to the Gentiles, that they should repent and turn to God and perform deeds worthy of their repentance. For this reason the Jews seized me in the temple and tried to kill me."

In his earlier review of these developments for Felix, Paul refers to the disruption which the Asian Jews initiated, but he does not actually provide any explanation as to their motive (23:18-19).

18. The note contained in 24:19 that the Asian Jews are absent from Paul's trial at Caesarea suggests that Luke may have understood them to have been in Jerusalem for only a limited time.

19. As Luke portrays his speech, Paul does not directly challenge the charges that have been brought against him. Instead he seeks to establish his standing as a dedicated Jew "brought up in this city at the feet of Gamaliel, educated according to the strict manner of the law of our fathers, being zealous for God as you all are this day" (22:3). By inference, if Paul is a loyal Jew, then the charges that he has been teaching against "the people and the law" and defiling the temple are false.

The sense of Luke's account is that this approach initially worked to Paul's favor. However, as noted in the text, the mention of a mission to the Gentiles proved too much for the crowd to accept. In portraying their reaction, Luke seems to indicate that they reverted back to their initial stance of extreme hostility toward Paul, presumably accepting all of the charges that had been made against him.

20. Luke most probably understands Paul's appeal in 22:5 as being directed to one of the high priests named in 4:6. Such a conclusion emerges from the consideration that both in the Gospel and Acts, the priest last listed as high priest continued to be the point of reference until a replacement is indicated (see Acts 5:17, 21,27 and 7:1)

and from the fact that Ananias is not introduced as high priest until 23:2.

While Luke does seem to depict Paul presuming that a high priest who knows his case is still alive and could testify on his behalf, Williams' suggestion, p. 370, that Luke may understand Paul to be making a kind of moral appeal to the Sanhedrin's "collective memory" also constitutes a possible interpretation.

21. Paul's willingness to appear before the Sanhedrin at this juncture is in marked contrast to his firm refusal to have his trial transferred back to Jerusalem in 25:9. While Luke has clearly portrayed the chief priests and others on the Sanhedrin operating destructively against the Jerusalem church, he has not portrayed Paul suffering at their hands up until this point. As noted above, Luke also does seemingly portray Paul holding that the high priest and the Sanhedrin are capable of remembering his previous relationship with them. (In the actual scene, however, the first words out of Paul's mouth cause him to be struck and Luke records no comments by any Sanhedrin members concerning Paul's previous service.)

22. From the standpoint of Ananias and those allied with him, the outcome which Luke portrays eventuating under Felix is one with both negative and positive features. The negative aspect is that they have not succeeded in their efforts to have Paul destroyed. The positive feature is that they do succeed in having him kept in Roman custody, out of circulation, for two years.

Chapter Six: Paul and the Roman Authorities in Greece and Asia Minor

1. As indicated in n. 6 and n. 14 of chapter five, commentators on Acts have discussed the possibility that Paul was in contact with the magistrates or comparable officials at Pisidian Antioch and Lystra. However, in neither case does Luke describe any sort of "official" activity taking place. Thus, while these passages do provide additional indications regarding the type of controversies that Paul experienced, they are not subject matter for this chapter in the same way that Luke's reports concerning Philippi, Thessalonica, Corinth, and Ephesus are.

2. H. Duckworth, "The Roman Provincial System," in BC-I, p. 195.

3. Sherwin-White, p. 177.

4. For an analysis of the extensive range of a Roman governor's *imperium,* see Sherwin-White, pp. 3-9.

5. Describing an event during Paul's sojourn in Athens, Luke reports that some of the populace took Paul "to the Areopagus" (*epi ton areion*) (17:19). This phrase might refer to a famous hill within Athens or to the city council (which itself possessed the same name as a result of its meetings on that hill). Williams, p. 303, argues that the council itself is meant, but the fact that Paul seems subsequently to be addressing a larger body ("Men of Athens" in 17:22) suggests that the setting is actually before a large group that has spontaneously assembled on the hill. Even if Luke does wish to indicate an appearance before the city council, he reports no "official" interaction as a result of Paul's address.

6. In his discussion of the magistrates at Philippi, Sherwin-White, p. 92, makes reference to coins from Corinth indicating that the Latin term for the magistrates of that colony was *duoviri iuri dicundo.* Sherwin-White believes that Luke's word, *strategoi,* actually renders the Latin *duoviri.*

7. J. Finegan, *The Archaeology of the New Testament* (Boulder, Colorado: Westview, 1981), p. 153, uses this phrase.

8. Williams, p. 322, states that the Romans called this province "Asia" because the

territory had recently been ruled by Attalus III, the king of Pergamus, and that the Attalids were known to the Romans as "kings of Asia."

9. Sherwin-White, pp. 85-86.

10. Sherwin-White, p. 90, lists the following as possible roles of the Asiarchs: annual presidents or ex-presidents of the provincial council of Asia; city delegates to that council; administrators of the various temples of the imperial council (these temples being under the charge of high priests appointed by the provincial council).

11. For a conveniently schematized chart of the Roman emperors and the kings and governors of Palestine along with the high priests of Israel and the legates of Syria, see DNT, p. 31.

12. As an illustration of the way in which city officials became increasingly accountable to the provincial governors, Sherwin-White, p. 84, cites admonitions from the civic speeches of Dio of Prusa, among them the following: "These riots will be reported to the proconsul. Nothing that goes on in the cities escapes the notice of the governors."

13. While it is clear that Luke indicates Philippi's status as a Roman colony at the end of 16:12, there is disagreement over which of two possible Greek texts is authentic in another part of that verse. The RSV opts for *protēs meridos tēs Makedonias polis* and translates "the leading city of the district of Macedonia." Sherwin-White, pp. 93-95, believes that the proper Greek phrase is *tēs protēs meridos Makedonias polis* in which case the translation would be "a city of the first district of Macedonia." Williams, p. 272, also holds the latter view.

14. It may have been preferable for the RSV simply to have utilized the Latin term, *duumvir,* as a translation for *stratēgos* instead of using the generic term, "magistrate." The fact that Luke portrays them accompanied by rod-wielding lictors suggests that officials of a particular rank are being described.

15. The Greek underlying the RSV's "the police" is *tous rabdouchous* (the same term appears in 16:38 and is implied in 16:22 where the magistrates order that Paul and Silas be beaten and *rabdizein* is the Greek word used). Bruce, p. 336, refers to the bundle of rods, sometimes with an ax inserted into them, which the lictors carried. These bundles, the *fasces et secures,* symbolized the magistrates' office and their right to inflict corporal and capital punishment.

16. Inter alia, Bruce, p. 340, notes that Luke did not present Paul referring to his status as a Roman citizen during the beating of the previous day. Bruce also notes that it is the "plain implication" of this passage that Silas is also a Roman citizen.

17. The Greek states that they have been beaten, *akatakritous,* translated literally by the RSV as "uncondemned." (Luke also presents Paul using this term in his reproach to Claudius Lysias in 22:25.) Haenchen, p. 498, states that the implied sense is that the scourging was carried out without any investigation or proof of guilt.

18. The RSV gives "apologized to them" as the translation for *parakalesan autous* in 16:39. In the estimation of Marshall, p. 275, this is an over-translation and he suggests that "conciliated" is closer to the sense of the Greek. So also Williams, p. 283.

19. Luke indicates in 17:5 that the unbelieving Jews originally intended to bring Paul and Silas before the *dēmos.* According to Sherwin-White, p. 96, this would be the popular assembly of the city.

20. In Acts 21:38 (Galatians 5:12 is the only other instance in which *anastatoō* appears in the New Testament writings) the reference is to political revolt. There the RSV renders the tribune's question to Paul: "Are you not the Egyptian, then, who recently stirred up a revolt [*anastatōsas*] and led the four thousand men of the Assassins out into the wilderness?"

21. So Marshall, p. 279.

22. In "The Decrees of Caesar at Thessalonica," *RTR,* Vol 30 (1971) pp. 2-5, E. Judge suggests that imperial edicts prohibiting public predictions about changes in rulers could plausibly be "the decrees of Caesar" that Paul's preaching might be considered to violate. Judge's suggestion has been favorably received by Marshall, p. 279. Nevertheless, the correlation between the edicts Judge cites and the decrees mentioned by Paul's opponents is, at this point, still conjectural.

23. What is here distinguished as a third allegation, other commentators have often considered to be a part of the second allegation, actually as a specification of the kind of activity by which Paul and his friends are violating the decrees of Caesar. So Marshall, p. 279, and Martin, p. 56. For assessments that indicate a distinction between charges concerning activities against the decrees of Caesar and the proclamation of another king, see Williams, p. 288, and Bruce, p. 344.

24. Bruce, p. 344, indicates the cumulative impact of Paul's opponents' charges in the following way: "Jason and the others were charged with harboring political messianic agitators—men who had been guilty of sedition and revolutionary activity in other provinces of the Roman Empire and had now come to Thessalonica with their propaganda, which was not only illegal in itself but actually proclaimed a rival emperor, one Jesus by name, to him who ruled in Rome."

25. This is Bruce's phrase, ibid.

26. The RSV's "were disturbed" may be too mild a translation for *tarassō*. When this word appears elsewhere in Luke-Acts, the translation is usually by stronger terms, i.e., "troubled," "stirred up." See Luke 1:12, 24:38, and Acts 15:24, 17:13.

27. Sherwin-White, p. 95 and p. 82 n. 2, refers to some of the procedures that the Romans adhered to in connection with *satis accipere* and *satis dare,* the giving of security; Sherwin-White holds that Jason is giving security for the "good behavior" of his guests. In contrast, Haenchen, p. 508, holds that Jason and his associates give bail for themselves. However, in light of the seriousness of the charges, it seems unduly restrictive to understand the bond as pertaining to only one group or the other. Rather it seems to be Luke's sense that the politarchs are demanding security against *any* transgressions comparable to those enunciated in the charges.

28. Williams, p. 310. Williams provides the following summary of Gallio's life: "Marcus Annaeus Novatus, as he was first called, was the son of Seneca the rhetorician and the brother of Mela (father of Lucan the poet) and of Seneca, the Stoic philosopher and sometime tutor of Nero. Born in Spain, he came to Rome during the reign of Tiberius, was adopted into the family of his father's friend, Lucius Junius Gallio, and took the name of his adoptive father (he was now Lucius Junius Gallio Annaeus)."

29. So also Schneider II, p. 252, and n. 54. In his explanatory footnote Schneider affirms that the breach of Roman law which is alleged here is to be compared with the breach of Roman law alleged by Paul's opponents at Philippi (16:21) and Thessalonica (17:7).

30. In rendering *anapeithō* (*hapax legomenon*) as "persuading," the RSV is seemingly under-translating the actual meaning. Various forms of "persuade" adequately render *peithō* when Luke uses that term in a variety of settings (cf. 18:4, 19:26, 21:14, 26:26). However something more forceful is seemingly required to capture the meaning of *anapeithō* here. Along with "persuade," BAGD gives "induce," "incite" (in something evil) as other meanings of *anapeithō*. In addition to meanings similar to "persuade," LSJ also gives "seduce," "mislead" as a third, well-attested meaning of *anapeithō*.

31. In general usage, *aneschomēn* and an accusative means "to bear with" someone.

However ZG, p. 413, points out that, in a specialized legal context, "accept a complaint" is a better translation. So also Bruce, p. 375 n. 34, citing a 1952 edition of W. Bauer's *Griechisch-deutsches Wörterbuch.*

32. In addition to "drive away," LSJ also gives "expel from" as a primary meaning of *apelaunō.* Haenchen, p. 536, notes that the term describes vigorous action on Gallio's part and implies that the sense of the passage is that anti-Semitism motivates this action. Williams, p. 311, states: "With all his Roman disdain of the Jews, he had his lictors drive the petitioners from his court."

33. Contra Haenchen, p. 536, and Bruce, p. 375, who suggest that a group of Gentile bystanders may have beaten Sosthenes, the passage does not indicate that anyone else is present at the time. A more likely, though still not secure, interpretation is that Luke understands some of the unbelieving Jews turning upon Sosthenes for having led them into such a humiliating outcome.

34. Martin, p. 62, terms the beating a "flagrant injustice" and holds that Gallio's indifference to it is consistent with his attitude throughout the proceedings: "he just couldn't be bothered."

35. Almost without exception the standard commentaries on Acts take the position that Gallio's actions constitute some kind of official exoneration or at least toleration of Paul. Thus, inter alia, Lake and Cadbury, pp. 228-229; Bruce, p. 375; Haenchen (obliquely), p. 536; Marshall, p. 298, and Schneider, II, p. 253. Williams, p. 306, goes so far as to state that Luke viewed the dismissal of the charge (sic) as "an important demonstration of the compatibility of the Christian faith with the Roman state."

36. In 19:30 Luke uses *dēmos,* a word which implies a more structured assembly than *ochlos,* his term in 19:33, 35, does. (See also n. 19, above, concerning the use of *dēmos* in 17:5.) Regardless of whether those assembled should be regarded as an unruly crowd or as a quasi-official popular assembly, it is clear that Luke's description of the scene inside the stadium portrays it as extremely tumultuous and confusing.

A point regarding Luke's portrayal of Paul should also be noticed here. In indicating that Paul wished to risk going into such a situation, Luke shows him manifesting a considerable bravery and a considerable confidence in his ability to overcome the tumult and give testimony to Jesus.

37. As Williams, p. 334, and others have pointed out, by indicating that the Asiarchs so counseled Paul, Luke does show that Paul's preaching had been favorably received by at least some persons of influence within the province. However, Bruce, p. 400, exaggerates and distorts this insight when he argues that this passage provides a sign "that imperial policy at the time was not hostile to Christianity and that the more educated classes did not share the antipathy to Paul which the more superstitious classes felt."

38. *Hierosulos,* the Greek word the RSV translates as "sacrilegious" is derived from *hieron* ("temple") and *sulaō* ("plunder"). Cf. ZG, p. 419.

39. The Greek reads *agoraioi agontai kai authupatoi eisin* and the reference to "proconsuls" in the plural has attracted considerable attention. It seems probable that Luke has used a "generic" or "generalizing" plural here (so Haenchen, p. 576) but the possibility of a reference to the two proconsuls of A.D. 54-55 cannot be ruled out (so Williams, p. 336).

40. The Greek term used here, *ennomō ekklēsia,* seemingly makes reference to an officially scheduled "regular" assembly. In contrast, in 19:32 and 19:41 Luke describes the gathering simply as an "assembly" (*ekklēsia* without any qualifying adjectives).

41. *Stasis* is used elsewhere in Acts in the sense of controversy or heated dissension

(cf. 15:2; 23:7, 10) but it may also have a stronger, more political meaning. In 23: 19, 25 of the Gospel Luke uses the term to describe Barabbas's violent activity and in 24:5 of Acts, *stasis* is the activity that Paul himself is charged with. For a further discussion see the analysis made in the next chapter regarding the charges against Paul at Caesarea.

42. The Greek underlying "no little stir" is *tarachos ouk oligos*. While *tarassō* appears fairly frequently in the New Testament and five times in Luke-Acts and *ektarassō* appears twice in Acts, there is only one other occurrence of the noun in the New Testament and that is at Acts 12:18. There the phrasing is exactly the same, *tarachos ouk oligos,* and so is the RSV's translation. However in that instance the sense is more of mental agitation, consternation (of the guards over Peter's miraculous escape). Here the meaning is more that of "commotion," "tumult."

43. At that juncture, Luke portrays Paul stating: "But this I admit to you, that according to the Way, which they call a sect, I worship the God of our fathers" (24:14). Then, in a narrative interlude, Luke indicates that Felix had prior knowledge in this area: "But Felix, having a rather accurate knowledge of the Way, put them off . . ." (24:22).

44. For an analysis indicating that "the Way," when used absolutely in Acts, is the way of Jesus and that this term designates a certain manner of acting as well as a new belief, see S. Lyonnet, " 'La Voie' dans les Actes des Apôtres," *RSR,* Vol 69 (1981), pp. 149-164, especially pp. 152-153 and 160-161. See also J. Pathrapankal, "Christianity as a 'Way,' " in AATRT. For a more general analysis of the origins of this term, see G. Ebel, *"Hodos,"* in TDNT. See also V. McCasland, "The Way," *JBL,* Vol 77 (1958), pp. 222-230.

Chapter Seven: Paul and the Roman Authorities in Jerusalem and Caesarea

1. The word "tribune" comes from the Latin, *tribunus,* and is a translation of *chiliarchos.* Literally *chiliarchos* means "commander of a thousand." In 21:31 this office is actually *chiliarchos tēs speirēs,* "tribune of the cohort." F. Gealy, "Cohort," in IDB states that the auxiliary cohort the Romans kept in Jerusalem normally consisted of 760 infantry with an attachment of 240 cavalry. So also Haenchen, p. 616 and n.10. In 21:32 Luke also indicates the presence of centurion(s) who were under the tribune's command.

2. In the self-serving letter which Luke subsequently portrays Lysias sending to Felix (see the analysis below), the tribune claims that he "rescued" (*exeilamen*) Paul. Perhaps as a consequence of this later claim, various commentators have interpreted the present passage with reference to "rescuing." Thus, for example, Walaskay/ Dissertation, p. 218 (see also Walaskay/*Rome,* p. 53), and Maddox, p. 94, who mentions in his discussion that Lysias took Paul into "protective custody."

3. Marshall, p. 349, correctly emphasizes that Paul is arrested because the tribune considers him to be the source of the trouble. So also Williams, p. 366.

4. Haenchen, p. 617, holds that the tribune's questions are addressed to the crowd. Marshall, p. 349, allows for this interpretation but also points to the possibility that the tribune began to question Paul only to have members of the crowd break in with their accusations and their own side of the story.

5. See Lake and Cadbury, pp. 276-277, Haenchen, pp. 619-620, and Williams, p. 368, for analyses of Josephus' references to the various revolutionary figures, including an Egyptian, with whom the governors Felix and Festus had to deal.

6. So Williams, p. 366, and Haenchen (citing Preuschen), p. 617. Haenchen in-

terprets this step as a fulfillment of the prophecy of Agabus that Luke had earlier described: "And coming to us he took Paul's girdle and bound his own feet and hands, and said, . . . 'So shall the Jews at Jerusalem bind the man who owns this girdle and deliver him into the hands of the Gentiles' " (21:11). Clearly, it is the Romans who here actually bind Paul; however the impetus for their action comes from the activities of the Asian Jews and the unbelieving Jews of Jerusalem.

7. Bruce, p. 447 n. 39, also holds that the sense of 21:33, 26:29, and 28:20 is that Paul was physically bound with a chain throughout his imprisonment in Palestine and also later in Rome. It should also be noted that Lysias' chaining of Paul fulfills Paul's earlier statement at Miletus (20:23) that "chains" (*desma*) and "afflictions" (*thlipseis*) await him in Jerusalem.

8. Maddox, p. 95, argues that Claudius Lysias is the most favorably portrayed of all of the Roman officials Luke describes. In some respects this is a defensible assessment. However Maddox does not take account of the self-serving character of Lysias' letter to Felix (23:26-30; to be discussed below) and he does not take account of the status of Herod Agrippa II and also of the city clerk at Ephesus as Roman officials.

9. H. Cadbury has provided the classic analysis of this gesture in his article, "Dust and Garments," BC-V, pp. 269-277.

10. Sherwin-White, pp. 27-28, distinguishes three levels of Roman beatings and states in passing that this beating (like that given by the magistrates at Philippi) was of the cautionary type. However Bruce, p. 445, and Williams, p. 378, interpret *mastixin anetazesthai* (literally "to be examined with a whip") as implying the more severe *flagellum.* Williams indicates that a whip of knotted cords or leather, sometimes weighted with pieces of metal or bone, could be used in the case of slaves or non-Romans; in contrast beatings given to Roman citizens were commonly carried out with rods.

11. With his 1939 work, *The Roman Citizenship* (Oxford: Clarendon) A. N. Sherwin-White provided a classic treatment of the procedures governing the Roman citizenship as they evolved over time. With specific reference to Paul's citizenship, the same author's 1963 work, *Roman Society and Roman Law in the New Testament,* is even more important. In the latter work see particularly the sections, "The Roman Citizenship and Acts," pp. 144-162, and the section, "Aspects of Roman Citizenship and the Question of Historicity," pp. 172-185.

12. BAGD gives "set free," "deliver," "rescue," as the primary meanings for *exaireō* in the middle voice. As indicated previously in the text, Lysias here claims to have rescued Paul; however such a claim is at variance with Luke's earlier description of the tribune *arresting* Paul in order to keep a full-blown riot from developing.

13. While the passage makes it clear that there was something in the magistrates' proposal that outraged Paul's sensibilities, Luke does not indicate precisely what it was about their proposal that so affronted him. Of the standard commentaries, Haenchen, p. 408, comes closest to a satisfactory explanation by suggesting that Paul actually envisioned the magistrates making a kind of restitution for the mistreatment they had inflicted. Building upon this idea, Luke's sense may be that Paul anticipated an honorable escort or some other form of public apology as his due and regarded the proposal for secret dismissal as insult being added to injury.

14. With a memorable understatement (for a discussion of "Lukan litotes" see Cadbury/*Making,* pp. 120-121) Luke here portrays Paul referring to Tarsus as "no mean city" (21:39) and the sense of this response is that it is his Tarsian citizenship, as opposed to his Roman, that Paul holds to with real pride. Lake and Cadbury, p. 278,

intimate that, within Acts Paul is only really proud of being a citizen of Tarsus. Sherwin-White, p. 179, states that within Acts Paul "thinks of himself first and foremost as a citizen of Tarsus."

15. See, for example, Haenchen, p. 635, Schneider, II, p. 327, and Bruce, pp. 446-447.

16. Sherwin-White, p. 155, deduces from the name, *Claudius* Lysias, that the tribune received his citizenship during the reign of Claudius as it was customary for those enfranchised to keep their own proper name as a cognomen but to adopt the praenomen and nomen of their patrons. Carried further, such a line of reasoning suggests that Lysias as only recently enfranchised, would have had far less standing than Paul in terms of years of citizenship.

Regardless of the exact time of Lysias' citizenship, Paul clearly was his senior in having possessed his own citizenship from birth; this factor leads Schneider, II, p. 327 and n. 27, to judge that Paul's answer drew attention to his higher status.

17. Drawing from a list of concerns proposed by Cadbury, Sherwin-White, p. 144, affirms that within Acts a subject of considerable importance is: "the effect of citizenship on a man's other loyalties, notably to his local community and to his cult." In reference to the three terms of allegiance that Sherwin-White indicates, it would be the conclusion of the present study that Paul's allegiance to the risen Jesus comes before all else and that, based upon 21:39, Paul attaches greater importance to his status as a citizen of Tarsus than he does to his status as a Roman citizen.

18. Drawing upon reports from Tacitus and Josephus, Bruce, p. 462, provides the following biographical sketch: "Antonius Felix, procurator of Judea from A.D. 52 to 59, was a man of servile origin, who owed his unprecedented advancement to a post of honor usually reserved for the equestrian order to the influence which his brother Pallas exercised at the imperial court under Claudius. Pallas was a freeman of Claudius' mother, Antonia, and so also (to judge by his gentile name Antonius) was his brother Felix. Before he succeeded Ventidius the procurator in A.D. 52, he seems to have occupied a subordinate post in Samaria under Cumanus from A.D. 48. His term of office as procurator was marked by increasing insurgent activity throughout the province, and by the emergence of the sicarii. The ruthlessness with which he put down these risings alienated many of the more moderate Jews, and led to further risings. Tacitus sums up his career in the biting epigram, 'He exercised the power of a king with the mind of a slave' (*Histories* V.9). Despite his low birth, he was remarkably successful in marriage; his three successive wives were all princesses, according to Suetonius (*Life of Claudius,* 28). The first of the three was a granddaughter of Antony and Cleopatra, the third was Drusilla, daughter of the elder Agrippa."

19. According to Sherwin-White, p. 55, Paul's response that he was from another province, Cilicia, could have theoretically afforded Felix grounds for sending him back to the jurisdiction of his native province. However, without specifying the governor's thinking on jurisdictional or related matters, Luke simply portrays Felix as being willing to proceed with the case.

20. Marshall, p. 373, indicates that this building was originally constructed by Herod the Great, but later served as the headquarters of the Roman governors. Haenchen, p. 649, allows for the possibility that there were rooms for guards and cells for prisoners within the palace.

21. Williams, p. 395, indicates that such a complimentary beginning was customarily an element of classical orations and makes reference to Cicero's *De Oratione* 2, 78. Haenchen, p. 657, comments that, as Luke records it, Tertullus' *captatio benevolentia* is

disproportionately long, three verses out of the seven which comprise the full speech.

22. Commenting on the sense of the charges in this passage, Sherwin-White, p. 50, argues that the intention was "to induce the governor to construe the preaching of Paul as tantamount to causing civil disturbance throughout the Jewish population of the empire. They knew that the governors were unwilling to convict on purely religious charges and therefore tried to give a political twist to the religious charge." By way of further elaboration, it can also be stated that, according to Luke's portrayal, Ananias and his allies are not so much threatened by Paul's preaching to the Gentiles as they are by the fact that it is Jesus whom he preaches.

23. Bruce, pp. 464-466, stands as an example of those commentators who treat Tertullus' statements that Paul was a ringleader of the Nazarenes as a separate charge. However, inasmuch as the statement does not indicate an additional infraction of the Roman order, it seems preferable to consider it as part of the first charge, actually as a note explaining the capacity in which Paul had been fomenting discord. See Schneider, II, p. 346, for a similar view.

24. The translation proposed in the text renders *loimon* considerably more strongly than does the RSV and also renders *kinounta staseis* somewhat more strongly. BAGD gives "pestilence," "plague," and "disease" as translations for *loimos* as a noun and comparable translations for adjectival forms. With reference to this particular verse, BAGD proposes the following translation: "We have found this man to be a plague spot." Explicit reference is then made to a passage in the writings of Demosthenes where *loimos* is used as a noun to designate a person dangerous to the public weal.

For *kineō*, BAGD gives a variety of similar meanings and suggests "cause," "bring about" as the word's meaning in this particular verse. ZG gives "set in motion, excite." Since *stasis* has the meaning of "revolt," "riot" (so ZG; BAGD holds for such a meaning in Luke 23:19 and Acts 19:40 but without explanation suggests "strife," "discord," "disunion" for the present verse and in Acts 23:7,10), the sense of Tertullus' words is that Paul is going among the Jews of the Diaspora "causing revolts" or "generating uprisings."

25. Note the distinction between the charge that Paul had actually profaned the temple and the charge that he *had attempted to* profane it. The Asian Jews raised the former charge in 21:28. The latter is what Tertullus alleges here. Various commentators have pointed out that Tertullus' next clause, " . . . but we seized him" (24:6b), seeks to convey the impression that the Sanhedrin authorities had intervened to prevent Paul from perpetrating this sacrilege. They also seemingly infer that they had Paul in custody when Lysias and his soldiers arrived on the scene. So Marshall, p. 375.

26. Citing Josephus' report (*Jewish War,* VI. 2,4) that the emperor had stipulated the death penalty for Gentiles (including Roman citizens) who violated the temple's precincts, Schneider, II, p. 346, seems to hold that Tertullus' charge envisioned direct Roman action against Paul on this basis alone. Martin, p. 78, also holds that Tertullus sought Paul's death on the grounds of the second charge. His view is that Tertullus actually envisioned the possibility of having Felix release Paul to Ananias and the others responsible for the temple. In support of such an interpretation, Martin cites a reading for 24:7 that the RSV relegates to the margin: "and we would have judged him according to our law."

27. Williams, p. 399, suggests that Paul was here underscoring the point that his opponents' whole case was conspicuously lacking in evidence. Such a response would also implicitly constitute a reply to the charge that he had caused uprisings among Jews throughout the world.

28. According to Josephus' various reports (summarized by Bruce, pp. 472-473), Drusilla was the youngest of the three daughters of Herod Agrippa I. She had earlier been given in marriage to Azizus, the king of Emesa, a small client-kingdom in Syria, by her brother Herod Agrippa II. However Felix persuaded her to leave her husband and marry him (as indicated in n. 18, above, she thus became his third wife). It should be noted that, in addition to appearing before her and Felix, Paul will also later appear before her brother and one of her sisters (Herod Agrippa II and Bernice; see 25:23ff).

29. In "Roman Law and the Trial of Paul," in BC-V, p. 307, H. Cadbury notes that one result of the situation Luke portrays is that Paul "suffered a kind of punishment through the delay itself."

30. Although the subject will be treated more comprehensively in a subsequent chapter, it should be mentioned at this point that commentators such as Haenchen, pp. 662-663 (see also Schneider, II, p. 353), reach significantly different conclusions regarding Luke's portrayal of Felix's handling of Paul's case. Haenchen's conviction that Luke actually wished to portray Felix as "the second of the four great witnesses for the Apostles's innocence" may be the foundational principle for his interpretation of Luke's account at this point. However, such an a priori concept of Roman officials as witnesses to the innocence of Paul, pervasive though it may be in the commentaries on Acts, is not substantiated in the case of Luke's presentation of Felix. Nor is it, as will be demonstrated below, an accurate concept for expressing Luke's portrayal of Porcius Festus.

31. According to Josephus's reports in *Jewish War* 2.13.7 and *Antiquities* 20.8.7,9, Felix was recalled to Rome by Nero as a consequence of his mishandling of a situation that had developed at Caesarea. The Jewish and Gentile inhabitants of the city had quarrelled and Felix had used his troops in such a way that the Jewish faction had suffered grave casualties. It was their complaint which prompted the recall and Josephus indicates that Felix would have been punished severely had it not been for the intervention of his brother Pallas. Among scholars there is considerable disagreement concerning Felix's dates in office. Marshall, p. 381 and n. 1, presents a concise summary of the principal positions in this debate.

32. At this stage Festus has not attempted to argue that it is more appropriate for Paul to be tried in Jerusalem because the charges related to Jewish law. However, the character of the reply that Luke shows him making suggests that Paul anticipated this as a possible pretext and wished to invalidate it in advance. Then at 25:20 Luke does show Festus implying to Agrippa that considerations of this kind were what prompted him to propose shifting the trial.

It should also be noted that Paul emphasizes that his opposition to the shift is rooted in the fact that it is a miscarriage of justice and not because of the fact that he himself fears death and is seeking to avoid such an outcome. The sentiments which Luke now shows him expressing are not, however, in the same key as the sentiments that Paul expressed earlier at Caesarea (21:13) when he responded: "For I am ready not only to be imprisoned but even to die at Jerusalem for the name of the Lord Jesus."

33. The RSV rendering of *me dunatai autois charisasthai* in 25:11 as "No one can give me up to them" fails to take account of an important nuance of meaning communicated by Luke's use of *charisasthai*. Again, here is a reference to the issue of "favors." The translation given by ZG, p. 441, "No one can hand me over to them *as a favor*" (emphasis added) better indicates that, by Luke's account, Paul perceived that Festus' motive in making this proposal was to do Paul's opponents a favor. (Similar considerations also apply to 25:16 where Luke portrays Festus com-

menting to Agrippa that it is not the Romans' custom to act in such a way.)

34. For a description of the republican origins of the right of appeal and the developments which took place in it under principate (when *provocatio ad populum* became *appelatio ad Caesarem*), see A.H.M Jones, "I Appeal unto Caesar," pp. 53-65 and "Imperial and Senatorial Jurisdiction in the Early Principate," pp. 69-98, in his *Studies in Roman Government and Law* (Oxford: Blackwell, 1960). Largely accepting Jones's analysis, Sherwin-White, pp. 63-69, provides several additional minor insights regarding the options that a provincial governor such as Festus had in such situations.

For two efforts to assess the consequences that Paul's appeal had for his relationship with the Sanhedrin parties (and for the Christian movement's presumed future relations with the Roman authorities), see M. Carrez's essay, "L'appel de Paul à César (Ac 25:11)," in his collection, *De la Torah au Méssie* (Paris: Desclée, 1981), pp. 503-510, and also H. Tajra, "L'appel à César: Séparation d'avec le Christianisme?" in *ETR* Vol 56 (1981), pp. 593-598. Both of these studies provide helpful insights; but, from the standpoint of the present work, each is seriously flawed because of a failure to take precise enough account of the particular circumstances under which Luke shows Paul making his appeal.

35. At this juncture, it is appropriate to provide some initial reflections concerning the degree to which Luke portrays Roman officials functioning justly and impartially in Acts. As has already been indicated in this study, Luke's description of the behavior of Gallio and Felix makes them out to be considerably less than models of just conduct.

It should be noted that such a conclusion is at variance with the interpretations presented in several widely used commentaries. For example, in reference to Paul's appeal to Caesar, Bruce writes (p. 478): "Paul has had encouraging experience of the justice and impartiality of Roman courts already, notably when he was accused before Gallio in Corinth. . . . If he was apprehensive about the result of a trial before Festus in Jerusalem, it was not because he had lost his confidence in Roman justice, but because he feared that, in Jerusalem, Roman justice might be overborne by powerful local influences."

The analysis of this passage presented by Haenchen also reflects such a view. Operating from the premise that Luke seeks to present Roman officials as "witnesses for the defense," Haenchen then encounters great difficulty in trying to explain why Luke does not present Paul insisting on the continuation of his trial at Caesarea instead of appealing to have it shifted to Rome (see pp. 668-670). However, once one drops the false premise that Luke wants to portray Roman officials taking Paul's part in various situations, the difficulties concerning the appeal passage vanish. For, read without presuppositions about political apologetic, the passage clearly shows Festus colluding with Paul's enemies. It thus comes as no surprise to Luke's readers that Paul acts to remove his case from Festus' jurisdiction.

36. Williams, p. 408, comments that the sense of Luke's account is that Festus was not particularly pleased to have Paul invoke his right of appeal. See below for an analysis of how Luke portrays Festus proceeding in an effort to have his own handling of Paul's case viewed favorably.

37. Additional attention will be given to Paul's address to the Jewish community of Rome in the following chapter.

38. Josephus provides information regarding Herod Agrippa II in four of his works: *Jewish War* 2.12.1; 2.12.7; 2.15.2; 2.16.4; 7.5.1; *Antiquities* 19.9.2; 20.5.2; 20.6.3; 20.7.1; 20.8.4; 20.9.6; *Vita* 65; *Against Apion* 1.9.

39. The RSV has translated *epikalesamenou tērēthēnai* as ". . . appealed to be kept

in custody"; but, following BAGD a more literal rendering would be; ". . . appealed to be kept under guard." As either of these translations makes clear, it is unmistakably the sense of Luke's Greek that Festus has distorted the record of events. The narrative does not provide any direct indication as to Festus' motive for such a distortion; but it may be Luke's sense that the governor wished to have Agrippa form the impression that Paul himself was not displeased about the manner in which Festus had handled his case.

Owing to the sublety of Luke's account at this point, it is easy to overlook the fact that he has portrayed Festus falsifying the record of events. However once this initial oversight is made, the way is open for further distortion. Thus, for example, Williams, p. 413, mistakenly accepts Festus's misrepresentation as an accurate statement and then "explains" it in the following way: "This wording throws a new light on the affair. Not only was Paul looking for Roman justice, he was appealing for Roman protection."

An additional feature of the present speech that should be noted in passing is the vocabulary used for the supreme authority of the empire. Luke first portrays Festus stating that Paul appealed for the decision "of the *emperor*" (*sebastou*) and then explaining that he kept Paul until he could send him "to *Caesar*" (*kaisara*). Further comments regarding Luke's references to the imperial office and the names and titles of those who held it will be made below in chapter eight.

40. As a background to the present section of the narrative, Williams, p. 171, stresses the Greco-Roman character of Caesarea and notes that the Roman governors had made it both the administrative and military center of the province. Commenting on the identity of "the prominent men of the city," he states that these may have included some Jews, but that the majority would have been Gentiles (p. 413).

41. Literally *to kyriō*, "to the lord," "to the sovereign." The contrast between allegiance to Festus' *lord* and allegiance to Paul's *Lord* will be analyzed in the next chapter.

42. It should be emphasized that, at this point in his speech, Festus is shown to be critical of persons (Ananias and his allies) who are not present to hear his criticism. According to the speech, Paul is innocent of misconduct and Festus has handled his case well, overcoming the incorrect information that Ananias and his allies gave him about Paul.

43. Williams, p. 422, states that 26:19 (which is seventeen verses into the speech) "marks the beginning of Paul's real defense."

44. The plural form of the pronoun shows that Paul's question is addressed to others as well as to Agrippa. Nevertheless, it is clearly Luke's sense that Paul intends to challenge Agrippa personally in asking it.

45. The RSV translates *parrēsiazomenos lalō* in v. 26 as "I speak freely." However, "I speak *boldly*" better preserves the sense of bold speech that Luke envisions in using various forms of *parrēsia*.

46. Here at 26:31 and also at 20:23, the RSV uses "imprisonment" to translate *desmōn* instead of the literal "chains." [In contrast the RSV uses "chains" to render *desmōn* at 26:29.]

47. In 26:31 an indeterminate "they" express their assessment of Paul's case to each other. At this point in his narrative, Luke clearly understands Agrippa to be the principal actor. Yet in this particular verse (in contrast with the following verse), he is not identified as the deliverer of the assessment. The assessment itself implicitly criticizes *Felix's* handling of Paul's case (Paul who has done nothing deserving of imprisonment has been kept in prison for two years).

48. 26:32 and 27:1 establish that Paul is not being set free and that his status is still

that of a prisoner. Luke's report at 28:20 indicates that Paul was still bound with a chain later on in Rome.

49. Luke does not provide a clear indication of the approach that Festus now adopted regarding the formulation of charges for Paul's case in Rome. As indicated in 25:26-27 Festus had originally hoped to have Agrippa's help in formulating such charges. Now, by Luke's account, Agrippa does not believe that valid charges exist.

50. BAGD identifies *kratistos,* the superlative form of *kratos,* as an honorary form of address with the meaning "most noble," "most excellent." That Luke himself understands this term as an honorific expression is apparent from the three other places in which it appears in his writings. In 23:26 he shows Claudius Lysias using this word to address Felix at the outset of his letter and in 24:2 he portrays Tertullus beginning his *captatio benevolentiae* with it. In addition, in his formal dedication at the beginning of the Gospel, (1:3), Luke addresses Theophilus as *kratiste.*

Chapter Eight: Paul, a Prisoner and a Witness in Rome

1. Cadbury/*Book,* p. 60, deduces from 17:1 that Paul and Silas were traveling on the Egnatian Way and from 28:13 that Paul was brought as a prisoner over the Appian Way. However, as Cadbury himself recognizes (p. 59), Roman achievements with respect to transportation are not explicitly mentioned within the Acts narrative. The noticeable lack of references within Acts to Roman accomplishments and culture, except for the realm of the explicitly political, is well attested to by the relative sparseness of Cadbury's "Roman" chapter (pp. 58-82).

2. This reference to "the Romans" will be analyzed at greater length in section four, below.

3. As discussed in chapter three of this study, the statement which Luke attributes to Peter and all of the apostles in 5:29 is also obviously relevant in the present discussion: "We must obey God rather than human beings." In chapter nine a more sustained investigation of Paul's stance in comparison with that of Jesus will be undertaken.

4. It is a remarkable feature of the latter part of Acts that Luke reports or portrays Paul witnessing "to the Lord" in at least seven different Roman provinces. Paul's ministry is, of course, also sometimes described in other terms, for example, "preaching the kingdom of God," and it should not be thought that the sense of Jesus' sovereign status is only present when the term "Lord" is used. Nevertheless, the frequency with which this specific term appears in the narrative is indeed striking; "the Lord" is used by Paul, or in association with Paul, more than forty times within the narrative of Acts.

5. Cadbury/*Book,* p. 58, notes that, in the latter part of the Acts narrative, Nero is not designated by name, but instead three characteristic contemporary titles are used to refer to him. Thus in 25:12 and 25:21 *Kaisar* (which the RSV translates as "Caesar"); in 25:21 and 25:25, *sebastos* (literally "revered one" or "majesty," it is translated by the RSV as "emperor"); and in 25:26, *kyrios* (translated as "lord").

Parenthetically, it is also worth noting that Cadbury's treatment of the *praenomen,* the *nomen,* and the *cognomen,* the three names possessed by Roman citizens, p. 69, paves the way for an appreciation of the way in which other Roman emperors are explicitly referred to in Luke-Acts. "Claudius" (Acts 11:28 and 18:2) is the nomen of Tiberius Claudius Nero. "Tiberius Caesar" (Luke 3:1) uses the *praenomen* and *cognomen* of Tiberius Julius Caesar. "Caesar Augustus" (Luke 2:1) combines the *cognomen* of Caius Julius Caesar Octavianus with the honorific title "Augustus." The meaning of this latter title is "revered one" or "worthy of reverence" (the Greek word is *augoustos* from the Latin *augustus* which itself translates the Greek *sebastos*).

In *Light from the Ancient East,* op. cit. A. Deissmann, pp. 349-357, traces the emergence of *kyrios* as an acceptable term for designating those who held the position of emperor. According to Deissmann the popular view among scholars has been that Augustus and Tiberius emphatically rejected *kyrios* as a term for designating themselves (such a term clashed with their conceptualization of the empire as a principate) with the result that it did not come to be popularly used until the reign of Domitian when the "principate" model was superceded. However Deissmann's own investigations convinced him that, especially in the East, *kyrios* was widely used as a designation for the emperor much earlier than the Domitian period, actually from the reign of Nero onward. Accordingly, Deissmann is inclined to view many Christian proclamations of Jesus as "Lord" as a "silent protest against other 'lords' and against 'the lord' as people were beginning to call the Roman Caesar" (p. 355).

Deissmann's methodology is considerably different from that which guides the present study and it is not at all clear how he understands the figure of Paul that Luke presents in Acts. Nevertheless, the treatment which he provides throughout his section "Christ and the Caesars: Parallelism in the Technical Language of Their Cults," pp. 338-378, does shed considerable light on the Acts narrative.

6. In 27:1 Luke indicates that there are other prisoners in Julius' custody besides Paul and his identification of Julius as a centurion of the "Augustan Cohort" (*speirēs sebastes*) suggests the presence of soldiers under his command, something explicitly indicated in 27:31.

7. The Greek is *bouloumenos diasōsai ton Paulon.* The "saving" of Paul described here is comparable to Lysias' intervention when, to protect Paul from his enemies' plot, he ordered his soldiers to bring Paul speedily to Caesarea (23:23-24).

8. The angel's words in 27:24, "Do not be afraid, Paul; you must [*dei*] stand before Caesar," represent the third instance in which Luke presents Paul receiving divine instructions regarding his journey to Rome. It should be recalled that in 19:21 Paul "resolved in the Spirit . . . I must [*dei*] also see Rome." Also at 23:11 the risen Lord appeared to him stating, ". . . for as you have testified about me at Jerusalem, so you must [*dei*] bear witness also at Rome."

While the note of necessity is indicated in all three passages (as evidenced by the Lukan *dei*), the present passage represents the first instance in which a call to witness specifically to Caesar is indicated (cf. 25:10). It will be made clear below that Paul does fulfill the general part of this mandate concerning witness in Rome; however this latter aspect, witness before the emperor, is not fulfilled in Acts.

9. Paul's report to his shipmates concerning the vision evidences his own sense of belonging to God. He indicates (27:23) that the vision came from "the God to whom I belong and whom I worship."

10. Paul's confidence in God is also reflected several verses later when he states to his shipmates: "Therefore I urge you to take some food; it will give you strength, since not a hair is to perish from the head of any of you" (27:34).

11. Luke's description of Paul's thanksgiving and breaking of bread in 27:35 has led some commentators to conclude that a Christian eucharist is implied (see Marshall, pp. 413-414, for a careful discussion of this question). In terms of the present analysis, the fact that a trusting thanksgiving to God is indicated, whether or not this thanksgiving took the form of a Christian eucharist, is a central point for emphasis.

12. For a nuanced presentation of the view that the sending of God's salvation to the Gentiles is the common theme of the sea voyage and the interval on Malta, see

S. Praeder, "Acts 27:1-28:16: Sea Voyages in Ancient Literature and the Theology of Luke-Acts," *CBQ*, Vol 46 (1984), pp. 683-706.

13. At 27:37, Luke gives 276 as the number of persons on board; there is, however, no specification as to the respective numbers of soldiers, crew, and passengers.

14. In his comments on the Acts passages which bear upon the situation Paul faced in Rome, Sherwin-White (see pp. 108-119, especially p. 111 and 118) presumes that Paul's is a capital case on appeal. Paul's own statement in 28:18 that "there was no reason for the death penalty in my case" also seems to attest that capital charges were at issue. Parenthetically it should also be noted that in the speech at Pisidian Antioch (13:28), the same words are used—*aitian thanatou*—when Paul affirms that Jesus was given over for capital sentence despite there being "nothing deserving death" in the case presented against him.

15. BAGD cites Acts 28:20 as an instance in which handcuffing is meant. (*Halusis* literally means a chain and the question is whether what is envisioned is a chain around the wrists.) So also Schneider, II, p. 415. The same word occurs in the plural in 12:6-7 (where the context makes it clear that the chains do bind Peter's hands) and at 21:33 (where Lysias had Paul bound "with two chains" in an unspecified fashion). On the assumption that Luke understands the same type of chaining in all three instances, there is justification for concluding that handcuffing, and probably handcuffing to the soldier guarding Paul, is the image that Luke wishes to communicate in the present passage. (As previously indicated in n. 46 of chapter seven above, the term used to designate Paul's bonds in 20:23, 26:29, and 26:31 is *desma(ōn),* literally "chains."

16. In section five of this chapter, it will be argued that the Roman Christians are among those designated by the word *pantas* ("all") in Luke's concluding summary.

17. ZG indicates that *xenian* usually means "hospitality" but that it can be understood in this context (28:23) as having the meaning, "lodging." This is, in fact, the translation that the RSV employs.

18. In the estimation of some commentators, Paul is making an oblique reference to Jesus' resurrection when he uses the phrase "the hope of Israel." See, for example Schneider, II, p. 415, who draws attention to 26:6 and also 23:6 and 24:15.

19. In addition to the two nuances of Paul's speech that are highlighted in the text, his familiar reference to "the people" (*tō laō*) in 28:17 and his statement in 28:17 that he had no charge to bring against "my nation" (*tou ethnous mou*) also serve to indicate Paul's bonds with his audience.

20. In sections two and four of chapter seven, above, it was stressed that Paul did not capriciously bring his Roman citizenship to the fore or casually avail himself of his Roman prerogatives. Indeed Paul's words in 28:19 were cited at that time as an explicit indication that he only appealed to Caesar when he was forced or "compelled" (*enangkasthēn*) to do so. It is now also clear that the Paul Luke here describes does not view himself as having entered into this appeal for the purpose of doing vengeance to the Sanhedrin leaders or in any way bringing harm to the Jewish populace of Jerusalem.

The view that Luke may well understand Paul to be stressing this point as a means of countering any efforts to use the fact of his appeal in impugning his Jewish loyalty is given additional plausibility by the Jewish leaders's response in 28:21. There they reply, as if to set Paul's mind at rest on this point, "We have received no letters from Judea about you, and none of the brethren coming here has reported or spoken any evil about you."

21. Paul's precise words are that he was delivered "bound" (*desmios*) into the hands of the Romans. As Munck points out, p. 258, Paul here describes events in language

strikingly similar to that used by Agabus in his prophecy concerning Paul's fate in Jerusalem (21:11).

22. Haenchen sees correctly, p. 727, that Luke presents Paul following a remarkably conciliatory approach. However, Haenchen's phrase, "really no one is at fault," does not quite capture the nuances that Luke indicates. For, in a close reading of Luke's report, Paul is not portrayed indicating that no one has culpability but rather as refraining from any criticism of those who have wronged him.

23. The substance of verses 28:22-23 indicates that Paul created a favorable enough impression with the Jewish leaders that they were willing to come to his lodging a second time and to bring with them other members of the local Jewish community. However, a note of caution is also recorded. The leaders' reply to Paul does indicate that they consider the Christian movement negatively as a "sect" (*haireseōs*). In full, they state (28:22): "But we desire to hear from you what your views are; for with regard to this sect we know that everywhere it is spoken against."

24. The reactions which similar preaching evoked within the Jewish communities at these three places have been previously analyzed in chapter five.

25. While agreeing that Luke's use of *ēpistoun* indicates that a number of those present emphatically rejected, "disbelieved," Paul's message, commentators differ over how favorably disposed Luke portrays the other members of Paul's audience. Bruce, p. 531, favors a translation of "believed" while conceding that *epeithonto* does not necessarily mean more than "gave heed." In contrast Haenchen, p. 723, holds that Luke does not indicate that any of those present accepted Christianity while conceding that Luke does portray differences of opinion within the group. The RSV itself translates *epeithonto* as "were convinced."

While it does not seem possible, given the available data, to determine whether Luke understood some of those present as having come to Christian faith, a point which needs to be emphasized is that Luke clearly does distinguish a second group different from those who adamantly disbelieve Paul's teaching. Indeed, his use of *asumphōnoi* at 28:25 (when he states that "they disagreed among themselves" as they departed) further emphasizes the existence of two different responses. Regardless of whether those in the first group should be considered as having come to faith, it is clear that there is a significant difference between them and those who fully reject Paul's words. As a consequence of this emphasized difference, it seems clear that those in the first group are not to be considered subject to the indictment that Paul now proceeds to deliver against those in the latter group.

26. In his report of events at Pisidian Antioch (13:46-48), Luke first describes Paul's strong criticisms against a (presumably large) group of unbelieving Jews and his announcement to them that he would thereupon turn to the Gentiles with his message (this mission to the Gentiles having been authorized by the risen Jesus). Luke then expressly states that the Gentiles of the area accepted Paul's preaching with gladness.

Nevertheless, despite the severity of Paul's rebuke to these unbelieving Jews and despite the fact that he seemingly initiated his preaching to the Gentiles as a kind of reproach to them (such being the sense of Luke's report), it is important to recognize that Paul does subsequently resume his ministry among Jewish communities of other towns and cities. And given Luke's subsequent reports concerning this activity, it is not possible to conclude from 13:46-48 that Luke understood Paul to be definitively ending his mission among the Jews for the sake of a new mission exclusively among the Gentiles. Similarly despite Luke's reports describing similar developments at Corinth (18:6-7), it is still evident that he does not understand Paul making a definite break with his mission among the Jews at that stage of his ministry either.

While the various factors that bear upon the character of Paul's missions among Jews and Gentiles have been analyzed at some length in chapter five, the conclusion of that analysis—that the Paul of Acts never definitively turns from a ministry among Jews to a ministry among Gentiles—needs to be carried forward and upheld in the present circumstances. For, in the present case, not only does Luke *not* understand Paul to be announcing a definite end to his preaching to Jews, Luke actually understands at least some of those Jews present to be in the process of responding favorably to Paul's preaching.

The literature on this question is voluminous, but a good overview of the principal interpretations can be found in J. Sanders, "The Salvation of the Jews in Luke-Acts," in LANP, pp. 104-128. However for the reasons indicated above as well as those presented in the text, Sanders' own attempted resolution of the matter cannot be accepted.

27. Additional comments on the significance of *pantas* will be made in the following section.

28. The Greek underlying the RSV's "and he lived there" is *enemeinen,* from *emmenō,* literally, "to remain."

29. Many standard commentaries and studies fail to take proper account of the fact that, as Acts ends, Paul is prohibited from his usual free-moving ministry (O'Toole/ *Unity,* p. 165, even states that Paul is in "an ideal situation"). To be sure, Luke does portray Paul making the maximum use of the opportunities he still possesses and highlights his undaunted witness. However, there is still a considerable contrast between the image of Paul inviting guests to his lodging and greeting them chained and under guard and Luke's previous images of him engaging in open ministry in the synagogues, streets, and public places of various provincial cities.

30. In 28:30 the RSV translators have rendered *misthōmati* as "at his own expense" and a similar translation is also proposed by Lake and Cadbury, p. 348. However, Haenchen, p. 776 n. 2, observes that *misthōmati* need not mean that Paul has paid for these lodgings and he himself seemingly does not wish to go beyond the sense that Paul had some role in "finding" his own quarters.

31. Williams, p. 452, aptly describes the character of Paul's confinement with this term. In comparison with his account of the circumstances of Paul's imprisonment in Rome, Luke portrays a much more severe (overnight) confinement when he reports that the jailer at Philippi, following the magistrates's instructions, "put them into the inner prison and fastened their feet in the stocks" (16:24). At Caesarea Paul was kept in chains and imprisoned in Herod's praetorium (23:35b). However Felix also issued the following instructions: "Then he gave orders to the centurion that he should be kept in custody but should have some liberty, and that none of his friends should be prevented from attending to his needs" (24:23).

32. In his section treating Luke's date of writing and location, Fitzmyer/*Gospel,* I, p. 57, emphasizes that speculation regarding Luke's knowledge of Paul's subsequent fate must not be allowed to diminish the interpreter's attention to what Luke has actually written. Fitzmyer's comment also anticipates a conclusion of the present study concerning Paul's boldness in Rome: "The analysis of that ending should begin with what is there instead of speculation about what it should have contained. The boldness of Paul in his preaching, even in Rome, the capital of the empire in which Christianity was then feeling its way, was more important to Luke than any foreshadowing of the martyrdom of his hero."

33. The appearance of the three names, "Lord," "Jesus," and "Christ" in sequence is relatively rare within Acts (otherwise only in Peter's speech at 11:17, in the Jerusalem leaders' letter at 15:26 and in Paul's farewell address to the Ephesian leaders at 20:21) and there is no other instance in Acts in which these three names appear in a single verse together with a reference to the kingdom of God. (However, cf. 8:12 where Philip does preach about both "the kingdom of God" and "Jesus Christ" and also 28:23 where, in his second meeting with the Roman Jews, Paul testifies regarding "the kingdom of God" and "Jesus.") The "kingdom of God" is itself not as frequently used within Acts (cf. in addition, 1:3, 1:6, 14:22, 19:8, and 20:25) as it is within the Gospel.

34. In the paragraphs which follow, all five instances in which *parrēsia* appears as a noun within Acts will be treated. However, for a fuller appreciation of how "boldness" figures as a characteristic of Christian discipleship, consideration should also be given to the various forms of *parrēsiazomai* which occur at 9:27, 9:28, 13:46, 14:3, 18:26, 19:8 and 26:26. Neither *parrēsia* nor any forms of *parrēsiazomai* appear in Luke's Gospel.

35. Martin, p. 89, has also noticed that the RSV's "quite openly" does not do justice to the Greek. Martin understands the present phrase to emphasize Paul's personal confidence and points to Philippians 1:20 where the Greek is *en pasē parrēsia* and the RSV translates, "with full courage."

36. The other instance in which this term appears in the Lukan writings is at Acts 9:1 where Luke describes Paul as " . . . breathing threats [*apeilēs*] and murder against the disciples of the Lord . . . "

37. Acts 28:31 represents the only occurrence of this adverb within the New Testament writings. Hòwever *kōluō*, the related verb, appears with varying shades of meaning six times in the Gospel and six times in Acts as well as in eleven other places within the New Testament. LSJ gives "unhindered" as the meaning of the adverb, BAGD gives "without let or hindrance," and, as noted in the text, the RSV translation is "unhindered."

As indicated in the text, it is important to recognize that, within the setting of Luke's closing words, *akōlutōs* is linked with the preceding adverbial phrase, *meta pasēs parrēsias,* in describing the qualities of spirit with which Paul continued in his ministry. Thus, as long as "unhindered" is understood as indicating a quality that Paul possesses personally, the quality of being unhindered in spirit, undaunted or un-intimidated, then "unhindered" serves as an appropriate translation for *akōlutōs.*

38. To understand "unhindered" to mean that the Roman authorities were not constraining, not impeding, not hampering Paul is actually to turn Luke's meaning by 180 degrees. Regrettably such a reversal of Luke's intended meaning is all too prevalent with the standard commentaries and in leading articles on the ending of Acts. For example, Haenchen, p. 726, states: "This 'unhindered' shows the tolerance of Rome at that time towards the Christian message. That Rome should continue this policy is Luke's passionate desire, the fulfillment of which he wished to promote precisely in these last chapters." Similarly, although they contain several useful insights, this general misappreciation for the meaning of Luke's ending and for *akōlutōs* in particular is also characteristic of "Das letzte Wort der Apostelgeschichte" by G. Delling in *NT,* Vol 15:3 (1973), pp. 193-204 and in "The Unhindered Gospel" by F. Stagg in *RE,* Vol. 71 (1974), pp. 451-462.

39. In adverting to the fact that, at the end of Acts, the word of God remains "unfettered" despite Paul's chains, Marshall, p. 425, and Williams, p. 455, verge upon bringing Luke's closing "image" into clear focus. What additionally needs to be

emphasized is that the work of God was "unfettered" precisely because of Paul's *boldness* and his refusal to be daunted or intimidated by his chains. For, as Luke actually presents the situation, it is Paul's internal conviction and fortitude, apart from the attitude and the conduct of the Roman authorities, that explain his continuation in "preaching the kingdom of God and teaching about the Lord Jesus Christ."

Chapter Nine: Jesus, the Disciples of Jesus, and Roman Rule

1. In terms of its basic methodology this chapter carries the line of analysis indicated in chapter two forward to its logical conclusion. In effect, an attempt is being made to take the portrait of the apostles' social and political stance and the portrait of Paul's stance as they are given in Acts and place them alongside of the portrait that Luke has given of Jesus' stance in the Gospel.

The idea of explicitly concentrating upon the face value of the portrayal that a given gospel writer provides is not new and was explicitly proposed by E. Hobbs in the 1950s in "A Different Approach to the Writing of Commentaries on the Synoptic Gospels," an essay in the collection, *A Stubborn Faith,* ed. E. Hobbs (Dallas: SMU Press, 1956). However, to analyze the pictures of an evangelist specifically from the standpoint of their social and political dimensions—that may well be the principal methodological innovation made in the present study. Many of the standard commentaries now provide treatments of the "*Paulusbild*" and frequently the "*Petrusbild*" of Acts and thematic studies such as O'Toole/*Unity* have analyzed the continuity between Jesus and the disciples as it is portrayed in Luke's writings. While important insights about Luke's portraits of Jesus, Paul, and Peter can be gained from consulting these studies, it has been my concern to pursue systematically the social and political dimensions that frequently receive less than full attention.

2. The analysis which follows will focus upon the respective *behavior* of Paul and Jesus at their formal trials before Roman governors. However a related point that is also relevant for the analysis to be made in section eight of this chapter is the *similarity in the charges* that are brought against Jesus and Paul by the chief-priestly group.

At 23:2 of the Gospel Jesus is denounced before Pilate in the following terms: "We found this man perverting our nation, and forbidding us to give tribute to Caesar, and saying that he himself is Christ a king." And at 23:5 these charges are elaborated: "He stirs up the people, teaching throughout all Judea, from Galilee even to this place." At 24:5-6 of Acts the following charges are made at Paul's trial before Felix (RSV translation): "For we have found this man a pestilent fellow, an agitator among all Jews throughout the world, and a ringleader of the sect of the Nazarenes. He even tried to profane the temple. . . ."

In this connection the charges made against Paul and his associates at Thessalonica (previously considered in chapter six) are also of interest. Made not by the Jerusalem chief priests but rather by the unbelieving Jews of Thessalonica, they were phrased in the following way (17:6-7): "These men who have turned the world upside down have come here also, and Jason has received them; and they are all acting against the decrees of Caesar, saying that there is another king, Jesus."

3. In this context reference should also he made to Stephen's death as the death of another leading disciple. However, inasmuch as there is a certain lack of specificity in Luke's reports about the Sanhedrin's involvement in Stephen's death, his demise, although no less treacherously accomplished, seems appropriately kept separate from the other official actions against disciples.

Chapter Ten: Not Political Apologetic or Ecclesial Apologetic

1. Although he himself is primarily concerned to argue for what will be described below as the "ecclesial-apologetic" position, P. Walaskay, both in his dissertation and in the monograph developed from it, provides an extended overview of the political-apologetic approach and describes the widespread support that this approach has historically had within New Testament circles. Following Gasque, p. 21, Walaskay/ *Rome*, p. ix, identifies C. Heuman as a commentator who articulated a version of this position over 250 years ago. Walaskay then identifies and treats the views of a number of scholars who have followed this approach in the 19th and 20th centuries, including H. Cadbury and H. Conzelmann.

2. While they may differ in assigning dates for the composition of Acts, scholars who adopt the political-apologetic position commonly affirm that the situation in which Luke wrote was such as to call forth an apology. Bruce, p. 20, believes that an apology was required simply because of Christianity's controversial origins and does not explicitly postulate the phenomenon of external persecutions. Nevertheless, his general statement could also be affirmed by those who hold that the Christians of Luke's day were suffering persecution: "When we examine the way in which Luke develops his narrative, we can hardly fail to be struck by his apologetic emphasis, especially in the second volume. He is concerned to defend Christianity against the charges which were popularly brought against it in the second half of the first century."

3. The presentation to be made in the sections which follow is thus intended to articulate the political-apologetic position in a far more developed form than can be found in the writings of Cadbury, Bruce, Conzelmann, Haenchen, Munck (pp. lvii-lviii), Martin (p.4), and other leading commentators who have accepted at least some version of this theory.

Maddox, p. 93, takes the following as characteristic elements of the political-apologetic approach: "The theory of a political apology in Luke-Acts rests on two contentions: first, that Luke emphasizes the political innocence of the Christians, from Jesus himself onwards; second, that Luke portrays Roman officials in a favorable light, or as friendly to the Christians (and thus indirectly urges the officials of his own day to follow the example of their predecessors)." In what follows, the two contentions identified by Maddox will be discussed as well as several additional points.

4. This phrase, sometimes taken as an indication of the fact that Luke was concerned to have Christianity be viewed as an above-board, public movement, was used by Paul in his response to Festus and Agrippa at 26:26. Hengel, p. 60, makes reference to this passage in stating:"Christians are not an anarchical, amoral, hole-in-a-corner sect, which shrinks back from public gaze" (Acts 26:26).

5. E. Haenchen, C. Williams, and H. Conzelmann are but three of many contemporary commentators on Acts who correctly affirm that Luke does not portray the disciples as revolutionaries, but then incorrectly leap to the conclusion that the disciples are thereby portrayed as socially and politically harmless. In his commentary, Haenchen affirms (p. 105): "Luke was most anxious to impress upon his readers that the Roman authorities treated the Christian missionaries with benevolence and acknowledged them to be politically harmless." And in a separate essay (see "The Book of Acts as Source Material for the History of Early Christianity," in SLA, p. 278), he states the following: "Rome, then, should not get embroiled against the Christians and their mission in which there is nothing subversive."

Similarly, in his comments upon the contents of Lysias' letter, C. Williams states (p.

252): "Luke stresses again that Roman officials found the faith harmless." (In a passing comment on p. 258, Williams also expresses a similar view.) And, in the same vein, Conzelmann/*Apostel,* p. 10, affirms that Luke shows the Christian message not "touching upon" or "engaging" the realm of the empire.

6. Drawing upon Ulpian (from whom comes the phrase, *pacata atque quieta*) and other Roman writers, G. de Ste. Croix, "Why Were the Early Christians Persecuted?" *PP,* Vol 26 (1963), pp. 6-38, especially p. 16, provides an insightful discussion of the attitude that provincial governors would have toward those who disturbed a province's peaceful and settled character. Such disturbers should be considered *mali homines,* and governors were advised to rid their provinces of them.

7. Cadbury/*Making,* pp. 311-312, is among those commentators who suggest that, from the Roman point of view, Luke took the edge off of his reports of the disciples' arrests by laying the blame upon Jews: "There is the constant explanation that the Jews took the initiative . . . Throughout the Book of Acts is emphasized the recurrent initiative of the Jews."

Conzelmann also voices a similar assessment, both in his *Theology* and also in his essay, "Luke's Place in the Development of Early Christianity," in SLA. In the former study appears (p. 144): "And in the background there is always the fact that it is the Jews who are continually causing public disturbances. It is they who need to be watched by the authorities, not the Christians." And in the latter (p. 301): "There is a certain contradiction between theory and practice which cannot remain hidden from the reader. Of course Luke takes care to eliminate it by presenting the Jews as the initiators of the persecution. In this he is a precursor of the apologists (Justin!)."

Similarly, Bruce, p. 21, also indiscriminately lumps Paul's Jewish opponents together and sees Luke laying most of the blame for disturbances at their feet: "How then, it might be asked, was the advance of Christianity attended by so much strife and disorder? Luke arraigns the Jewish authorities as responsible for this. It was the Jerusalem Sanhedrin who prosecuted Jesus before Pilate and Paul before Felix and Festus; and most of the disturbances which broke out when the gospel was proclaimed in the Roman provinces were fomented by local Jewish communities, who refused to accept the gospel themselves and were annoyed when their Gentile neighbors believed it."

8. Because the point itself is a significant one and because it is also important to distinguish the conclusions reached in the present study from those which are commonly held by leading commentators on Luke-Acts, it is well to indicate at some length the analyses that scholars such as Cadbury and Haenchen have made in this regard.

Clearly the findings made in the preceding chapters of this study contravene many of the specific and general conclusions that Cadbury/*Making,* pp. 308-309, 313, relies on in arguing that Acts portrays the disciples of Jesus receiving exoneration: "Still more patent is Luke's defense of Christianity from charges brought against it as breaking Roman law" . . . "Luke appears to be interested in the charges, but he is more interested in the verdict. The Romans find no fault in Jesus or his followers." . . . "The Roman magistrates recognized that it was a Jewish controversy. The matters were not justiciable, or were so obscure that procurators and proconsuls could not fathom them. So Gallio drove Paul's Jewish accusers from the judgment seat while the procurators Felix and Festus tried to put them off with delays and alternatives much as Pilate had tried to do."

In the same way the findings made in the preceding chapters contravene many of the assertions (the general statement and many of the specific assertions) made by Haenchen in the following passage (p. 102): "On the other hand Christianity does not imply any transgression of Roman laws. Consequently the intelligent representatives of Rome always took a benevolent view of the Christian mission: the procurator Sergius Paulus lets himself be converted; the procurator Gallio dismisses a Jewish complaint against Paul; some of the Asiarchs (whose office it was to promote the cult of the emperor) are friendly with Paul; the town-clerk of Ephesus defends the Christians against the charge of profanation; the tribune of Jerusalem, Claudius Lysias, likewise the governors Felix and Festus, refuse to condemn Paul out of hand; and as a prisoner in Rome Paul is allowed to carry on his missionary work unhindered—indeed that very word, *akōlutōs,* is the last word in the book, standing as the summation of past experience and a recommendation in respect of future policy."

Significantly, although he adds a note bidding the reader to consider the assessment just quoted from Haenchen, J. Jervell himself rightly expresses reservation about this interpretation (p. 157): "But more important is the portrayal of Roman officials which Luke presents in Chapters 22ff. According to common opinion, Luke describes the Romans as well-disposed toward the church. It is clear, however, that the Roman officials frequently appear in a somewhat unfortunate light in Luke's work—a curious way of proceeding vis-à-vis the court whose understanding or protection is being sought."

It should also be noted that, although Jervell does not systematically develop his own analysis in this area, he clearly does have misgivings about other conclusions traditionally reached by proponents of political apologetic (cf., p. 167).

9. Walaskay/*Rome,* p. 50, is not alone in the view that Luke was especially concerned to exploit the fact of Paul's standing as a citizen: "As a Roman citizen Paul was the perfect spokesman to defend Christian political loyalty in a Roman court."

10. Roman officials who valued their own citizenship and expected citizens facing such circumstances to declare their identity could only have been disoriented by Paul's failure to do so in this instance. Presumably these readers' sympathies would have been with Lysias some verses later when the tribune is shocked to find out that Paul is indeed a citizen. Why did Paul not reveal this when Lysias was initially investigating? Did Paul not realize that Lysias needed this information in order to know that he could not proceed to handle Paul's case as that of an ordinary provincial?

Haenchen, p. 635, argues that Luke actually constructed these scenes so as to highlight dramatically the fact that Paul possesses citizenship and also sees Paul's response about possessing his citizenship from birth as contributing to Luke's emphasis. But what group does Haenchen think that Luke is trying to impress with such a presentation? Seemingly, although this is not explicitly stated, Haenchen understands Luke's Roman readers to be the interested recipients of this information. However, such a view requires Luke to have thought that his readers would not look upon Paul with suspicion for having initially withheld this information from Lysias. Such a view also requires that Luke be altogether unmindful about the way in which other elements in his narrative would have generated reservations and misgivings about Paul in his Roman readers' minds.

11. The significance of the charges that Luke portrays Paul's opponents making against him at Thessalonica (17:7) has been underscored above in chapter six. However it is not inappropriate to state again at this juncture that there is "the color of truth" to the charge that Paul is loyal to "another king." Encountering this charge in the context of Paul's own numerous references to Jesus as his "Lord," Luke's Roman readers could

only have found reason to wonder about the exact character of Paul's loyalty to their own "lord," the emperor.

12. It is in connection with his own view that Luke is writing to Christians to instruct them regarding right conduct toward the Roman state (this line of analysis will be given further attention in the concluding "ecclesial-apologetic" section of this chapter) that Maddox, p. 96, summarizes Paul's stance toward the Roman state. However this summary can also be regarded as expressing an assessment that is congenial to the political-apologetic approach: "[Luke] is emphasizing that Paul, though accused of civil disruption by both Romans and Jews . . . and the object of violent jealousy on the part of Greeks, . . . had always behaved with honor and respect towards the state."

While not totally lacking plausibility in terms of the text of Acts (for as observed above, Paul is generally respectful and cooperative in his dealings with Roman officials), general summaries of this sort must still ultimately be rejected on the grounds of failing to capture the essence of the approach that Luke portrays Paul following. For such an assessment implies that Paul's fundamental stance was to accommodate his preaching and his ministry to the expectations and policies of Roman officials. And, as argued above, Paul's fundamental stance was not accommodation.

13. A straightforward articulation of this assumption is given by H. Conzelmann who states: "In the end it is confidence in the justice of the Emperor that forms the great climax of the narrative. There is no suggestion whatever of any weakening of this confidence" (Conzelmann/*Theology,* p. 144). From a slightly different perspective, a similar view is also adopted by Walaskay/Dissertation, p. 244.

14. It has been pointed out by Cadbury (see n. 5 of chapter eight above) that, while using several different terms to refer to the emperor to whom Paul appeals, Luke never indicates the *name* of this emperor. Indeed, his failure to do so is all the more noticeable given the fact that he has mentioned Augustus (2:1) and Tiberius (3:1) by name in the Gospel and Claudius by name at 11:28 and 18:2 of Acts.

While there are certainly other explanations for such an omission, it is conceivable that such an omission (if it was a conscious omission) indicates misgivings on Luke's part regarding this particular emperor (Nero). At the very least, the fact that Luke does not give the name of this particular emperor calls for additional investigations concerning the precise "Kaisarbild" of Luke-Acts.

15. Paul's use of this term at 28:19 has already been analyzed in section four of chapter eight.

16. Haenchen, pp. 106-197, affirms that Luke has artfully achieved a favorable portrait of Roman justice from Gallio at Corinth to Festus at Caesarea. Similarly, Cadbury scarcely seems to advert to any Roman failings in offering the following assessment of the circumstances under which Paul sailed to Rome: "For the biographer such details more than cancel the superficial impression that Paul suffered as a malefactor. His journey to Rome is recorded not as the commitment of a criminal, but as the appeal to the supreme court of an innocent man enjoying from Roman officials all the privileges of citizenship" (Cadbury/*Making,* p. 314).

Also, although he wishes to remain at a certain distance from those who affirm political apologetic, Walaskay too is convinced that Luke has described just treatment being accorded to Jesus and Paul: "*The empire which has exonerated Jesus and saved Paul* can continue to sustain the work of the church through its public administration and services, legal apparatus and protection" (Walaskay/*Rome,* p. 66; emphasis added).

17. In a number of cases the contrast between "Roman justice" and "Jewish

justice" or "Roman order" and "Jewish disorder" is expressed subtly or implicitly. Marshall (who generally exercises a certain reserve in the subject area of political apologetic) does not emphasize this contrast when he treats Paul's appearances before Gallio and the Jerusalem Sanhedrin. However, in commenting upon Paul's treatment by Festus and Agrippa, he states the following: "The effect of the scene as a whole is to emphasize the uprightness of Roman legal proceedings against the partiality and injustice of the Jews . . ." (p. 386).

A similar emphasis upon the higher standards of Roman justice can also be seen in the assessments that various commentators make of Gallio's performance. In such cases the proconsul's anti-semitism is frequently disregarded and it is simply summarized that Luke presents Gallio as a model dispenser of Roman justice who administers Paul's case in such an evenhanded way that Paul's opponents are thrown into confusion. (See, for example, Conzelmann/*Apostel,* p. 107, who also wishes to argue that Luke is suggesting to his Roman readers that they take Gallio's response as a model to follow in disputes involving Christians and Jews.)

18. In presenting his own "ecclesial-apologetic" interpretation, Wilson, p. 38, explicitly affirms that the apostles' two statements before the Sanhedrin run counter to the political-apologetic position. Indeed, as a sign of the importance he attaches to them, Wilson quotes both statements in his text at this point.

19. Barrett, p. 63, states perceptively that much of Acts would have seemed to be so much "theological and ecclesiastical rubbish" to Roman officials and on this basis he argues against the political-apologetic position. From the standpoint of the present analysis, Barrett is correct to affirm that much of Acts would have been confusing to Roman readers and correct in taking this factor as grounds for arguing against the political-apologetic position. However, as indicated above, there are even more substantive reasons for arguing against the political-apologetic position: elements and statements which are so obvious within Acts that they would not have been overlooked by Roman readers even though these same readers might have found other parts of the narrative confusing.

20. The argument concerning Luke's "Zealot" reference is admittedly much stronger on the supposition of a post-70 A.D. date for Acts. Nevertheless the argument still has force in the context of an earlier date of composition if it is assumed that information regarding the Zealots and their activities had reached Rome in the years prior to the fullscale uprising in A.D. 66.

21. See Cassidy/*Jesus,* p. 130.

22. At various places in the present study and in *Jesus, Politics, and Society,* it has been emphasized that Luke does *not* portray Jesus and his followers adopting the violent approach of the Zealots. Nevertheless a point to be noticed in the present context is that, within Acts, Luke does portray Herod Agrippa I treating two of the apostles, James and Peter, as though they were highly dangerous. (In addition to his report that Agrippa I executed James, it is significant that Luke portrays the king keeping Peter under high security with "four squads of soldiers to guard him.")

While such references do not undermine Luke's portrait of Jesus and his followers as nonviolent, they, along with Luke's mention that Simon possessed a Zealot connection, do show that Luke was not scrupulously concerned to distance *his* Christians from events and associations that might possibly be disquieting to Roman officials.

23. It should be observed at the outset that the position that has been referred to in the text as the "ecclesial-apologetic" position is not necessarily incompatible with the political-apologetic position even though each position affirms a distinct line of "movement."

As indicated previously, what the political-apologetic position affirms is that Luke wrote to the officials of the empire to show them the "goodness" of Christianity. In contrast,what the ecclesial-apologetic position affirms is that Luke wrote to his fellow Christians (*ad ecclesiam*) to show them the "goodness" of the Roman system. But could Luke have combined both kinds of apology in a single work? It can be argued that such an enterprise is theoretically possible and P. Walaskay is an example of a commentator who seems to verge on adopting such a view. As indicated in the notes below, Walaskay argues energetically on behalf of the ecclesial-apologetic position throughout his works. However, at the same time, he also seems to accept key arguments made by proponents of political apologetic (see Walaskay/*Rome,* p. 37 and pp. 65-67).

Obviously, individual commentators on Acts will differ in the degree of support that they accord to one or other of these positions and will sometimes alternately affirm aspects of both positions without necessarily distinguishing the lines of "movement" that their support for a given aspect tends to imply.

It should also be noted that there are commentators who, at least implicitly, point to still another line of "movement." Talbert, for example, argues (on p. 95, after having cited points pertaining to political apologetic and ecclesial apologetic) that Luke views Paul's appeal to his citizenship in order to avoid whipping as providing later Christians with authorization to invoke their legal rights as a protection against injustice. In effect,Talbert is thereby arguing that Luke wrote to his fellow Christians to instruct them *regarding their conduct in the empire.* As such this argument is clearly distinct from the argument that Luke wrote to his fellow Christians to persuade them about the goodness of the empire (the ecclesial-apologetic argument).

Similarly while affirming aspects of the ecclesial-apologetic and political-apologetic positions, O'Toole/*Unity,* p. 166, also states the following: ". . . Luke advocates taking full advantage of the Roman policy. His principle would be: Christians should use every available legal means to protect themselves."

24. It should be noticed that the arguments which Walaskay, Wilson, and Maddox make on the subject of Roman justice in Acts are at once similar and dissimilar to those made by leading proponents of political apologetic. The similarity arises from the fact that appeal is made to many of the same passages in Acts. The dissimilarity arises from the fact that Luke is now alleged to be counseling his fellow Christians to look favorably upon the Roman empire because the empire affords them fair and just treatment.

On Luke's portrayal of Roman justice Walaskay thus writes the following (Walaskay/*Rome,* p. 59): "The fair and just legal system of the empire, only hinted at in Jesus' trial, was clearly presented in the trials of Paul. Time and again when Paul and his companions were brought to the authorities for disciplinary action, they were protected by the process of Roman law. Even when due process was neglected, as in Thessalonica, the magistrates quickly remedied the situation when challenged by Paul." And on the implications of this portrayal, Walaskay writes the following (ibid., p. 58): "From beginning to end, Luke has designed his work to aid the Christian community in its understandings of the workings of the empire so that the church may begin to develop a dialogue with the local magistrates. Christians, like Paul, need not feel intimidated by untrue accusations nor anxious about being dealt with fairly."

In the same vein Wilson, p. 39, also alleges Luke's favorable portrayal of Roman justice and Luke's intention of urging cooperation (within certain limits) with the Roman state: "On this view the message would be that the Roman authorities are just and fair; they treat all citizens with impartiality and will not allow anyone to be arraigned on false charges. Christians have no need to fear civic authorities, and if they get on quietly with their own business, Rome will leave them alone. The great figures of the past stand as examples of good Christian citizenship. However, if things go awry, and there is an attempt by political authorities to ban them from confessing and propagating their faith, they are bound to stand by their prior commitment to God."

Finally, although he does make the qualifying observation that Luke shows the death of Jesus to be due in part to "the failure of Roman integrity" and also introduces other qualifications, Maddox, p. 96, still does affirm that, in Luke's portrayal, Jesus and the disciples "respect the state and seek to collaborate with its constructive purposes, and indeed entrust their own safety to its justice." Maddox then summarizes, p. 97: "This, I think, provides an adequate explanation of Luke's care to draw attention to the political innocence of the Christians, and to take on the whole an optimistic view of the imperial government. And it is an explanation which fits in harmoniously with what we have so far learned from the study of other aspects of Luke's purpose. Luke wishes to reveal to his fellow-Christians in his own day the nature of their life and calling in Christ. The proper business of Christians is to live at peace with the sovereign power, so far as is possible, and not to play the hero. In order to encourage such an attitude, it was necessary for Luke to hold up before his readers the example of their great leaders, especially Jesus and Paul, and (like Paul and the author of 1 Peter) to take the best possible view of the regime."

25. As with Roman justice, the position on the Roman military that is adopted by Walaskay, a leading proponent of ecclesial apologetic, is at once similar and dissimilar from the position adopted by proponents of political apologetic. Many of the same passages concerning the Roman military in Acts are cited. However, in this case, the argument is not primarily that the Roman officials would be pleased to see their military portrayed so favorably. Rather it is that the Christians of Luke's day were being encouraged to view the Roman military positively and appreciatively. See Walaskay/ Dissertation, pp. 250-251, and Walaskay/*Rome*, p. 62, on these points and also on the specific point that Luke saw the cooperation of Paul and Julius "in fulfilling their mutual salvation" as a model for the Christians of his day.

26. In the context of a much longer list of Acts passages which he cites in arguing that Luke wishes to indicate to his fellow Christians that a cooperative stance toward the empire was desirable, Wilson, p. 36, makes mention of the fact that the centurion Cornelius becomes a Christian in Acts 10-11 and the proconsul of Cyprus a convert in Acts 13:6-12.

Haenchen, writing from the perspective of political apologetic, attaches even more significance to these passages and what he writes can, *mutatis mutandis,* also be considered from the standpoint of ecclesial apologetic. Commenting on Luke's account of Sergius Paulus' conversion, he writes as follows (p. 405): "Luke's story . . . serves several purposes. First it shows that at the outset of the Pauline mission the highest Roman authority of a province, the proconsul 'came to the faith.' What better *apologia* for Christianity could there be? . . . But we could actually refer back to the story of Cornelius: the first Gentile convert was actually a Roman officer."

At this juncture, while discussing the general issue of the portrayal of Roman officials/officers within Acts, it is also desirable to make mention of the position adopted by J. O'Neill. O'Neill does not argue that Luke portrayed Roman leaders coming to faith in order to encourage other Roman officials to tolerate Christianity (a political-apologetic argument). Nor does he argue that Luke shows them embracing the faith in order to persuade Christians to recognize that the Roman empire provided them with favorable climate for expansion (an ecclesial-apologetic argument). Rather it is O'Neill's contention, p. 58 and pp. 169-173, that Luke actually presented such accounts because he wished to persuade large numbers of educated Romans to become Christians.

The following statement thus expresses O'Neill's view (p. 171): "But Acts was not only designed to show that Christianity had a far greater claim to recognition than Judaism; it demonstrated by the examples of Cornelius and Sergius Paulus (and Publius, Acts 28.7ff) that some well-placed Romans had already adopted it as their faith in the earliest days. . . . What the Jews had rejected was now an open possibility for the Romans. The fact that educated Romans could believe and had believed was a strong argument for others to follow their example."

Having reached this conclusion (it should be noted once again that, like many others who focus on the passages concerning Sergius Paulus and Cornelius, O'Neill pays scant attention to the other passages in Acts in which Roman officials respond to the Christian message in less favorable ways), O'Neill then proceeds to argue that Luke furthered his evangelistic purposes through other means as well, including that of political apologetic (see pp. 172-173 for his argument that political apologetic should be regarded as subsidiary to Luke's primary evangelistic concern).

27. As the citations contained in n. 24 above indicate, there is a tendency for commentators to concentrate so intensively upon what is said in Acts concerning Roman legal *procedures* that they neglect to give proper attention to the fact that Acts also shows that just *outcomes* do not materialize from these procedures. In the end, to establish the existence of apology *ad ecclesiam,* it is not sufficient to emphasize that Luke shows Roman procedures enabling Paul to avoid a whipping and to make a personal appeal to the emperor. Far more significant is what actually happens to Paul once he is under arrest. For longer than four years he wears a Roman chain and is restricted from his former ministry. And as Acts ends Paul has still not been effectively vindicated.

28. It is the burden of this note and the one which follows to emphasize that Luke shows Paul witnessing to Jesus and to the message of Jesus regardless of whether he is constrained or abetted by the actions of Roman officials and Roman officers. Clearly Paul is aided by Julius the centurion in several instances. However within Luke's framework, it is clearly the sovereign power of Jesus and Paul's faithful response to Jesus as his Lord that are of primary importance in an explanation of how Paul came to witness in Rome. Thus, contra Walaskay/Dissertation, p. 250, and Walaskay/*Rome,* p. 62, the gospel was not, in any meaningful way, "saved" by Julius, an agent of the empire.

29. Walaskay/Dissertation, p. 251 (see also the modified statement in Walaskay/*Rome,* p. 62) thus moves well beyond the sense of Luke's narrative in stating: "Paul must (*dei*) bear witness in Rome and Julius would make sure that he did. The representative of the state and the representative of Christ have worked together not only for their mutual salvation but for the preservation of the Christian message and imperial justice."

30. As indicated in the text, attempting to number Tiberius Felix among the Roman officials who respond favorably to Christian preaching immediately dilutes the force of the argument. Similar considerations also come into play with respect to the possibility that Herod Agrippa II could be assigned to such a group. (At 26:27 Paul does attempt to bring Agrippa to faith. However, the reply Agrippa gives in 26:28 can hardly be taken as an expression of belief.)

In the end, then, there are only two Roman officials/officers who respond positively to the Christian message. Luke details Peter's conversion of Cornelius the centurion at great length and he also reports that Sergius Paulus, the proconsul of Cyprus came to believe in the wake of Paul's preaching and his vanquishment of Bar-Jesus.

31. It is thus the case that the pattern which Luke shows in the response of Roman officials is not materially different from the pattern that he indicates for Jews and for Gentiles who are not Romans. In all three groups there are those who respond favorably, those who are unmoved, and those who respond in a hostile manner.

Chapter Eleven: Allegiance to Jesus and Witness before Kings and Governors

1. This point has previously been adverted to but bears repeating in the present context. Similarly, it is also appropriate to refer again to Harnack's characterization of Luke as "an enthusiast for Christ" (see Cassidy/*Jesus*, p. 7 and n. 26).

2. The argument that Christians and those drawing close to faith comprised the core of Luke's intended audience will be presented in somewhat fuller form in section two, below. However, at the present juncture it is worth observing that one consequence of the rejection of the political-apologetic theory is that Luke's prefaces should be regarded as primarily directed to Christians. (In this view Theophilus himself is a Christian or someone proximate to faith.) When the prefaces are so regarded, Luke's words, particularly in the Gospel preface, are easily understood to mean that he wishes to write an account that will strengthen his readers and hearers in their faith and confirm them in their allegiance to Jesus.

3. A definite implication of the present study is that Luke held Jesus' approach to be of fundamental consequence for the Christians of his day. However, as observed in chapter nine and in other places in the preceding chapters, Luke does not portray the apostles or Paul adopting the approach he has attributed to Jesus in every facet, e.g., he does not portray them carrying forward with Jesus' ministry to tax collectors and sinners. Presumably, then, the Christians of Luke's day also possessed a certain latitude with respect to the manner in which they would appropriate Jesus' approach.

4. It should be observed at this point that the present theory has been formulated in such a way as to leave open the question of whether Luke and/or any of those in his immediate audience were in situations in which persecutions were being mounted by the Roman authorities. Throughout this chapter the perspective adopted is that Luke was interested in communicating to his readers that Jesus and his leading disciples had witnessed faithfully before a variety of Roman officials. However, assuming a situation in which the Christians of Luke's day were suffering systematic persecution is not a precondition for asserting that Luke was concerned to emphasize the faithfulness of Paul and the faithfulness of Jesus and the apostles in their testimony before various officials.

5. In addition to wanting his readers to be familiar with instructions pertaining to trial witness that had come from Jesus, Luke also presumably wished them to be knowledgeable concerning the approach that Paul had adopted in his own encounters with the political authorities.

The fact that Luke portrays Paul interacting cooperatively with his judges on various occasions has already been commented upon at several junctures. It had also been noted above that, under special circumstances, Paul sometimes availed himself of rights that he possessed as a citizen under Roman law. Similarly Luke also describes one instance in which Paul forcefully rebuked a Roman governor for failing to handle Paul's case properly. Conceivably these specific points (along with the major theme of Paul's faithfulness) may also have been on the list of concerns that Luke wished to share with his readers.

6. When the reader of Luke-Acts takes time to review systematically all of Luke's reports concerning Jesus, the apostles, and Paul before various political officials, one of the principal insights which emerges is that there is no particular pattern as far as the *outcomes* of these proceedings. In other words, Luke's accounts do not show either that the central Christian figures invariably experienced a harsh outcome or that they inevitably experienced a safe passing through. My own sensitivity to this aspect of Luke's descriptions has been greatly enhanced as a consequence of my presence at trials and proceedings involving members of Christian peace groups, particularly those of Fr. Thomas G. Lumpkin. For his consistently nonviolent civil disobedience, Fr. Lumpkin has: 1) been convicted as dangerous to the public order and sentenced to prison; 2) been convicted and given a suspended sentence; 3) been found not guilty of the charges and 4) had the charges against him dismissed on procedural grounds.

7. While the focus of this particular study is almost exclusively upon the allegiance-witness theory, it is not the position of the present writer that concerns in the area circumscribed by the theory were the only concerns influencing Luke. Perhaps the most effective way for quickly gaining a sense of the variegated concerns that Luke undoubtedly possessed is to consult one of the recent surveys of literature on him. (See, for example, E. Richard, "Luke—Writer, Theologian, Historian: Research and Orientation of the 1970s," *BTB,* Vol 13 [1983], pp. 3-15.) Nevertheless, it *would be* the present writer's view that, before any purpose is accepted as authentically Lukan, it should first be critically assessed according to an explicitly articulated set of methodological criteria.

The three methodological questions utilized in the present evaluation are certainly not the only criteria which can be employed in such an evaluation. (For example, despite the fact that Luke's prologues are framed in general terms, there is merit to W. Gasque's stipulation, p. 303, that Luke's prologues be taken seriously before a given purpose is ascribed to him. See also S. Brown, "The Role of the Prologues in Determining the Purpose of Luke-Acts," in PLA, pp. 99-111, and R. Dillon, "Previewing Luke's Project from His Prologue (Luke 1:1-4)," *CBQ,* Vol 43 (1981), pp. 205-227.) However the present three criteria do provide a basis for a systematic and orderly assessment and, for this reason, warrant serious consideration.

8. It was for this reason that in chapter ten no effort was expended in discussing the political-apologetic and ecclesial-apologetic theories according to the other two methodological criteria. Proponents of both theories have attempted to show that each congrues well with the presumed circumstances of Luke's audience, but this putative congruence cannot be sustained given what is actually present within Luke's text.

9. If Paul's testimony before Claudius Lysias and the witness that he gave to Julius throughout his journey to Rome are added to this estimate, the phenomenon of Paul's witness before Roman officials in Acts (military as well as political officials) is even more striking.

10. While this statement correctly highlights the fact that Paul's ministry after Ephesus failed to produce full-fledged converts, it should not be forgotten that Luke does describe Paul's subsequent preaching as having a considerable impact upon different audiences, e.g., some of the Gentile inhabitants of Malta and some of the Jews who visited Paul in Rome.

11. Maddox, pp. 66-67 and p. 76 (citing C. Burchard), observes that the image of Paul as missionary and maker of converts recedes as the Acts narrative moves forward and suggests that Luke wished his readers to remember Paul the prisoner even more

than Paul the missionary. From one standpoint Maddox's analysis is congenial to the present interpretation; however a significant difference resides in the fact that Maddox treats the block of material from 21:27 to 28:31, the material from Paul's arrest onward, as constituting a separate and distinct category. Such a separation fails to recognize the significance of the testimony that Paul has given before various political officials in the preceding chapters of Luke's account. Indeed Maddox classifies this earlier material under the heading of Paul's "missionary" activity.

12. The possibilities for dates and places given in the text are meant to be suggestive rather than exhaustive. Although individual commentators frequently argue on behalf of specific dates and/or places, almost all recognize that certainty in these matters is not achievable. See, for example, Williams, pp. xxiv-xxvi.

13. The subject of the communities for which Luke wrote and/or the community structures which Luke reflects in his writings has attracted considerable attention in recent scholarship (see for example, R. Schnackenburg, "Lukas als Zeuge verschiedener Gemeindestrukturen," *BL,* Vol 12 [1971], pp. 232-247; E. LaVerdiere and W. Thompson, "New Testament Communities in Transition: a Study of Matthew and Luke," *TS,* Vol 37 [1976], pp. 567-597; and especially R. Karris, "Missionary Communities: a New Paradigm for the Study of Luke-Acts," *CBQ,* Vol 41 [1979], pp. 80-97). As a consequence, a number of stimulating proposals have been advanced relative to the internal character of these Christian communities and their presumed external relationship with Judaism and with the surrounding Hellenistic culture.

While the accent of the present analysis falls upon the presumed impact of Roman rule upon those who comprised Luke's audience, such an accent should not be taken to indicate any lack of appreciation for other influences that were undoubtedly operative upon the Christian communities of Luke's day. Indeed as a means of emphasizing this latter point, the words of Paul Minear are again appropriately adverted to: " . . . Luke was responding to multiple problems with multiple 'intentions.' His conversation with his readers moved on several levels" (from P. Minear, "Dear Theo: The Kerygmatic Intention and Claim of the Book of Acts," *INT,* Vol 27 (1973), p. 132; cited in Cassidy/ *Motive,* p. 147).

14. That Jesus' "scandalous" crucifixion carried significant consequences for Luke and his fellow Christians has previously been adverted to in Cassidy/*Motive,* pp. 146-147. What can now be elaborated is that these consequences were presumably both "internal" and "external" to the life of the Christian community. Seemingly Christians intent on clarifying their own self-identity would almost necessarily have valued information concerning the circumstances of Jesus' crucifixion. And it must also be supposed that Jesus' crucifixion would have been a primary subject in their contacts, hostile or benevolent, with Roman officials and others in the populations around them.

15. When the subject of Luke's sources for Acts is viewed from the perspective of the allegiance-witness theory, a number of factors present themselves for consideration. Clearly there is a great amount of material in Acts documenting Paul's appearances before Roman officials and, as argued above, it seems highly probable that Luke possessed a definite personal interest in such reports.

But did Luke's sources also evidence such an interest in the subject of Christian testimony before political officials? While such a question cannot ultimately be resolved, it is indeed an interesting one for speculation. In effect, the issue is whether there were disciples at Philippi, at Thessalonica, at Corinth, and at other centers of Christian life who provided Luke with reports that especially emphasized Paul's dealings with the political authorities of those places. For it is conceivable that Luke may have found that his own interest in such matters was nurtured and affirmed as a consequence of the very reports that were entrusted to him.

16. Cassidy/*Jesus,* pp. 1-4. However, see J. Tyson, "Source Criticism and the Gospel of Luke," in PLA, pp. 24-39, for a study which effectively delineates the difficulties involved in trying to determine Luke's sources for his Gospel.

17. As discussed in Cassidy/*Jesus,* pp. 60-61, the task of unraveling Luke's process of composition is further complicated by the fact that Luke previously portrayed Jesus giving similar instructions in 12:11-12, a passage which lacks a precise parallel in Mark. Nevertheless it is still possible to presume that Luke had access to Mark 13:9-13 when he wrote 21:12-19. And on this assumption it is significant that he did elect to incorporate substantial elements from Mark's report in his own final version. Indeed had Luke done *nothing more* than incorporate Mark's report without alteration, such a step would in and of itself have provided support for the allegiance-witness theory.

18. Because of the complex nature of the relationship between the two passages, readers are advised to assess the analysis which follows with a gospel synopsis in front of them. It should also be noted at the outset that, over and beyond the alterations which Luke may be presumed to make for his allegiance-witness purposes, there are also a number of other changes which can be observed. (See Fitzmyer/*Gospel,* II, p. 1328 and p. 1340 for an explanation of why Luke may have omitted the material contained in Mark 13:10 and why he may not have been satisfied with Mark's reference to the Holy Spirit's role in 13:11.) Nevertheless, most of the modifications and additions which Luke accomplishes do seem to be readily explicable within the framework of the allegiance-witness theory.

First, in contrast with Mark 13:12-13, Luke 21: 16-19 makes it much clearer that Jesus is referring to experiences which will befall the disciples themselves, e.g., Luke's Jesus is much more explicit on the point that the disciples will experience betrayal by family members on the occasion of their trials and he is much more explicit on the point that some of them will experience death.

Secondly, Luke's Jesus also gives a much more definite counsel regarding the approach that the disciples should follow at the time of their interrogations. They are consciously to adopt the approach of not planning beforehand what to say. In Mark, Jesus' words are not quite so explicit and emphatic on this point.

Finally, there are also a number of lesser changes which also may reflect the sensibilities of a writer with allegiance-witness concerns. Luke changes Mark's "governors and kings" to "kings and governors." Does this change indicate that Luke viewed kings as lesser in rank and therefore appropriately listed first? And more significantly, does Luke's arrangement in 21:12 reflect the concerns of a writer who wishes to place more emphasis on *secular* as opposed to religious persecution? Luke's Jesus refers to deliverance before synagogues and *prisons* and a bringing before kings and governors while Mark's Jesus refers to deliverance to councils (sanhedrins), *beatings in synagogues,* and a standing before governors and kings.

19. "But before all this" *(pro do toutōn pantōn),* the phrase which Luke attributes to Jesus at 21:12 has no counterpart in Mark's version and enriches the meaning of Luke's passage in a way that is highly congenial to the allegiance-witness position. For inasmuch as the disciples will be brought before kings and governors in a different, earlier period, this experience possesses its own unique identity and requires its own unique response. It is not simply one phenomenon among many cataclysmic phenomena occurring at the end.

And secondly, as a consequence of the fact that they are *temporally* distinct from them, there is also a basis for regarding the disciples' experiences with the political authorities as *qualitatively* distinct from the other strictly negative phenomena of wars, famines, and earthquakes. Indeed, Jesus' statement in the following verse, "This will be a time for you to bear testimony," can be taken to confirm such a distinction. For the seeming implication of these words is that the interrogations and trials which the disciples will undergo do have a positive aspect to them: they afford the disciples with positive opportunities for testifying on Jesus' behalf.

20. Since it cannot be known whether Luke possessed passion sources besides Mark, the process which he followed in developing his own final version cannot be determined with certainty. (See Neyrey, pp. 69-79, for a recent analysis which emphasizes Luke's redaction of his Markan source but still remains alert to the possibility that Luke possessed other sources for at least part of the passion, e.g., the trial before Herod Antipas.) Nevertheless, on the assumption that Luke did have Mark's text in front of him as a reference, it must be recognized that he consciously elected to move beyond what Mark had supplied in the two areas now being analyzed: the charges made against Jesus and an appearance before Herod Antipas.

21. See Cassidy/*Motive*, p. 149 and n. 21.

22. Within the present study, "the ending of Acts" refers to everything that Luke relates concerning Paul's witness and ministry in Rome from 28:14 to 28:31, but especially to those elements of the narrative which pertain to Paul's situation as a Roman prisoner due to appear before the emperor. This "Roman" dimension of the ending of Acts is particularly to be stressed in light of the approach that J. Dupont has followed in his essay, "La Conclusion des Actes et son rapport à l'ensemble de l'ouvrage de Luc" in Dupont/*Nouv. Etudes*, pp. 457-511.

Effectively interpreting Paul's interactions with the Jews of Rome in the light of Luke's reports at the conclusion of the Gospel and his reports at the beginning of Acts (as well as in light of material included at other points in both works), Dupont nevertheless separates out from the body of his study the material in the concluding verses of Acts which refers to Paul's circumstances as a Roman prisoner. For this reason, while his study provides many helpful insights on the subject of the Christian movement's stance vis-à-vis Judaism and vis-à-vis the Gentile world, it should not be regarded as a study analyzing all major elements in Luke's ending.

23. In earlier as well as in more recent studies it is not unusual for the ending of Acts to be characterized as "abrupt" or "enigmatic" (see, for example, Cadbury/*Making*, p. 321, and Munck, p. liv) and more frequently than not such observations derive from the author's assessment that Luke's conclusion is lacking in terms of climax and/or completeness. Indeed, as the paragraphs which follow indicate, there is a way in which— without the benefit of the allegiance-witness perspective—the interrelated qualities of climax and completeness could seem to be missing from Luke's ending.

24. The existence of a Christian community in Rome prior to Paul's arrival is indicated in 28:15. This feature of Luke's ending plus the fact that Luke does not portray Paul winning converts in Rome have led some commentators to conclude that Paul's ministry in Rome actually falls short of the expectations that Luke has engendered through his reports of Paul's achievements in various provincial settings. See, for example, Haenchen, p. 731, who also asserts that Luke consciously strove to overcome these factors and sought to end with the image of Paul as a successful missionary.

25. That Luke was concerned to show that Jesus' disciples witnessed "to the ends of the earth" in accordance with the Lord's prophetic statement in 1:8 and that he shows this prophecy authoritatively fulfilled with Paul's arrival in Rome have frequently been

remarked upon in the introductory sections of commentaries on Acts. Such an observation is congenial to the present analysis; but, especially in light of the contents of the second vision, it cannot be regarded as a fully adequate rendering of the "movement" that Luke actually describes in Acts.

For, in terms of the present analysis Paul is not only called to proclaim the message of Jesus in Rome with great authority and integrity. He is also called to a special type of witness not entrusted to anyone else: he is specifically and precisely called to testify on Jesus' behalf before the emperor. Paul is, in other words, the first witness of Jesus called to *judgment* before the emperor's tribunal (in the estimation of BAGD this is the precise meaning of *parastēnai* in 27:24) and the first disciple called to testify regarding the Lord Jesus Christ in that setting.

26. For a listing and evaluation of five solutions for what he terms the "familiar question" about Luke's failure to report the outcome of Paul's trial, see Walaskay/ *Rome*, pp. 18-21. It should be noted, however, that none of the proposed solutions, including the proposal favored by Walaskay, takes account of the perspective and insights afforded by the allegiance-witness theory.

27. Although Luke does not subsequently mention that any official report was entrusted to Julius or sent to Rome by any other means, the clear implication of Festus' conversation with Herod Agrippa II in 25:26-27 is that the governor regarded the submission of such a report as an important part of his responsibilities. And, on the general subject of communication between Jerusalem and Rome, it should be recalled that the response of the Jewish leaders of Rome in 28:21 alludes to the possibility of letters or verbal reports being sent from Judea. In Paul's case, however, no such letter or report had been received.

28. In effect, by having recounted Paul's previous faithful testimony before various Roman officials and by indicating that Paul's similarly faithful testimony before the emperor was a foregone conclusion, Luke had provided his readers with a significant word regarding any form of opposition (religious and cultural as well as political) to the Christian message. For no matter what intimidating circumstances he faced, including in the end, the circumstances of the imperial tribunal, Paul had ever remained faithful to his Lord. And so too, by implication, must Luke's readers be guided and strengthened by this heritage of fidelity. For what human authority, what human agency could exist that would ever have the power to sway them from or to compel them from their allegiance to Jesus?

29. Because it provides the key to the issue of climax, the element of Paul's faithful (and, in principle, complete) testimony before the emperor has been stressed in the text up until this point. Nevertheless, Luke's penchant for engaging his readers on several levels makes it fully appropriate to suggest that he would also have been pleased with his closing description of Paul for what it enabled him to indicate to his readers regarding their own ongoing "ordinary" witness on behalf of Jesus.

Paul had indeed received a special call from the risen Jesus to give testimony before the emperor, but this "special" witness was not the only form of witness to which the risen Lord had called him. Indeed Luke's final verses make it abundantly clear that Paul continued steadily and faithfully in his usual ministry of hospitality, preaching, and teaching, right up until the time of his "summit" appearance before the emperor.

Presumably Luke would have found it appropriate to impart just such a word to his readers at the end of his work. For few, if any, of his readers would ever be called to give testimony before the emperor as Paul was. Yet which one of them did not have the calling of witnessing faithfully to the risen Jesus through such ongoing activities as hospitality, preaching, and teaching? And was it not important for every one of them to know that Paul was disposed to engage enthusiastically in these aspects of his ministry for as much time as the Lord entrusted to him?

30. From the perspective of the present theory, then, the ending of Acts is far from being ill-considered or inappropriately related to what has preceded. Luke presumably gave considerable thought to what he wished to achieve through his conclusion and eventually evolved an ending that was fully congruent to both the Gospel and Acts, works with the abiding themes of allegiance and witness.

Bibliography

The bibliography which follows lists works cited in the text (but not listed in the Abbreviations) as well as other selected works. For more complete listings in each of the topic areas, the bibliography given on pp. 202–18 of *Jesus, Politics, and Society* should be consulted.

Studies in Luke-Acts

Bailey, K. *Poet and Peasant/Through Peasant Eyes*. Grand Rapids: Eerdmans, 1983.

Bauernfeind, O. *Kommentar und Studien zur Apostelgeschichte*. Introduced by M. Hengel. Tübingen: Mohr, 1980.

Franklin, E. *Christ the Lord*. Philadelphia: Westminster, 1975.

Hanson, R. *The Acts*. Oxford: Clarendon Press, 1967.

Karris, R. *Luke: Artist and Theologian*. New York: Paulist, 1985.

Marrow, S. *Speaking the Word Fearlessly*. New York: Paulist, 1982.

Mattil, A. *Luke and the Last Things*. Dillsboro, North Carolina: Western North Carolina Press, 1979.

Mussner, F. *Apostelgeschichte*. Würzburg: Echter Verlag, 1984.

Tyson, J. *The Death of Jesus in Luke-Acts*. Columbia, South Carolina: University of South Carolina Press, 1986.

Other New Testament Studies

Carrez, M. *De la Torah au Méssie*. Paris: Desclée, 1981.

Hahn, F. *Mission in the New Testament*. Translated by F. Clarke. London: SCM, 1965.

Hobbs, E. (Editor), *A Stubborn Faith*. Dallas: SMU Press, 1956.

Schmithals, W. *Paul and James*. Translated by D. Barton. London: SCM, 1965.

Studies Pertaining to Roman Rule

Deissmann, A. *Light from the Ancient East*. Translated by L. Strachan. Grand Rapids: Baker, 1927.

Finegan, J. *The Archaeology of the New Testament*. Boulder, Colorado: Westview, 1981.

Jones, A. *Studies in Roman Government and Law*. Oxford: Blackwell, 1960.

Judge, E. *The Conversion of Rome*. North Ryde, Australia: Macquarie University Ancient History Association, 1980.

Magie, D. *Roman Rule in Asia Minor*. 2 volumes. Princeton: Princeton University Press, 1950.

Sherwin-White, A. *The Roman Citizenship*. Oxford: Clarendon, 1939.

Index of Names and Subjects

81, 96, 99–100, 107, 129; choosing of Silas by, 67–68; citizenship of, 69, 101–02, 109, 147, 150–52, 184n.1, 198–99nn.14, 16, 17, 213n.10; collection of money by, 28–29, 56; conversion of, 51, 52, 54, 59, 64, 80, 81, 113, 178n.7, 184n.1; in Corinth, 59, 76, 83, 85, 91–93, 120, 129–30, 152, 162; in Cyprus, 66–67, 75, 76; in Derbe, 76; disagreement between, and Barnabas, 66–67; in Ephesus, 55–57, 74, 76, 83–86, 93–95, 96, 120–21, 129, 141, 162; and forgiveness, 67–68; and Gentiles, 58–60,70–75, 78, 98, 140, 207–08n.26; in Greece, 60, 77, 83–95; and high priest, 63, 65, 66, 75, 77, 79, 141; in Iconium, 74, 75, 76, 120; imprisonment of, 56, 73, 78, 80–81, 88–89, 96–116, 118–35, 143–44, 146, 149, 162, 168–70; in Jerusalem, 59–60, 66, 71–73, 75, 77–79, 96–116, 141, 152, 162; and Jews of Diaspora, 60, 70, 75–77; loyalty of, to Jewish tradition, 127–28; in Lystra, 52, 61, 67, 75; in Miletus, 53, 55, 61, 140; persecutions by, 30, 38; and Pharisees, 142; in Philippi, 53, 58, 68–69, 74, 83–89, 100–03, 119, 120, 121, 141, 162; in Pisidian Antioch, 62, 75, 76, 120, 129–30, 141; addressing Porcius Festus, 61, 66; in Rome, 60, 73, 118–35, 142, 167; in Samaria, 58, 140; and Sanhedrin, 61–65, 75, 78–81, 98, 99, 119, 141, 142, 162, 169; and scribes, 142; social stance of, 51–69; and Stephen, 66; in Syria, 59, 77; in Tarsus, 76; and taxation, 146; and Tertullus, 80; in Thessalonica, 58, 83–86, 89–91, 120, 124, 141, 162; in Troas, 53, 77; in Tyre, 53

Pentecost: address of Peter on, 33, 46; Holy Spirit and, 22, 29

Peter: address of, on Pentecost, 33, 46; Ananias and, 22, 139; in chains, 23, 134; and chief priests, 23, 32, 34, 39, 61; Cornelius and, 32; healings of, 22, 24, 137; imprisoned by Herod, 23, 47–50, 138, 143, 149, 154, 161, 184nn.17, 18; and Jerusalem church, 28, 31; and money, 25; and Sanhedrin, 32, 34, 37,

39, 41–46, 61, 138, 149, 154; Sapphira and, 22, 139; Tabitha and, 22

Pharisees, 7, 14, 16, 71, 139, 142

Philip, 22, 23, 24, 27, 30–31, 137

Philippi: ministry of Paul in, 53, 58, 68–69, 74, 83–89, 100–03, 119, 120, 121, 141, 162; women of, 58, 87, 89, 140

Pisidian Antioch: ministry of Paul in, 62, 75, 76, 120, 129–30, 141; women of, 76

politarchs, 84, 85, 162

Pontius Pilate: authority of, 86; Herod Antipas and, 19; interaction of Jesus with, 1, 12–13, 17–20, 133, 142; massacre of Galileans by, 9; role of, in death of Jesus, 33, 62

poor (*ptóchos*), 24, 54, 139, 177n.3

Porcius Festus: authority of, 83, 86, 96, 123, 128–29, 150; Paul addressing, 61, 66, 98, 119, 141, 151; trial of Paul before, 80–81, 106, 107–16, 142, 146, 162, 169

prayer: Jesus and, 7; and sovereignty of God, 10–13, 21–23, 51–54, 134

Priscilla, 59, 140, 185n.12

proconsuls, 84

ptóchos (poor), 24, 54, 139, 177n.3

Publius, 53, 54, 125

Q source, 165

Rome: imprisonment of Paul in, 73, 78, 118–35, 142, 168–70; ministry of Paul in, 60, 167

Sadducees, 18, 39

Samaria: Paul and Barnabas in, 58, 140; Philip in, 22, 23, 24, 30–31

Samaritans: acceptance denied to, 3; in Acts, 57–58, 140; kingdom of God and, 29, 31, 137, 140

Sanhedrin: authority of, 14, 15–16, 39–41, 44, 48–50, 161; corruption of, 61–65; John and, 32, 34, 37, 39, 41–46, 149, 154; Paul and, 61–65, 70, 75, 77, 78–81, 98, 99, 119, 141, 142, 147, 162, 169; Peter and, 32, 34, 37, 39, 41–46, 149, 154; Stephen and, 35, 37, 40, 49–50, 61–62, 64, 181n.2, 181n.28; trial of Jesus before, 12–13, 18, 33

Sapphira, 37, 138, 178n.9; Peter and, 22, 26–27, 139

scribes, 18, 34, 39, 139, 142

Index of Scriptural References

233

Biographical Note

Father Richard Cassidy's educational background includes graduate work in history and economics as well as in theology. In economics he holds an M.A. from the University of Michigan in Ann Arbor. In theology he has received the S.T.L. from the Gregorian University in Rome and a Ph.D. from the Graduate Theological Union in Berkeley.

Ordained for the Detroit Archdiocese in 1967, Fr. Cassidy recently completed eight years' service as the director of the Archdiocesan Justice and Peace Office and now teaches New Testament Ethics and Christian Social Ethics at St. John's Provincial Seminary. He is active in The Catholic Biblical Association of America and The Society of Biblical Literature, serving as a member of their task forces on Luke and Acts. Among his previously published works are *Jesus, Politics, and Society: A Study of Luke's Gospel* (Orbis, 1978) and *Political Issues in Luke-Acts* (co-edited with Philip Scharper; Orbis, 1983).

Prepublication Statements on Society and Politics in the Acts of the Apostles

"The attitude of the disciples to society and politics in Acts does not deviate, the author shows, from that of Jesus himself as set forth in Cassidy's earlier work *Jesus, Politics, and Society.* He argues that Luke's purpose in Acts is not political apologetic. Of special interest is the discussion of Paul's relation to the Roman Empire: his Roman citizenship was subordinate to his Jewishness and especially to his vocation as a witness and servant of Jesus Christ, and there was an element in his preaching and activity which did present a threat to Roman society. This aspect of the book in particular is worthy of serious attention."

F. F. Bruce
Emeritus Professor of Biblical Criticism and Exegesis
University of Manchester, England

"Father Cassidy offers a masterly analysis of Acts, in beautifully intelligible language. It culminates in the refusal to accept either of two popular character-izations of the book—as a defense of Rome to the Christians or as a defense of Christianity to the Romans. Rather, Luke intended to promulgate his commit-ment to Jesus and exhort others to follow, providing them with guidance on how to bear witness in the prevailing political structure. The result is surely right. It means that the author of Acts was leading the church into history, yet one whose essence transcends this world."

David Daube
Emeritus Professor of Law
University of California, Berkeley

"This work completes with distinction the previous work of Richard Cassidy on Luke: *Jesus, Politics, and Society.* The contemporary reader will not be able to remain indifferent to the social and political attitudes of the first disciples of Jesus or of Paul. Readers will particularly appreciate Cassidy's concern with emphasizing the different aspects of the problem. His book should receive the attention of both interpreters of Acts and historians of Christianity's origins."

Jacques Dupont, O.S.B.
Monastère Saint-André, Ottignies, Belgium

"Attentive to complexes of social data and thematic patterns throughout Luke-Acts, Cassidy presents a fresh perspective on the disputed issue of Luke's purpose. An effective critique of conventional views is coupled with an engaging counter-thesis that Luke-Acts aimed at strengthening Christians on trial by linking their situation and steadfastness to the experience of their apostolic predecessors and the risen Lord.

"Its comprehensive survey of the data and its judicious assessment of scholarly opinion make this a timely contribution to one of the burning issues of Lucan research."

John H. Elliott
Professor of Theology and Religious Studies
University of San Francisco

"Once again Richard Cassidy has used his comprehensive knowledge of New Testament studies and his concern for the witness of the church in our day to illuminate greatly our understanding of the Lukan writings. This work will both further the desire of contemporary scholarship to obtain a more precise analysis of the social setting of first-century Christianity and provide a model for future research. I take pleasure in commending his work to the public."

W. Ward Gasque
Sheppard Professor of Biblical Studies
Regent College, Vancouver, BC, Canada

"With clarity and perception, Richard Cassidy not only himself touches the heart of the matter but invites his readers to do likewise. Cassidy places the religious issues within the context of the geographical, social, and political world of Luke, a context that helps explain 'theological' issues such as witness, discipleship, opposition versus allegiance to Jesus, authority and dissent. This well-written book exemplifies interdisciplinary scholarship and represents a provocative challenge for those who seek to understand the message and the implications of Christianity today."

Mary Ann Getty, R.S.M
Assistant Professor of New Testament
Catholic University of America

"In this latest volume, Richard Cassidy continues his disquieting role in Lukan scholarship, shaking up the *status quo post Conzelmann et Haenchen*. Luke's 'political apologetic' in Acts has long been self-evident to me, and probably to most scholars. Yet Cassidy patiently, thoroughly, and most of the time persuasively dismantles the infrastructure of that theory, as well as the 'ecclesial apologetic' theory, replacing them with his 'allegiance-conduct-witness' theory of Luke's purpose in writing. I find Cassidy's book worrisome—exceedingly so!"

Edward C. Hobbs
Professor of New Testament
Wellesley College

"Following the methodology he employed in writing his earlier *Jesus, Politics, and Society,* Richard J. Cassidy has carried through to completion his project of delineating the Christian social outlook developed in the New Testatment writings of Luke. This book presents a clear and detailed analysis of what Cassidy understands to be Luke's vision of the social and political stance of the apostolic church and its principal leaders in relation to the stance of Jesus himself, as analyzed in his first book. His most original contribution lies in offering an allegiance-witness theory of Luke's purpose in writing as opposed to the presently more widely held apologetic theories. The book deserves a careful and thoughtful reading by all who are interested in the social, political, and ethical implications of the New Testament writings." **J. Warren Holleran**
Professor of Sacred Scripture
St. Patrick's Seminary, Menlo Park, California

"In this very readable sequel to *Jesus, Politics, and Society*, Richard Cassidy adds a new dimension to the purpose of Acts by suggesting that Luke wanted to show Christians how to live in the Roman Empire and specifically to give them examples of how to cope with being tried before political officials. This is an interesting and stimulating study." **I. Howard Marshall**
Professor of New Testatment Exegesis
University of Aberdeen, Scotland

"A challenging work of Cassidy presenting the church in the Acts as a community committed to an uncompromising testimony to Christ. The socio-political stance adopted by Jesus of Nazareth towards the Roman order was courageously followed by the Jerusalem community until it reached its climactic affirmation in the ministry of Paul. A convincing presentation of the social thrust of the Word of God in our time." **Joseph Pathrapankal**
Professor of New Testament
Dharmaram Vidyakshetram, Bangalore, India

"Fr. Cassidy knows the Lukan theology from a theoretical and practical point of view. In this marvelous book he analyzes the beginnings of Christianity in order to explain its spiritual and political significance in confrontation with the political authorities of the day. As a result the reader gains a new perspective on an early Christianity ready to denounce every social and political stance contrary to the message of Jesus." **Antonio Salas, O.S.A.**
Director de la Escuela Biblica
Madrid, Spain